My Place at the Table

MY PLACE AT THE TABLE

*A Recipe for
a Delicious Life
in Paris*

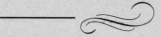

ALEXANDER LOBRANO

A Rux Martin Book
Houghton Mifflin Harcourt
Boston   New York
2021

For information about permission to reproduce selections
from this book, write to trade.permissions@hmhco.com
or to Permissions, Houghton Mifflin Harcourt Publishing Company,
3 Park Avenue, 19th Floor, New York, New York 10016.

hmhbooks.com

Library of Congress Cataloging-in-Publication Data
Names: Lobrano, Alec, author.
Title: My place at the table : a recipe for a delicious life in Paris /
Alexander Lobrano.
Description: Boston : Houghton Mifflin Harcourt, 2021. |
"A Rux Martin Book."
Identifiers: LCCN 2020044144 (print) | LCCN 2020044145 (ebook) |
ISBN 9781328588838 | ISBN 9780358307099 | ISBN 9780358311249 |
ISBN 9781328585219 (ebook)
Subjects: LCSH: Lobrano, Alec. | Food writers—France—Biography. |
Dinners and dining—Paris—France. | Cooking, French.
Classification: LCC TX649.L63 A3 2021 (print) | LCC TX649.L63 (ebook) |
DDC 641.5944092 [B]—dc23
LC record available at https://lccn.loc.gov/2020044144
LC ebook record available at https://lccn.loc.gov/2020044145

Book design by Kelly Dubeau Smydra

Printed in the United States of America
1 2021

For Bruno Jean Roland Midavaine, my spouse;
my dearly missed friend Judith Devreaux Fayard,
who gave me so many chances;
and everyone who has ever cooked for me

What we notice in stories is the nearness
of the wound to the gift.

— JEANETTE WINTERSON
(from an interview)

CONTENTS

Acknowledgments   xi

1. The Little Footprint   1

2. The First Supper   4

3. Words and Whey   15

4. On the Shores of Memory   25

5. Cracking My Shell   35

6. A Map of My Palate   55

7. At My Tutor's Table   64

8. The Old Lady's Place   78

9. Seductions   88

10. The Talk of the Town   106

11. My Tour de France   117

12. The Game of Fame   128

13. Becoming a Parisian   141

14. Earning My Way with a Fork and Pen   156

15. The New Bistro Is Born   169

16. The Naked Truth   180

17. Ruth   193

18. The Two Gifts   203

19. The Harvest   213

     My Little Black Book   225

ACKNOWLEDGMENTS

My eternal thanks to my mother, for lighting the wick of my curiosity, and my father, for his sense of fun and the harshness that made me strong.

Also to my grandmother Jean, for the love, wit, intelligence, and generosity that guided me through my early years, and the dozens of brilliant teachers and professors who made my mind their garden: Mrs. Hogenauer, Miss Gorham, Miss Armitage, Mrs. Lewis, Mrs. Robotham, Miss Fleissig, Professor Holdreith . . . the list is much too long to be fully unpacked here. To Ruth Leahy at the Weston Public Library, who comforted, nurtured, and groomed me.

To Tom Crane, for teaching me to cook and for his patience, and Marc Parisot, for the day he took me into the église de la Madeleine in Paris.

To the editors who gave me work and the fellow writers with whom I've shared a career, including Joe Fox at Random House, Julia Glass, Michael Luther, Gary Walther, William Sertl, Ruth Reichl, Beth Kracklauer, Kevin Doyle, Debi Dunn, Barbara Fairchild, Malachy Duffy, Catherine Bigwood, Stephen Brewer, Natasha Edwards, Karen Albrecht, Christine Muhlke, Ted Moncreiff, Hanya Yanigahara, James Oseland, Andrew Powell, Deborah Gottleib, and many others. To all of the friends who've shared meals with me, including Elizabeth Lobrano, Joel Paul,

Laurie Eastman, John Philip, Kato Wittich, Ken Buck, Lisa Bannon, Christa Worthington, Judy Fayard, Nanette Maxim, David Lebovitz, Claire and Denis Quimbrot, Alexandra Marshall, and many more. To Deborah Ritchken, Susanna Porter, and Christopher Steighner, with whom I published *Hungry for Paris* and *Hungry for France.* To my wonderful agent, Jane Dystel, and my brilliant editor, Rux Martin, for bringing this book into the world with me. My sincere thanks to Susanna Brougham for her superb copyediting.

My Place at the Table

1

THE LITTLE FOOTPRINT

The gray pencil script on the soft sheet of ruled yellow paper was my own embarrassingly loopy second-grade handwriting. I started reading "The Very Best Sandwich":

The BLT is the most perfect sandwich. The bacon brings it salt and the rich taste of pork. The tomato is sweet and juicy, and the lettuce is crunchy. The mayonnaise makes them all friends. Mom likes them made with toasted white bread, but I prefer rye bread, because of the little sweet seeds called caraway. Iced tea is a good drink with them.

I found the little essay in a bulging brown accordion file marked ALEC that my mother had given me when she moved to an assisted-living community. Filled with snapshots, clippings, report cards, and vaccination records, it was a time capsule of my first seventeen years. I so clearly remembered the May morning when I'd written my ode to a sandwich, I could almost smell the chalk dust in the air of that grade-school classroom as the sun poured in through its tall windows.

"Today I want you to write me a paper about one of your very favorite things," said Miss Armitage. "Your subject might be your dog, or a song, or a game. It could even be a flower." She smiled at me. "It can be anything you choose — except for books, which we'll keep for book reports, but it should be something you really like a lot. I want you to explain to me why you like it so much too. You have thirty minutes to complete this assignment, so keep track of your time." She nodded at the clock on the wall. "And I don't want you doing a lot of erasing. Think before you write."

I stared at the bouquet of frilled pink peonies in the heavy glass vase on the corner of Miss Armitage's desk. When I'd come into the empty classroom early that morning, I'd found her trimming their stems before she arranged them, and I'd told her that peonies were my favorite flowers. She said they were hers too.

I wouldn't write about them, though. Flowers weren't an appropriate interest for boys — too girly. That's what my father had told me after I'd asked my grandmother for some tulip bulbs as a birthday present the previous October.

I thought of writing about going to the beach because I loved the briny smell of the sea and the calm that came from sitting at the edge of a body of water I couldn't see the end of. I hoped there was some unknown place beyond it where no one knew me, and that place would make me free. Then I had another idea — I'd write about my favorite sandwich. I picked up my pencil. Would Miss Armitage think this was a silly subject? I hesitated. I could also write about the old apple tree I liked to climb up into and read. I was sure she'd like that. Ten minutes had already gone by. I decided to risk the sandwich.

At the end of the following day, just before we left the classroom to go home, Miss Armitage distributed our essays. Glancing at my grade, I ran home from school and found my mother reading in the living room.

"I'm very proud of you!" she said after she'd seen my A. "What was the assignment Miss Armitage gave you, sweetheart?"

I explained.

"You really do love to eat, don't you?" she said with a smile, and gently shook her head.

That night, after my father had come home from his office in New York City and changed out of his suit, my mother poured him a short glass of cocktail sherry. He'd put on his "good luck sweater" from college, the old ivory-colored tennis pullover with bands of navy and maroon at its V-neck; he'd never lost a game when he wore it. Now he stood at the desk in the living room, glancing through the mail. I watched him through the open door of the TV room.

"Alec had a very good day today," I heard my mother say as she handed my father my essay.

He read it, then dropped it into the wastepaper basket. "Alec!" he shouted, and I came to the doorway. "How could you write such a dumbbell paper? It makes you sound like a real dope."

"Miss Armitage gave him an A, Sandy," my mother protested.

He ignored her. "The next time you write about your favorite thing, it should be ice-skating, baseball, or football," he said. "Or your dog, or going fishing, or climbing a tree."

"I almost wrote about climbing a tree," I told him.

"Why didn't you?"

I shrugged. "I decided it would be more interesting to write about a BLT."

My father glared at me and shook his head.

What I didn't know then was that food would become my muse, my metaphor, and my map for making a place for myself in the world and finding my place at the table.

THE FIRST SUPPER

The Eiffel Tower craned over the city like a giant toy giraffe. I was viewing it from a bridge over the Seine on a warm Indian-summer evening, and on either side of me, people were stopping to snap its photo. Me, I didn't need to, because I wasn't a tourist anymore. This thought was as exciting as it was intimidating. I still couldn't believe that I was actually living in Paris. Just a month earlier, I'd turned my whole life upside-down. I'd been working as a freelance writer in London for more than a year, and I was up for an appointment at the British Consulate. So I'd returned to New York City to apply for a UK residency permit.

After an excruciating two-hour interview with the consul general, I was waiting to cross Third Avenue when I bumped into Nancy, a friend from the days when we were both editorial assistants at Random House. Over coffee, she said she'd just been thinking about me. Her sister was an editor at Fairchild Publications, publishers of *Women's Wear Daily* and *W,* a glossy magazine featuring celebrities and aristocrats, and she had just mentioned that a position for a menswear editor was open in the company's Paris office.

"Can you call your sister and find out if the job is still available?"

What I'd just said surprised me.

"But Alec, you just applied for residency in the UK."

"I'm supposed to go back to London tomorrow night, so I need to get an interview immediately."

"You're not interested in fashion, Alec."

"I've always wanted to live in Paris."

Forty-five minutes later, I was shaking hands with John Fairchild, whose smirking boyish face and cold blue eyes instantly made me wary.

"Parlez-vous français, Alec?"

"Je le parle assez bien."

"And what do you know about menswear?"

The honest answer would have been "Absolutely nothing." I had about as much natural aptitude for fashion journalism as I had for jet-engine mechanics. But I said, "Right now, I don't know very much about fashion —"

"I could tell by the way you were dressed when you walked in."

Though he'd interrupted me, I plowed ahead. "But I'm sure I'll learn, and I think having studied art history will help me . . ."

"Forget the art history. Forever," he said, and stared at me for a while. Finally he asked, "Do you have anything else to say for yourself?"

I smiled and shook my head.

"Can you start a week from tomorrow?"

I nodded and thanked him.

As I was leaving, he said, "And don't worry, Alec. If it doesn't work out, that's easy. I'll fire you."

Since arriving in Paris, I had been living, at Fairchild's expense, in a two-star hotel not far from the company's office on the rue Cambon, in the heart of the city. The most surprising thing about my new life in France was that it was so hard to eat well.

I managed lunch alone with no problem because there was an excellent *traiteur*, the French version of a delicatessen, right out the door. The taciturn proprietress sold hand-carved slices of juicy ham, which she smoked in the chimney of her house in Burgundy, and an array of excellent homemade salads, including my favorites—céleri rémoulade (grated celeriac in a light mustardy mayonnaise dressing) and salade piémontaise (potato salad with hard-cooked eggs, pickles, chopped tomato, and chunks of ham). Depending on the weather, I'd happily eat my takeout in the Tuileries Garden, at the end of the street, or at my desk.

Dinner, however, had been difficult. The café at the corner near my hotel did a decent omelette that came with some salad, to which I added an extra order of frites. This always made the café's sturdy fifty-something waitress smile. "You can eat those fries because you're as skinny as a cat, but if you keep it up, you'll end up like me!" she'd say with a snort.

One night she looked at me and shook her head. "You again! It's a little sad, no? You're young! You have money in your pockets!" she scolded. "You have the whole city of Paris to discover, not just this one café!"

My cheeks blazed, and briefly I thought of walking out. Instead I ordered the usual omelette and avoided her gaze while I wolfed it down.

Walking back to my hotel, I was angry at the waitress because she'd not only embarrassed me: she'd been right. The debut of my new life had a flaw, one that I kept to myself, that was even worse. How would she react, I wondered, if I told her that on weekends, when the café was closed, I lived on a little stash of Baby Bonbel cheeses wrapped in red wax, slices of a gnarly sausage with a white mildewed rind, crackers, and apples. These I kept hidden in a plastic bag in my locked suitcase (food was explicitly forbidden in the hotel's rooms). Why? Going to a good restaurant by myself was unimaginable. The waitress's reprimand had made everything clear, though. With a sinking feeling, I recognized the fallacy at the heart of the fantasy of living in Paris, which I'd nursed for so many years. Somehow I'd just assumed the city would make me someone else, someone very different from the man I was when I'd stepped off a train from London at the Gare du Nord a few weeks earlier, on a rainy September night in 1986.

Now that the waitress had called me on it, I cringed at the obvious. There would be no such effortless metamorphosis. Just being in Paris wasn't enough. I'd have to work at it. With a rush of adrenaline, I knew exactly how I'd begin to build a real life here. The next day, I went to a bookstore and bought four guides to Parisian restaurants, two in English and two in French. I'd make Paris my home by eating it.

All week long, I read the books and made a list of the restaurants that appealed to me. Both the banana-yellow Gault & Millau, in French, and the American Express guide, in English, described Au Quai d'Orsay on the Left Bank in glowing terms: "charming" and "fashionable," with "excellent traditional French cooking, especially the mushroom dishes in season." I made a reservation for myself for Saturday night.

In one of the other English-language guidebooks, Frommer's or Fodor's, I came across some advice: "Parisians think nothing of going out for a meal on their own, and you will almost always be well-received if you have made a reservation and are correctly dressed. Some people feel more comfortable if they bring along something to read. You might also consider doing a crossword puzzle, or even some discreet needlework." This latter suggestion struck me as ludicrous, but I did tuck a magazine into the foppish briefcase that had been a gift from the English boyfriend I left behind when I moved to Paris. I also brought along my map of Paris and a small softcover English-French dictionary.

Once I'd crossed the Seine, the excitement I'd felt when leaving my hotel had wilted. Inside the restaurant, I lingered by the open reservations book at the end of the service bar, but no one came. When I attempted to flag down a waiter, he said, "We're full tonight," and rushed away, holding his tray aloft on strong steepled fingers. Across the way, a woman in a sleeveless coral dress glanced at me and said something to the man sitting across the table. After he'd eyeballed me, his lips moved, and they both chuckled. At last an older woman, with a toffee-colored chignon and a pair of glasses on a chain atop her ample bosom, sauntered back to her post.

"May I help you?"

I gave her my name.

"You're late," she said, and I worried I might be sent back out into the night. But she escorted me to my table and asked if I'd like an aperitif. When I asked for a vodka tonic, she shook her head. "We don't serve cocktails. Would you like a glass of Champagne?"

I nodded, and wondered why she'd been so dismissive. When the Champagne came, I noticed that the small tight bubbles rising in the narrow flute were a perfect metaphor for my anxiety. But the first sip was ecstasy. A waiter arrived with the menu, which I studied intently, eventually pausing to glance around the room. No one was wearing a tie, so I surreptitiously removed from my neck the narrow knitted burgundy noose, a hand-me-down from an older cousin, and stashed it in my briefcase. I undid the top button of my shirt too.

Though I'd read that this restaurant was well known for serving mushrooms, nowhere on the menu did I see the word *champignons*. There lots of words I didn't know, so I extracted the little dictionary from my briefcase. *Pintade* turned out to mean "guinea hen," which wasn't much help, since up to this point I'd eaten only three types of fowl: chicken, turkey, and, infrequently, duck.

A handsome woman nearby had short, wavy nut-brown hair and alert brows that reminded me of my adored late paternal grandmother, Jean. She'd traveled a lot, even as a very elderly woman, and often alone, and I wondered how she'd managed solitary meals like this one. She didn't much care about food, though, so it was easy to picture her in the bar of some grand hotel in Cairo or Delhi in the middle of the afternoon, off in a corner, sitting in a leather club chair with a glass of dry sherry and a toasted cheese sandwich before her and a mystery novel as her sole companion. "You can always get a cheese sandwich," she'd said once, when I'd asked her what she'd eaten during a long trip to India.

Like everyone else in my family, my grandmother Jean had found my passion for food puzzling, even a little embarrassing, but the last time the subject had come up, she surmised it might be explained as "a form of edible anthropology." Despite the slightly patronizing tone, her words sounded gentle, offering a thoughtful diagnosis.

The waiter was at my elbow. He had black hair, neatly slicked back, and was wearing a white apron below a snugly fitted black vest. When I looked up, I saw his expression subtly change: first wry, then assessing, and finally politely entertained. He wordlessly cleared the second place setting on my table, returned, and opened his order book.

"It's the beginning of the mushroom season, sir. I hope you like mushrooms?"

Yes, I liked mushrooms, a lot. But the plural form of the word puzzled me.

"Do you like cèpes? We have cèpes from the Ardennes tonight, the first ones of the season."

I'd thought I was on solid ground when a conversation turned to mushrooms, those nice, white, round-capped fungi I'd grown up with. As a child I'd eaten them after they'd been drained from a little can with the image of a green-faced Pennsylvania Dutchman peering out in a friendly way. But now cèpes had been mentioned, and I was lost. I did gather, however, that they were some kind of mushroom.

The waiter excused himself and returned with a small straw basket lined with a napkin. Pulling open its folds, he showed me the cèpes, meaty-looking mushrooms with thick umber-brown caps and fleshy ivory stems; little clods of earth and moss were still attached to their feet. He motioned me closer, and their wild bosky aroma assailed me.

I loved the seriousness involved in constructing my meal, as though it was a very important project, and I was grateful for the waiter's willingness to try to understand my mangled French. I'd have the cèpes to start, and then the guinea hen, which was stuffed with duck foie gras, and trompettes de la mort, another kind of wild mushroom. My little dictionary ominously translated its name as "death's trumpet." I hoped the kitchen knew what it was doing.

"And will monsieur have some wine?" the waiter asked. I picked up the heavy black leather-bound wine list with what must have been obvious dread. But the waiter remained unperturbed: "May I suggest a half bottle of Vouvray, a nice white wine from the Loire Valley that's dry enough to flatter the cèpes but round enough to pair well with the guinea hen."

I nodded enthusiastically.

"*Et de l'eau — plate ou pétillante?*"

I stalled again.

"You would like water with bubbles or not the bubbles?"

It was bubbles for me.

"Chateldon?"

He got another blank look.

"Chateldon is a mineral water from the Auvergne. It was carried in tanks on the backs of donkeys to Versailles because it was the favorite water of Louis XIV. It has small bubbles and is good for the digestion."

I nodded. If the water had been good enough for the Sun King, it would be good enough for me.

I'd just ordered my first solo dinner in a real Paris restaurant, and under the tutelage of the patient and perceptive waiter, I was actually having a wonderful time. The magazine I'd brought along remained in my briefcase, since the crowd in the dining room offered much better entertainment.

They were mostly middle-aged couples, the men in corduroy trousers and tweed jackets in heathered colors. The women wore blouses, wool skirts, and sturdy pumps, and my maternal aunts had a hairstyle just like theirs — a short bob held in place with a barrette over each ear. These couples were apparently resigned to sitting for long periods in the sad yet civil silence of marriage gone mute. In the corner I noticed a jovial-looking, barrel-bellied elderly man with a head tonsured like a monk's, his napkin tucked into his shirt collar and a full bottle of wine on his table. Could this be a vision of my future self, happier and completely comfortable in Paris?

The waiter returned with a ramekin centered on a paper doily on a plate. "Your amuse-bouche, monsieur, a mousse of roasted peppers," he said as he expertly removed the cork from my half bottle of wine. With one sip, Vouvray became a favorite quaff, and the king's water, its label featuring a gold medallion of the sun, was regally refreshing too. The worthlessness of my little French-English dictionary was confirmed when I looked up *amuse-bouche:* "mouth amuser." The tidbit was pretty, a pale terra-cotta-colored mousse ornamented by four shiny silver diamonds of — something.

"Those are raw sardines," my ever-observant waiter told me when he arrived with the breadbasket. Sardines. My childhood aversion to seafood twitched, but I decided these tiny pieces of raw fish would provide the perfect punctuation to an evening that was about boldness and rising to new challenges. The mousse was smooth and slightly sweet, flavored by the pepper's caramelized juices and a whiff of char. The sardines added salt, oily bass notes, and texture. They made perfect sense.

"Would you like me to hang your jacket?" the waiter asked as he cleared the mouth amuser's plate from the table. I slipped off the blazer, and the man who'd chuckled earlier, when his wife had said something about me while I was waiting to be seated, smiled and gave me a thumbs-up. His wife turned and made a fanning motion. So their amusement hadn't been caused by the fact that I'd been standing there alone, but rather that I'd been so overdressed on a warm night.

The cèpes had been cut into quarters and evenly seared to a dark-caramel color; they were seasoned with a nearly invisible veil of finely chopped parsley and garlic. Whatever name these mushrooms went by, they were the best I'd ever eaten. Fleshy and funky, they tasted of rut, and it struck me that I already knew this taste, or at least a version of it. When I was living in New York City and had first become interested in cooking, I'd occasionally bought cellophane packets of dried porcini mushrooms as I cooked my way through Marcella Hazan's first cookbook. I deduced that the French word for porcini was *cèpe*, but this connection left me feeling more dim-witted than clever. It laid bare the immensity of everything I didn't know about France's language and food.

Plated with a little mound of wilted spinach and three waxy white potatoes that had been perfectly whittled into small rounded bobbins, the rolled and sautéed breast of guinea hen sat in a shimmering puddle of golden sauce. The foie gras gave the fowl luxurious succulence, and the chewy black trompettes de la mort mushrooms amplified the rustic flavors of both the bird and the duck liver — but it was the sauce of wine and reduced cooking juices that made the dish so delectable. I was quietly wondering which wine had been used to deglaze the pan the guinea hen had been cooked in when the waiter refilled my wineglass.

"Are you enjoying it?" he said.

I nodded vigorously and asked if the sauce had been made with Marsala, the Sicilian wine.

"No, no, it's vin jaune, from the Jura, in the east of France. It has the flavor of walnuts." A yellow wine "with the flavor of walnuts" — what a beautiful phrase. But what was the flavor of walnuts? Something woody, buttery, nutty, ever so slightly bitter — that would be the skin of the nut. So yes, the wine did taste of walnuts, but it would never have occurred to me to parse this subtlety myself. In the world I came from, it was enough if something tasted good. At our family table, this was the rote goal of cooking, to make something flavorful. But beyond a murmur or two of approval, culinary success had never been deemed worthy of discussion, much less lyrical description.

"Et voilà!" said the waiter as he placed in front of me a quivering, eggy yellow soufflé with a brown cap dusted with powdered sugar. I'd almost forgotten I'd ordered dessert, an apricot soufflé, made, as I'd been told, with the last of the season's apricots from Provence. Rising from a ribbed white-porcelain ramekin, the soufflé was magnificent. The waiter came back with a silver-plated canister, a bowl of water on a plate, and two silver spoons. He set the canister on the table, and then, with one spoon, he pierced the soufflé to create a smile-shaped incision. Next he lifted the lid off the canister, rinsed the spoon he'd just used in the bowl of water, and plunged the spoon into the canister, eventually extracting a perfect egg-shape of very pale green sorbet, which he then gently fed to the mouth he'd made in my soufflé.

"Lemon verbena sorbet," he said. I didn't know what lemon verbena was, but the sorbet's vivid citrusy-herbaceous flavor was a perfect foil for the sweet-tart, musky taste of the apricots. With each spoonful, the casual elegance of this dessert excited me, but this pleasure also made me anxious. Suddenly I wanted this meal to be over so that nothing could spoil it, and I could be alone with my almost painful jubilation.

I declined coffee and asked for the check, and when it arrived, I left 300 francs on the small rectangular tray, pocketed the perforated receipt, pulled on my jacket, and thanked the waiter effusively when I passed him as I hurried through the restaurant. The bracing coolness of an early autumn night was an ecstatic relief.

Several times I laughed out loud as I walked back to the hotel. Cutting through the relentlessly well-groomed gardens of the Champs-Elysées, I startled a couple sitting on a bench and kissing, but they quickly returned to their embrace after I passed by. Their ardor briefly punctured my giddiness. I wanted to be necking on a park bench with someone too, but maybe that would happen someday soon. Still, even without any friends or a lover, I'd found a way to make Paris mine, and I couldn't wait to get back to my stuffy hotel room and decide which restaurant to visit the following night.

When I got there, I didn't know what to do with my elation. I noticed a notebook on the second twin bed, which I was using as a desk. I picked it up, sat down, and started to write about every detail of this perfect evening in Paris.

3
WORDS AND WHEY

My new office, which I shared with the staff photographers, overlooked an airshaft. When I arrived for my first day of work, the gray Formica-topped desk was piled high with mail addressed to Richard Buckley, the popular, handsome man who had previously held my position. Buckley had been promoted to a big job at Fairchild's home office in New York City.

I'd gotten in early on this drizzly morning after walking the entire perimeter, twice, of the mournfully leafless Tuileries Garden. I did this to unknot my nerves. Each time one of my colleagues got coffee from the machine on the waist-high refrigerator in the closet next to my office door, I tried to introduce myself. Twice I'd gotten a chilly "*Bonjour,*" once a clipped "*Ciao*"—all from other Americans. Finally a smiling woman offered a fleeting but polite "Welcome to Paris, I'm Anne." I later learned that she was from the Bay Area.

Having left my door ajar, I discovered that I was the object of a sartorial critique whispered by an unseen man. "Did you see that the guy who replaced Richard Buckley? He's wearing a new Armani suit? It's so pathetic!"

I didn't know why my suit was pathetic, but it made me angry with my English boyfriend, who'd bullied me into buying it. He'd reasoned, wrongly it now seemed, that if I was going to be a fashion editor, I had to dress the part. The suit had cost a fortune.

By mid-morning, I had the sinking feeling that I might have made a terrible mistake. Beyond my elation at being in Paris, this job, as an almost comically miscast fashion writer, would be my daily reality. Michael Luther, the editor I reported to in New York, had told me my first assignment was to go down to Milan and interview the designers for a story that previewed the main trends in the next season of Italian menswear. I had no idea who these designers might be, so I looked at the ads in a copy of *Vogue Hommes* and made a list of the Italian ones. I was in the midst of my fourth call with the press department at Giorgio Armani in Milan — at least I knew who he was — trying to set up an appointment for the following week, when Christa Worthington, the bureau chief, came in. "We're having our weekly editorial meeting in a few minutes, Alec. It would be a good time for me to introduce you to everyone," she whispered.

When I entered to join the others around the big table in the room next door, one of the few other male editors eyeballed me from head to toe. "Oh my God! Is that Armani?" he exclaimed in mock awe. I recognized the voice; it was the one I'd overheard earlier. Several people chuckled.

"Alec Lobrano, who's just moved here from London, is taking over from Richard Buckley," Christa explained. The group discussed the production schedule, and then it was time for new story ideas.

"OK, Alec, do you have anything?"

Mercifully, the jolt of adrenaline I experienced from being put on the spot brought one to mind. "Well, yes, maybe I could do a story about Androuet, the most famous cheese shop in Paris." I'd been there twice with my family during my first trip to Paris fourteen years ago.

"Why would that be a good story?" Christa asked.

I explained that, when he opened his shop in the rue d'Amsterdam in 1909, Henri Androuet had been the first person in Paris to sell cheeses from all over France. Before that, Parisians mostly ate cheeses from the Ile de France, such as Brie; a few Norman cheeses, including Camembert; and hard cheeses, like Mimolette, from the north of France. This made Androuet the father of modern French cheese culture. Subsequently run by his son Pierre, the shop and restaurant continued to age the cheeses they sold in cellars built into the limestone under the rue d'Amsterdam.

"That sounds interesting. Go for it," said Christa.

That weekend, I laboriously translated my questions for Pierre Androuet into French and wrote them on numbered index cards. They would help me avoid language problems. At least that was the plan.

When Patrick, who was one of the Fairchild photographers, and I showed up at his shop, Monsieur Androuet was wearing a baggy gray cardigan and worn brown-corduroy trousers. He had the gentle face of a Cistercian monk. After he'd served us coffee, I read the first of my index cards. A rough English translation would go something like this: "Thank you for your beautiful cheeses for which I have admiration and will be loving to eat. I am so glad to learn of cheese. Today I would like to be your cheese student. So instead of asking you very many questions, I would like you to tell me about your cheeses in the most intimate way."

He smiled and nodded. *"Bien sûr,"* he said. Out of the corner of my eye, I saw Patrick shaking his head.

Monsieur Androuet handed us shower-cap-like bonnets to wear over our hair and disposable plastic galoshes to cover our shoes, explaining that these items would protect the cheese cellars from unwanted bacteria. We followed him down a worn stone staircase to the aging cellars, which had a pleasant mossy smell. He gestured at his chèvres, the first word of his that I'd understood since *bonjour*. He stopped and pointed at a small cheese wrapped in a folded brown leaf and tied up with raffia twine. Then he fondled the cheese gently while speaking a torrent of French, from which I could skim only a few words. In a panic, I scribbled in my notebook, "Something about goats, cheese wrapped in a leaf." I smiled and nodded, and wrote, "Help! Help! Help!" to keep up the illusion that I was studiously recording his words.

Fortunately, some of the shelves had name tags, so at least I could see what the cheeses were called. We visited a few more little goat cheeses, including Cabécou from Rocamadour in the Dordogne, Pélardon from Lattes in the Languedoc, and Chavignol from the village of the same name in the Loire Valley. From a straw mat, Monsieur Androuet picked up a very small ivory-colored cheese with a mottled skin and held it out for me to sniff. It had a faint but unmistakable scent of dried urine.

"These are Boutons de Culotte, and they come from the area around Mâcon in southern Burgundy."

I nodded, scribbled some more, and raised my eyebrows to express interest, though I continued to understand almost nothing. Did he just say "The buttons of underwear?" That couldn't possibly be right, but I wrote "underwear buttons" in my notebook, along with a string of "Oh God! Oh God! Oh God!" When we reached *les vaches*, cow's-milk cheeses, he lifted a wooden lid and held out a cheese for me to smell. It was punchingly pungent.

"Some people do not like Epoisses from Burgundy because they say it smells like *le pénis d'un vieil homme*."

The photographer guffawed. I smiled and nodded. Monsieur Androuet couldn't possibly have said what I thought he'd said, which I added to my notebook: "Smells like an old man's penis? Epoisses from Burgundy. Oh, dear Lord help me, help me, help me!" Happily, I lacked any experience that might qualify me to confirm or dispute Monsieur Androuet's olfactory observation, a thought that made me chuckle to myself. The relief at having been spared was fleeting, however, and I continued scrawling in my notebook and making slow, purposeful nods to gratefully acknowledge the information I was pretending to receive from Monsieur Androuet and understand.

Finally we reached a dim corner of the cellar where Monsieur Androuet announced, *"Les brebis."* The sheep? This was perplexing. Did sheep produce milk? They were mammals, so I guessed the females did.

"This is the world's best Roquefort — Gabriel Coulet, but Papillon black label is an outstanding cheese too," he said. The cheeses were wrapped in fine aluminum foil. "Roquefort was France's first AOC, in 1925."

"AOC?" I wrote. I had no idea what he was talking about, so I said, *"Oh, oui, c'est très jolie."*

Monsieur Androuet giggled, and Patrick muttered something under his breath. I'd look up AOC later — it stood for Appellation d'Origine Contrôlée, a designation certifying the cheese had been produced according to strict rules in a specific geographic location.

"Now let's go upstairs to taste some cheese," said Monsieur Androuet.

I gestured at the cheese around us in the cellar and said, *"Au revoir, mes amis,"* which made Monsieur Androuet chortle.

Back upstairs, we went into the restaurant where I had eaten with my family long ago. When I told Monsieur Androuet, *"J'ai mangé ma famille ici,"* Patrick muttered, *"Putain!"* — "Fuck!" Suddenly, I realized I'd just told Monsieur Androuet that I had actually eaten my family.

Unperturbed by this confession of cannibalism, he smiled kindly and poured Patrick and me glasses of white Mâcon. "A round white wine is better for a cheese tasting than a red one because the tannins in reds can mask the subtler flavors of a cheese," he told us, and put a white plate on the table before us. "On the plate you build a clock, a cheese clock," he said.

Then he started filling the plate with cheese from the glass display case. At noon was a Sainte-Maure de la Dragonnière, a creamy Loire Valley chèvre with a lactic tang; then a slice of heart-shaped Neufchâtel, a runny cow's-milk cheese with a velvety white rind that's been made in Normandy for more than a thousand years; a washed-rind Abbaye de Cîteaux cheese from the Burgundian abbey of the same name; a three-year-old Comté, a firm cow's-milk cheese from the Jura; a dab of Epoisses, the odorific cheese of Burgundy; and finally some Roquefort, the strong blue-veined cheese made from raw sheep's milk in the Aveyron region of southwestern France. Even with my feeble understanding of French, I grasped the idea that a good cheese plate starts with the mildest cheeses, usually goat cheeses, and then moves clockwise through gradually stronger ones to eleven o'clock.

I asked why raw milk was better than pasteurized, and Monsieur Androuet explained that the heat in the pasteurization process kills the bacteria the cheese needs in order to ripen, the process that gives it its texture and flavor. Only vaguely understanding what he meant, I jotted down, "Germs are good for cheese?"

"What is your favorite cheese, Alexandre?" he asked. Having recently lived in England, I loved Stilton, but that didn't seem an appropriate answer in Paris's best cheese shop, so I mumbled something about Cheddar and Swiss. He agreed that Cheddar was a very nice cheese but asked which Swiss I liked best, which stumped me, since the only Swiss cheese I knew was the hole-bored, plastic-wrapped blocks from the Stop & Shop supermarket in Westport, Connecticut.

"*Je suis fait de fromage! Ma tête est pleine de fromage!*" I babbled. What I'd really wanted to say was that I really loved his cheeses and that I had learned so much in the time we spent to-gether. Before we left, Monsieur Androuet signed a copy of *The Encyclopedia of Cheese,* a book he'd written, and another one about the history of his shop, both of which were, to my vast re-lief, in English. He also gave me a bag of cheeses.

My response in French, as we shook hands, was awkward but heartfelt: "Thank you so much! I will always be a cheese, and your cheeses should be nailed to the walls of the Louvre!" I was trying to say that his cheeses were masterpieces, or small edible works of art.

In the cab on the way back to the office, Patrick exploded: "Jesus, Alec! Your French is a train wreck! Do you have any idea what you just said?"

I turned away and looked out the window.

"You just told him you were made of cheese and that your head was full of cheese. Did they think you spoke French when they hired you in New York?"

They did, I told him.

Patrick grudgingly took pity on me that afternoon and told me some of the more interesting and important things Monsieur Androuet had said. A few hours later Christa, the bureau chief, came into my office with a big grin on her face.

"How did it go this morning?"

"Pretty well," I fibbed.

"Did you really tell that guy that his cheeses should be nailed to the walls of the Louvre?" she asked, and started laughing un-controllably.

That night when I got home, I opened the white paper bag Monsieur Androuet had given me. It contained several types of Swiss cheese, including Gruyère and Appenzeller, marked with little red-and-white Swiss flags; also, a thick slice of Roque-fort; a Camembert—the white-mold-flocked cheese he'd called the edible emblem of France; and another little one I didn't know, nestled into a brown-glazed ceramic ramekin—

Saint-Marcellin, L'Etoile du Vercors, according to the label. I looked up Vercors in my atlas and learned it was in the Isère department of southeastern France, between the cities of Valence and Grenoble. When unwrapped, it released a chalky lactic scent and was very soft when I poked it with my fingertip. I cut into it. It was so ripe, it had the consistency of very thick cream. Smeared on a torn hunk of baguette and accompanied by a swig of white wine, it was so immediately the best cheese I'd ever eaten in my life that I was moved. I decided I'd write to Monsieur Androuet and thank him, for the Saint-Marcellin and the other cheeses, but most of all for making me his student in the kindest of ways. But I'd have to find someone to help me with the letter, lest I inadvertently end up telling him that I'd smeared myself with Saint-Marcellin or committing some other linguistic faux pas.

That weekend, I read both of the books he'd given me, which I found fascinating, and then I wrote and rewrote my story. On Monday morning, I left it on Christa's desk — she reviewed all copy before it was sent to New York. At the end of the day she came into my office.

"This is really nice," she said. "You find graceful ways of explaining the technical stuff so that it's not boring. Oh, and don't worry about your French. Mine was crappy when I first moved to Paris too. You'll see, it'll just come along all on its own."

I certainly hoped so.

A few weeks later I wrote a story about eating oysters in Paris, in which I attempted to clarify the mind-bending complexity of a French oyster menu. Unlike the system used in the United States, which usually categorizes bivalves according to their provenance only, French oysters receive a more involved classification. First, they are tagged based on their shape: either *plates* (flats) or *creuses* (having convex shells). *Plates* may also be called Belons or Marennes, after the Atlantic coastal regions where they're cultivated, while *creuses* are occasionally billed as *portugaises* or *japonaises,* the two main types.

Then come the numbers. The shellfish are calibrated on a scale of 000 to 6, with the smallest number indicating the largest size, a system that could make sense only to a people whose word for ninety-nine is *quatre-vingt-dix-neuf,* which translates as "four times twenty plus nineteen." But wait, there are at least another dozen terms to contend with. Though Spéciales follow the standard sizing scale, these oysters are slightly larger and meatier. Fines de Claire spend two months in salty *claires,* or marshes. French oysters are also often identified by geographic origin, including, rather ghoulishly, Utah Beach in Normandy, or the name of the producer. Some of the latter are luxury brands well known among French oyster lovers, such as Gillardeau, purveyors of oysters so precious, the shell of each one is engraved with a G to distinguish it from counterfeits. Cadoret, a Breton company that has been in business for five generations, is most famous for its Belons. Happily, eating these sublime mollusks is a lot easier than ordering them.

The editors in New York liked the oyster piece as much as the one about Androuet, so a month later one of them called to ask me to do a critique of L'Ami Louis, the most famous bistro in Paris. "The idea is to tell the world what this place is really like," said the editor. I was grateful that I would get to discover this exorbitantly priced restaurant on an expense account, and I invited Natasha, an English friend who'd also never been there, to join me for lunch.

Both of us were shocked by the musty-tasting foie gras we shared to start. A lukewarm emaciated roast chicken for two came to the table with a side dish of cold, greasy potato straws. When we asked for more bread, the waiter reached over to the not-yet-cleared table next to us and dumped its half-full breadbasket into ours, which made us both laugh.

"Oh, Alec! This place is just too ghastly!" said Natasha.

What fascinated me most about this restaurant was why any-one would pretend to like it. I mulled over my meal for a few days and finally got to work:

> The pleasure of a meal at L'Ami Louis isn't gastronomic, because the food at this small shabby bistro in the 3rd ar-rondissement with a mythic reputation just isn't very good. Instead, what makes this place exciting to those who love it is that it's so perfect for preening in the company of other equally wealthy and deluded people who've been willingly inducted into the same cult . . . L'Ami Louis isn't about food, it's about a certain type of communal conspicuous consump-tion that bonds powerful people with its smugness.

I sent the piece off to New York. When, a few days later, on a Sunday, my phone rang rather late at home, I assumed it would be my mother or my sister.

"I just read what you wrote about L'Ami Louis," said John Fairchild. "And you don't know what the hell you're talking about. It's one of the best restaurants in the whole world! Fix this story tomorrow morning!" he said, and hung up.

Even though everyone in the office knew that I was writing about L'Ami Louis, no one had bothered to tell me that it was Mr. Fairchild's favorite restaurant in Paris.

Unwilling to extol its food, I made the piece as blandly repor-torial as possible. But even this lackluster restaurant was a vastly more interesting subject than menswear, and I continued to an-gle for every food assignment I could get.

4

ON THE SHORES OF MEMORY

L ong before Paris, there was the eternity of my childhood
in Westport, Connecticut, on Long Island Sound, fifty miles
northeast of New York City.

My mother always said we lived there because of its excellent public schools, but I think summer was the real reason. It
was my father's reward for his daily commute by train to his job
as an executive at a series of different textile companies in New
York City. An eternal fraternity boy whose happiest years were
those he'd spent at Amherst College, he loved to sail, play tennis,
and host cookouts. Though he'd probably have denied it, I think
he even liked the suburban marching drill of pushing a noisy
lawn mower back and forth, or at least the results of his labor. A
freshly mown lawn showed the world that order and discipline
reigned at his house.

My father was also almost shockingly handsome, tall and
lean, with chestnut-brown hair and eyes and a perfect Roman
nose. When he sent me into the hardware store to pick up the
paint or screws he'd ordered by telephone, the lady behind the
counter, her dark eyes outlined in turquoise eye shadow and her
hair piled high in a beehive, always asked, "Your father isn't
coming in?" When I shook my head, she'd sigh. "Your father's
the best-looking man I've ever seen in my whole life," she'd always say, a remark that made me uneasy.

Once my father had finished the lawn, my brother John and I had to rake up the grass clippings. The tedium of this chore early on Saturday mornings was broken only by the occasional sharp allium scent of the grass, which came from tiny onion seedlings gone wild. Before being pulled into the web of New York City suburbs, Westport had been an onion-farming town, as we'd learned in a local history lesson at school. Schooners with big canvas sails took on loads of onions from docks built out into the muddy tidal Saugatuck River and brought them to New York. The image of sailing ships full of onions fascinated me; it made my prim, quiet, well-groomed hometown, a place where nothing ever happened, seem more interesting. Even though I'd never lived anywhere else, I already wanted to.

My parents had moved to Connecticut from a New York City apartment shortly after I'd been born. Unlike my Boston-born mother, I loved Manhattan, eagerly looked forward to our infrequent trips there, and envied my cousins who lived in the city. Other than that, though, I was a lot more like my mother than my father.

She loved to read, had no interest in sports, and was passionately interested in politics, history, and art. Even though she had four children, with me the eldest, followed by my two brothers and my sister, she was dismissive of domesticity, making an occasional exception only for cooking because she loved good food. Instead, she regularly reminded the world she'd studied philosophy and art history at Mount Holyoke College and worked at Harvard Business School before getting married. She was involved in all sorts of local organizations, including a program to pair Westport families with those of UN diplomats for mutually elucidating weekend picnics, the library board, and groups supporting other causes. She was insistently not a housewife. "I don't think of you as my children," she would say to us. "I think of you as my friends."

Tall, blonde, and patrician, she was the kind of woman state police officers tipped their hats to — attractive, smiling, a mother who was admired at a polite distance by the mailman, the pharmacist, and the few other men to be found in Westport on weekdays, after the early-morning trains had transported the rest of the husbands to their offices in Manhattan.

If you saw my privileged, sociologically compatible parents together, you'd assume they were the perfect match. But they weren't — not at all. One of the rare things they agreed on was their love of the beach on hot summer Saturdays, under bright blue skies, after the chores were done. I loved it too.

In the heat of a summer's day, the tarred road that led down to the beach got gummy, so I had to walk on the sharp crabgrass along the shoulder, next to the muddy bank of the fish-stinky salt marsh after I'd decided to go home before my family did. On the other side of the road, a cement wall, painted white, was backed by a tall, overgrown privet hedge in flower, which gave off a fetid honey scent, like perfume applied to disguise sweat.

When I got to the main road, I would pause by the sign that said "Burying Hill Beach. Town of Westport, 1835" and choose my route. I could take the low road, which led past the Greens Farms train station, a small clapboard building painted barn-red. Or I could head up the hill past the big Victorian house with wide verandas, where, apparently, no one ever sat. The high road was longer but I often chose it because there were a lot of mean dogs along the low one, and it also passed by my Aunt Bette's house.

One day when I was ten, I decided to risk the shorter route on my way home, and my aunt surprised me. Her dark-blue Buick pulled up and its automatic window slid down. "Hello, sweetheart, can I give you a ride?" she said, smiling but looking a little alarmed. Since saying no was not an option, I climbed in and sat on the vinyl-covered bucket seat, chilled by the air conditioning. Aunt Bette was nice, but I knew she was a bit worried and uncomfortable. She had a horror of creating any sort of awkward situation with her sisters, including my mother.

"What are you doing out here, darling?"

I told her I was going home.

She fumbled in her pocketbook and gave me a round red-and-white-pinwheel peppermint wrapped in plastic. A successful real-estate agent in our well-heeled suburban town, she always carried these mints. "Were you down at the beach?" she asked.

"Yes."

"Did you tell your mother you were going home?"

I nodded.

"Are you not feeling well, dear?"

"No, I feel fine." I could see she was now completely confused.

"Too much sun then?"

I shook my head.

"Is your father at home?"

"No, he's at the beach."

Driving very slowly, she shook a cigarette from the pistachio-green quilted-leather cigarette case that rested on the transmission strip. Then she pushed in the dashboard lighter.

"Just too hot for you down there then, I guess," she said. She lit her cigarette and inhaled deeply. We drove along in silence for a minute. Then she said, "Say, why don't we go get an ice cream cone."

I didn't want an ice cream cone. I wanted to be alone in the hot empty house, the place where I'd invented a secret existence that summer. But I knew it would hurt her feelings if I said no. So I nodded, and we went to Carvel's on the Post Road, where I declined her tempting offer of a sundae; as much as I loved the salty pecans drowning in thick, slightly bitter chocolate sauce, it would take too long to eat. I really wanted to get home.

We licked the chocolate-dipped vanilla ice cream while sitting in the car, which smelled of my aunt's Coty perfume.

"I never eat the cone," she said. "It tastes like wet newspaper, don't you think?"

I nodded.

"Not that I've ever eaten wet newspaper," she said, trying to coax a chuckle out of me with one of her own. I got out of the car and threw the emptied cones away.

"I could run you back down to the beach if you'd like, sweetheart. A swim might be nice right now."

I told her I just wanted to go home. Her reluctance was palpable, and I felt sorry for her. She dropped me off at my house, waited until I got to the front door, waved at me, and drove away, feeling, I knew, as though she had failed.

What I couldn't explain to her, or myself, was that this bright day was just too painful for me. I really wanted to be alone in the shadowy rooms of my own very warm, occasionally creaky, empty house. I didn't want to swim with the other children at the beach or smell the sea or talk to anyone. Hiding was the only way I could make my big sadness go away when it came.

My mother would reluctantly agree when I told her I wanted to leave the beach and go home. She felt an embarrassed empathy for me, even when my actions didn't quite make sense to her. One day when I got home from school the previous fall, I had burst into tears and told her that sometimes I felt so sad, I wished I could just stop breathing—a confession that made her turn white. She'd asked me exactly why I was sad but seemed relieved when I said I didn't know.

Today she'd tried, just once, to encourage me to stay at the beach. "Are you sure you want to go, dear? It's such a lovely day."

Silence.

"Well, all right then, but be very, very careful," she said, and I'd nodded and set off on the two-and-a-half-mile hike home.

Tired after the long walk but elated by my solitude, I foraged and feasted, drinking maple syrup from the bottle, eating Cheddar cheese with Triscuits. When I was alone like this, I'd sort of cook, making the foods I craved, ones with hard, strong acidic tastes. I liked food that stung, even hurt, because this sharpness pricked the trance of normalcy.

Sometimes there was a slice of leftover pizza in the fridge. When there was meatloaf, I'd make a sandwich with lots of mayonnaise and Tabasco. Sometimes I went for a Chef Boyardee spaghetti kit — a box with a packet of spaghetti, a can of tomato sauce, and a smaller one filled with clumps of grated Romano cheese. My mother used to buy these kits for the Saturday nights when she and my father went out. The Chef Boyardee tomato sauce was actually sort of good, since it had tiny shreds of mushroom and wasn't too sweet. Because I loved garlic and mushrooms, I'd give it a boost with canned Pennsylvania Dutchman mushrooms sautéed in butter, lots of garlic powder, and a glug of Italian salad dressing.

Occasionally, I'd look at the heavy leather-bound album containing my parents' wedding photographs — my mother with a lace cap and veil leaving Trinity Church in Boston, my father in his morning suit with a white carnation pinned to his lapel. Then the reception at the Brae Burn Country Club, where the determined cordial enmity between my two grandmothers became intriguingly legible as they stood side by side before a sort of arc of acanthus leaves decorated with gardenias, my mother's favorite flower. Grandmother Jean, the New Yorker, looked chic in a suit, a blouse, and a fitted black hat, while Grandmother Drake, wearing a diamond brooch on her taffeta dress, had the air of a wealthy matron.

Sometimes I'd go upstairs and sit at my mother's dressing table, examining the contents of her jewelry box. Once in a while,

I'd put on some lipstick and some mascara too. All the while, I felt furtive and strange. I was sensing a difference, still opaque, and as terrifying as it was thrilling.

Most of the time, though, I'd lie on the couch in the living room and read. That summer I was working my way through a series of books from the public library called "The Land and the People of . . . ," which took me to places like Paraguay, Ghana, and Burma. Interspersed with these titles were others from a collection of books that my aunt, an editor at William Morrow in New York City, had given me. Each of these beautifully illustrated volumes was focused on a particular country, such as Norway, Ireland, or Spain, and a brother and sister living there. I found the depictions of their daily lives compulsively interesting. Although there were no reindeer or waterfalls plunging into sapphire-colored fjords in southwestern Connecticut, the Norwegian children picked wild strawberries just like we did in the meadows of the abandoned farm across the street, and of course the children who lived in Rome loved pizza as much as we did.

I returned to one book in this series over and over again. It was the story of two Parisian children sent south by train to visit their grandparents, who owned a hotel in Nice. In the dining car, they had vegetable soup, roast beef, and chocolate tarts. Their grandparents were waiting for them at the station in Nice, and when they reached the hotel, they saw mimosa flowering in the garden. But what was mimosa?

When I found a photograph of this flower with the help of the local librarian, I became obsessed with it. This is why one of the best and kindest presents my father ever gave me was two sprays of these yellow-gold blooms, wrapped in purple tissue paper, from a florist shop near his office in New York City. The fuzzy little yellow balls had a saffron-like perfume, and they instantly transported me to Nice and the bedroom the children shared, which had terra-cotta tile floors that were cool underfoot, French doors leading to a small balcony, and a bathroom with a claw-foot tub and mint-green tiles.

Every day the children went to the market in the Cours Saleya with their grandmother or the hotel cook and helped carry home baskets filled with tiny artichokes, zucchini flowers (to be turned into beignets), tomatoes, olives, lemons, and herbs. They spent a lot of time in the kitchen helping the hotel cook with small tasks, such as peeling onions to be caramelized as the topping for pissaladière, a sort of Niçoise pizza garnished with black olives and anchovies. The children were also sent to the bakery down the street several times a day to bring home armloads of freshly baked baguettes. The birthday of Françoise, the little girl, fell during the stay with her grandparents, and the cook made les petits farcis — baby vegetables, such as onions, tomatoes, and round zucchini, stuffed with bread crumbs, ground veal, garlic, and herbs. The book's pen-and-ink drawing of les petits farcis was irresistibly titillating to me, and that year I asked my mother if she could make them for my birthday dinner.

When she found a recipe in a cookbook from the public library, I was ecstatic. But in the kitchen, she said that the dish seemed like an awful lot of work, what with spooning stuffing into several dozen small hollowed-out vegetables, and that the dish varied from her meatloaf only in terms of presentation. "And in any event, darling, they don't have baby vegetables at the A & P." So I settled for artichokes — my mother would ask my father to bring some home from New York. He was usually willing to go on this occasional errand since he loved artichokes too. Maybe he was making a gastronomic feint at his New Orleans ancestry — my great-great-grandfather had, according to his obituary in the *New Orleans Picayune,* grown them in the garden of his house in the Faubourg Livaudais. The rest of my birthday meal never changed: wiener schnitzel with capers (I loved capers), noodles, and a maple-walnut cake.

But something about my yearning for les petits farcis had irritated my mother. She challenged me on it. "You know we have some very nice things to eat in the United States too."

"Like what?"

She paused. "Maple syrup, corn on the cob, good steaks—the beef in France is like shoe leather—and . . . chocolate-chip cookies and apple cider." Even though I liked everything she'd just mentioned, the list she offered somehow lacked the allure of les petits farcis.

That night at dinner, my mother said to my father, "Your son has become obsessed by the idea of French cooking."

"Where did that come from?" he asked me.

"I don't know. Maybe the book Aunt Dottie gave me about the French children who go to Nice."

The next day I couldn't find the book, which I'd left on an end table in the living room. I looked everywhere, asked everyone. No one knew where it was. When my father came home from work that night, I asked him too.

"I've put that book away for a while. You've read it a dozen times already, and you should read something new instead."

I think he reasoned that depriving me of the book would achieve some kind of bitter cure. But since I'd nearly memorized the story, I continued to draw pictures of Jean-Marc and Françoise sitting on the beach in Nice, wearing rubber sandals so that they could walk on *les galets* (the large smooth stones that cover the main beach), and though I only vaguely sensed it, a seed was germinating in my imagination—I'd make my own escape.

Eventually, my mother persuaded my father to give the book back to me, and he grudgingly did so. "You'll find out someday," he said when he handed it to me. "There's just no place like home."

And though I was only ten and couldn't have explained the concept, I wondered if he wasn't being ironic.

I was lying on the couch — reading, for the hundredth time, about how much Jean-Marc and Françoise looked forward to a snack of socca, a thin crepe made with chickpea flour (what was a chickpea?) and heated on a large round metal pan, when they went to the market with their grandmother — when someone spoke my name. My heart jumped like a rabbit.

"Come, Alec. We're going back to the beach," my father said.

As we drove by the dairy farm, where a hot breeze wafted the fecal scent of baked cow pies toward us from the rolling green pastures, he spoke.

"Why do you do that?"

I shrugged.

"I want you to explain to me why you go home in the middle of the day like that. It's just not normal, and you're not doing it ever again. Do you hear me?"

I nodded as faintly as I knew how.

"Ever! And I mean not ever again!"

At the beach, people looked up as I crossed the hot sand with my father. So they knew that he'd gone to get me. My mother patted a place next to her on the bedspread, and I sat down.

"I'm sorry, sweetheart," she said quietly. "But don't worry. Someday you'll have a nice big suitcase, and you'll be free as a bird to go wherever you like."

5

CRACKING MY SHELL

When I went away from home for the first time, two sum- mers later, it wasn't with a big suitcase, but a heavy backpack with an aluminum frame. After my mother and I had finished packing it, I slung it onto my back for the first time, and she saw me wince, because it dug in hard.

"Well, I suppose you can always just carry it by its straps or something," she said. "Now go down to the beach and have sup- per with your cousins and everyone else." The following morn- ing, my parents would drive me to Wayne, Pennsylvania, the Philadelphia suburb that was the departure point for Camp Ad- venture, a two-month traveling camp for boys. They had en- rolled me in it.

The sun hadn't set yet, but we were eating early because my cousins from California had just arrived that morning and were supposed to be tired. But they weren't. My mother had picked up a bucket of Colonel Sanders fried chicken, potato salad, and coleslaw for the kids' dinner. The adults would be eating lob- sters and corn on the cob after we'd gone to bed.

"Are you excited about your trip?" my cousin Nancy asked me, when I sat down on the old flowered bedspread with her and the others.

"A little bit," I said, and took the paper plate of food my grandmother had served me, along with a plastic fork and knife and a napkin. I nibbled at the chicken, but I wasn't hungry, and the liquid that sluiced out of my coleslaw into the middle of the plate had a sharp, sweet taste that nauseated me.

Grandmother Drake watched us from a folding chair, and though she had the local newspaper in her lap, she wasn't reading. It was stressful for her to be tasked with keeping an eye on seven children — me, my two brothers and sister, and my three cousins, at the beach. We all watched the kites in the pale blue sky as a June dusk crept over Long Island Sound. The kites ducked and weaved as boys ran along the beach at the water's edge, trying to keep them aloft in the warm, slackening breeze.

We were so happy to see our cousins, Nancy, Richard, and Barbara. Richard, very blond and wearing thick black-framed glasses, kneeled and turned his soda bottle into a microphone. "Tonight in Phnom Penh, there were bombs falling from low-flying planes and lots of people were killed," he said, aping someone he'd seen on TV. "The Viet Cong are all over the place too," he said with a laugh. He was wearing a Hang Ten shirt, the kind favored by surfers; its logo was a pair of tiny bare feet. But that was only one of the reasons I envied Richard. The California cousins lived in a house with a swimming pool and palm trees, and they went to Disneyland often. California was sunny, new, and glamorous, unlike Connecticut, which was cold, old, and eager to scold. Their family had moved west when my uncle's company had left New York City for Los Angeles.

"Alec, come sit next to me," said Grandmother Drake. When I settled in, cross-legged, next to her, I entered the invisible tent of her perfume. "You should eat some more, dear. Tomorrow's the beginning of your big adventure," she said, nodding at the fried chicken leg and the biscuit I'd perched on the edge of my plate, to keep it dry. She was so pretty, my grandmother, and it was still a shock to see her on the beach, in front of the summerhouse she'd rented for a month, wearing neatly ironed cornflower-blue culottes, a white blouse, and a straw hat. Parlors were her natural habitat, with their porcelain bibelots, crystal candy dishes, precious jade and ivory carvings, thick oriental carpets, and sofas, stuffed with feathers and covered in damask, that sighed when you sat on them. Best of all, the closet in her television room was stocked with jars of buttery Macadamia nuts from Hawaii. We children weren't supposed to eat them, but we did. Grandmother Drake had lived in a big house in Boston but moved down to Connecticut to be closer to us — Uncle Grant, Aunt Bette, and Aunt Janet, though Aunt Janet and her family had eventually gone to California.

"Oh no!" said my brother John, pointing at the sky. We looked up to see a fancy magenta-colored box kite, with a long streaming tail, rising higher and higher into the deepening blue sky of early evening.

"Oh, what a shame," said my grandmother. "That poor little boy. He should have been more careful."

My sobs came so suddenly, I heard them as if they were someone else's. My sister was by my side immediately. And Nancy and Barbara came and sat next to me too.

"Alec, are you all right? Are you OK? What's the matter?" asked my sister.

"Maybe the kite will land somewhere, and he'll get it back," said Nancy.

I couldn't stop crying.

My grandmother stood and held out her hand. "Alec, come with me now." To my siblings and cousins she said, "I'll be back in a minute. You finish eating your dinner, and don't leave this blanket for any reason."

My grandmother was embarrassed. She knew my tears had nothing to do with the lost kite, but she would never have said so. As we walked across the sand, people looked up, puzzled. The mothers were concerned. What had happened? But I saw one of the fathers shake his head. There was no skinned knee or elbow to explain my tears.

In the kitchen, the window was streaked with condensation. The two big aluminum pots on the stove awaited the corn that my mother and Aunt Janet were husking at the table. The blue smoke from their cigarettes rose from a clamshell midway between their glasses of cocktail sherry.

"Mother, you shouldn't have left the children alone on the beach," said Aunt Janet as she rushed out the door.

"Come," said my mother, and she brought me upstairs to a room under the bare wooden eaves, which smelled of salt and cedar. We sat on the bed. "What's the matter?"

I didn't know the answer to the question that had brought my tears: Was I going away or being sent away? "Whose idea was it to send me to camp anyway?" I finally sobbed.

My mother pushed her hair back from her forehead, got up, and turned on the fan. "I think it was all of ours, and maybe even a little bit yours too," she said.

We'd been preparing for my trip for months, or ever since Mr. Shaw, a junior high school science teacher who ran the camp, drove up from Pennsylvania to have lunch with us one Sunday. He'd brought slides, which we watched in the den. There were pictures of excited boys in inflatable boats riding the rapids on the Colorado River, sitting around a campfire with what looked like a real tepee in the background, and swimming in a big, still blue lake, which was doubtless ice cold. The metallic rattle of the projector as it displayed each new image was exciting but also alarming. As much as I loved seeing these pictures, it was impossible for me to imagine myself among these gangs of grinning boys.

We ate a fancy Sunday lunch — roast beef with roasted potatoes, creamed onions, red currant jelly, green-bean casserole made with cream of mushroom soup, salad, and pineapple upside-down cake, with a maraschino cherry plugging the hole in each slice of the canned fruit.

"There will be hiking, fishing, archery, horseback riding,

canoeing, even a little bit of mountain climbing," Mr. Shaw, a bachelor, told my parents. "Lots of fresh air and exercise, but of course we'll also be visiting some monuments and museums too, especially when we get to Mexico. Alec, have you ever heard of the Aztecs?"

My twelve-year-old mind reeled at the stupidity of his question, and my mother kicked me gently under the table. "Their leader was Montezuma before the Spanish destroyed their empire," I said, and caught a flicker of surprise on his face, where the red wine he'd eagerly gulped at lunch had brightened the starbursts of rosy veins on his cheekbones.

After lunch my mother made coffee, and Mr. Shaw and my father went into the living room. "Why don't you kids go over to the field for a while," my mother said, referring to the abandoned farm across the street. My parents were going to tell Mr. Shaw that something bad had happened to me while they were on a Mediterranean cruise paid for by my grandmothers. "Your parents are going away to get to know each other again," my paternal grandmother had explained to me, when me, my brothers, and my sister went to stay with her at her summerhouse on Long Island while they were away. I hated that Mr. Shaw would know the secret when I myself couldn't remember exactly what had happened.

Later in the afternoon, just before he left, Mr. Shaw cupped my shoulder in his strong hand and squeezed it. "You're going to have such a great time with us this summer, Alec," he said, and ruffled my hair with obvious pity.

We'd be camping out for the whole two-month trip, which would take us across the country to Colorado, down into the Southwest and Texas, over the border into Mexico, and then back to Wayne. This list of equipment I'd need included everything from an aluminum canteen in an olive-colored canvas sling to a rubber sheet to put under my sleeping bag when it rained.

My mother decided there was no reason I couldn't use some of the Boy Scout camping equipment belonging to my older cousins who lived in nearby Ridgefield. So instead of the backpack with a sturdy H-shaped frame that had been specified, I went away with a triangular one, which had been explicitly discouraged. ("They dig into your back and often break" was the notation, written in Mr. Shaw's neat purple hand on the mimeographed page, and eventually it did.)

Like most trips, this one wasn't anything like what I imagined it would be. As we campers pulled out of the school parking lot, our parents stood by their cars, waving goodbye, and fifteen minutes later on the Pennsylvania Turnpike, Mr. Shaw said, "OK, boys, USA, here we come!"

I was sitting in the third seat of a pale-blue International Harvester station wagon, and my thighs stuck to the vinyl seat. I listened as the other boys chatted and joked among themselves. There were fifteen of us — Mr. Shaw, two counselors, and twelve boys who mostly came from New Jersey, New York, and Pennsylvania — traveling in two cars. All of the boys, except for me and Tim "Tiny" Rosen from Brooklyn, had done Camp Adventure before. Tiny and I were also the only twelve-year-olds; in fact, I wouldn't be twelve until October. The others were fifteen or sixteen.

Tiny was sitting next to me, so I made an attempt at conversation, asking him something about school. His answer was monosyllabic. I volunteered that I was from Connecticut, which elicited no response. I persisted, and learned that his father owned a chain of shoe stores in Brooklyn. I told him I wanted to go to Coney Island someday.

"It's not that great," he replied.

We hadn't gone even a hundred miles, and already I feared the trip would be a failure. No one had said it, because no one needed to, but I knew the hoped-for outcome of this experience:

that I, a shy, bookish introvert, would be transformed into a regular boy.

The car radio was on, and "Tighten Up," by Archie Bell and the Drells, came on. Once again I took the conversational plunge. I loved this song, and so did Sally, our nice cleaning lady. She wore a stiff wig and swayed her hips while ironing shirts, skirts, and handkerchiefs in the kitchen once a week in a hiss of steam.

"Do you like this song, Tim?"

"It's OK." When I started to say something else, he held up his hand. "It's too hot to talk, OK?"

The shadows under the trees that lined the Pennsylvania Turnpike were darkening to purple, and just as I felt a flicker of melancholy, I heard the clinking of the turn signal. We were getting off the highway, which was sort of exciting, and were heading somewhere to spend our first night. We drove for a while and reached a state park, where we pulled up to a sentry box faced with logs sawn in half. In it stood a lady wearing a green shirt with epaulets, and Mr. Shaw paid her. She leaned forward, smiling, and peered into the car. "You all get a move on, and you can swim in the lake before the lifeguard goes off duty!" she said.

That night there would be no time for a swim because once our gear was unloaded and a counselor had made a couple of thermoses of lukewarm orange Kool-Aid, Mr. Shaw blew a whistle. We sat down in the grass around a flame-blackened circle of rocks and a heap of dead ashes and scorched beer cans.

"Boys," he announced, "as most of you know, every night when we stop to pitch camp, there will be chores — getting water, doing KP duty, pitching tents if rain is expected, doing the dishes." He continued with specific guidelines. The counselors would assign us our tasks and when they needed to be done, and we were to follow their instructions. No one was ever to leave the group, aside from going to the toilet, or, in the morning, for a wash, without telling a counselor. That night there was no KP because we'd be having a cookout, with ice cream afterward, so we were free until the whistle blew again. The older boys immediately divided into two groups and took off with their Frisbees. Tiny and I stood off to one side and watched until Mr. Shaw saw us and blew his whistle.

"Tiny, you go with this group, and Alec, you go with the other."

I walked toward my group and told the counselor I needed to go to the bathroom and would be back in a minute. Then I headed down the path, past the bathrooms, and walked deep into a field of tall, warm grass. I sat on the ground cross-legged, pulled from my pocket the little orange leatherette diary with a silver globe stamped on the cover, the symbol of the 1964–65 New York World's Fair. I opened it with the tiny brass key that I kept on a large triangular paper clip, which I'd taken from my father's desk.

"May 30, 1966. Somewhere in Pennsylvania," I wrote. I described the day and listed the names of all the other boys. I wrote about how much I already missed everyone back in Connecticut, how I'd seen a car with a North Dakota license plate, and how I hoped Tiny and I might be friends.

"Alec, come help me make dinner," said Mr. Shaw, looking down at me with a furrowed brow as I sat in my nest of crushed grass. I walked behind him, and then he stopped and turned.

"Why didn't you want to play Frisbee with the other boys? Were they not nice to you?"

"No, no, I just needed to write some things down."

We walked in silence for a minute, and then he paused and leaned toward me. "It'll take some time to get to know everyone, Alec. But you'll see, we'll all end up being good friends."

I nodded. Then he picked me up and gave me a hard, whiskery kiss on the mouth. He smelled of lime cologne, sweat, and

beer, like my dad sometimes. His kiss was disgusting and exciting. I couldn't explain why, but it hadn't surprised me.

"From now on, you should call me Joe." He walked behind
me. "Alec, are you afraid of snakes?"

I nodded.

"Well, then it's not a good idea to wander off by yourself like
that, because in the places we'll be going, there might be snakes.
Lots of snakes."

When we got back to the camp, everyone else was sitting
around a fire that was burning in the circle of rocks. "Alec went
up to the phone booth in the camp office to call his dad and
wish him a happy birthday," Mr. Shaw said. We ate hot dogs and
canned baked beans with inedible jelly-like chunks of fat, and
we toasted marshmallows on sticks and had bowls of melted
strawberry ice cream from one of the coolers. As we ate, the
boys who'd done Camp Adventure before told funny stories
about other trips, about a boy who'd fallen into a latrine and
someone else who had been bitten on the bottom by a spider.
Then Mr. Shaw announced, "Lights out, boys. Sleep well."

We slept out in the open. In my sleeping bag, it was too hot,
but when I unzipped it, the mosquitoes came, and so it went all
night, though I was occasionally distracted by the stars and a recurring lump in my throat.

Whatever the next few weeks might bring, there was nothing
I could do about it. As much as I wanted to be like my handsome
half-Argentine second cousin Bart, who had a cherry-sized Ad-
am's apple and a Firebird convertible and made his girlfriends
squeal in the chauffeur's apartment over the garage of Grandmother Jean's summerhouse, I realized, with a sinking feeling,
that I'd still be me. Even something as extreme as a two-month
camping trip wasn't going to change that. My wishful thinking was as futile as alchemy. If there was one thing I hoped the
trip might accomplish, it would be to spare me the fate of being

"a bit of a fruit loop," as I'd once overheard my father ruefully describe me to a bunch of other equally beery Cub Scout troop leaders. I intuited that "fruit loop" meant that I wasn't enough of a boy's boy. It was sad and exhausting to be such a disappointment. It was confusing too.

On Friday nights I'd stay up late with my father and keep him company after everyone else had gone to bed. We watched old westerns on the black-and-white TV and ate popcorn; both of us liked best of all the burned kernels that stuck to the bottom of the popper. He drank Ballantine ale, one after another, and I was allowed a Pepsi or two. I listened while he rambled, often telling the same stories about going trout fishing with his father at the camp they had on a lake in the Adirondacks and how they'd sit in silence for hours, waiting for a nibble. Or he'd talk about the time he'd spent in Japan in the occupation army, or as a student at Amherst College, the best years of his life, he often said. Or about an inventor he'd met named Clancy, who'd come up with a new way of making yarn that was going to make us very rich.

"Sandy, please come upstairs now, and let Alec go to bed." Mom was standing in the door, with white cream on her face.

"We'll be right up," he'd say. "Let me spend some time with my boy, Ducky." They called each other by their college nicknames, Sandy and Ducky. We always stayed up until the screen went blank. In the morning, though, everything was different, and once, when he overheard me telling a story to some friends in the backyard, he called me inside and said, "I wish I could pull your imagination up like a weed and throw it away!"

After a few weeks on the road, no one looked for me anymore when I disappeared after we'd stopped for the day. On rainy days, I'd spend hours sitting at a sheltered picnic table and writing. When it was sunny, I'd walk as far away as I dared and draw pictures of plants. I pressed flowers and leaves in my diary and I listened to my transistor radio. I wrote dozens of postcards and looked forward to every prearranged mail stop, where I got a few letters and cards. In Connecticut, my cousin Richard had finally tried a lobster — "They look like monsters, but they're good!" — and my sister was hating Brownie camp. Grandmother Drake, Mom's mom, sent a monogrammed AGD (Agnes Grant Drake) note card with a ten-dollar bill in it, and so did Grandmother Jean, Dad's mom, along with a "lazy little letter":

> Thinking of you, darling, and loving you very much. Camping can be a bit uncomfortable, so look up at the stars, enjoy the good fresh air, and write down everything you see and think in your diary so we can talk about it when you get home. Your aunt is here and playing tennis over at the Coleses' every day, and your cousins come up from NYC next week. I'm thinking of you driving through endless fields of corn and wheat and sitting by the fire at night. I wonder if there's some storytelling before you go to bed? If there is, you should join in, because you know how to tell a tale.

We drove for days, and after miles and miles of corn, we crossed the Mississippi River, and I saw the huge, gleaming steel Gateway to the West in Saint Louis. During a rainy week, we slept in a hangar at an air force base in Kansas, where the other boys climbed into the cockpit of a fighter jet. We saw a wolf one night just after we got to Colorado, and a week later, we woke up at dawn on the edge of the Grand Canyon after traveling all night and had a campfire-cooked breakfast of bacon and eggs instead of the usual cereal. In New Mexico, we slid down huge dunes of white sand that squeaked and was almost as fine as flour, and in Texas, there were derricks, big metal birds that relentlessly pecked the ground and pulled oil out of the earth.

We stopped in a dusty little town for supplies, and Mr. Shaw announced that it was a "free lunch," which meant that we were on our own for an hour or two to eat. I went into a luncheonette that had a red counter marked with cigarette burns. I perched on a mud-colored Naugahyde stool and ordered a grilled cheese with bacon and an iced tea. I was writing in my new diary, a notebook with a marbled cover I'd bought after filling up the old one, when a man wearing a big black cowboy hat sat down next to me.

"So where are you from, son?"

"Brazil."

"Is that right? You sure don't look like a Brazilian."

"Well, we've been living in Connecticut for a while now."

"That's way up north, isn't it?"

I nodded.

"You're a long ways from home, aren't ya? Did ya run away?"

I shook my head and gave him an outline of our group's itinerary.

"That's quite a trip you got in front of ya there, boy," he said. Then he told the waitress, "Give this Brazil nut a piece of that pie, baby."

She was a sturdy lady in a mint-green nylon dress. She giggled, took a cherry pie from the plastic pie keeper, and sliced me a wedge.

"You have a good trip then, son," said the man after he'd finished his coffee, and we shook hands. He paid up, and after the screen door had slammed behind him, I felt proud of myself for participating in such a grown-up conversation.

The waitress lit a cigarette. "Now aren't you a strange little critter," she said. "What did you do that made them send you away like this? So far from home, and you look like a little bird." She shook her head.

I rubbed the condensation off my water glass and hated her.

"You want some vanilla ice cream on that pie?"

I shook my head.

"So what's it like back where you're from?"

I told her there were lots of trees in Connecticut, which was not at all like Texas, where everything was dried out and dusty, and that we went to the beach a lot and my father worked in New York City and took a train there every day.

"New York City! Would I ever like to get up there one day and see a show! I don't think I'd like it much, though—too many people—but just to see a show and do some shopping. Of course, thing is, they say almost no one up there speaks English, they're all foreigners, from all over, maybe even Brazil, like you." She chuckled. "Far as I've ever been was one time up to Albuquerque to get a tooth pulled." She cleared the dishes left by the man who'd been sitting next to me and wiped the counter with a sponge. "Must be costing a whole bunch of money, this fancy camp thing you're doing," she said.

"My grandmothers paid for it," I explained. She offered me some more iced tea, and I said no, because I had to be back at the car by 3 p.m.

"Do your mom and pop know you're going to Mexico?"

I nodded. "This trip was their idea," I told her. I paid for my meal and left a quarter on the counter as a tip. I got down from my stool and started walking toward the door.

"Hey, you! You get back here!" The waitress came out from behind the counter and hugged me so hard, it knocked the wind out of me. "You be real careful now, you hear me? Mexico, now that's one crazy place! Even for a Brazilian!"

Just as boys did at home, the others left me alone. They were polite but that was all, which really didn't bother me, since I was so busy writing in my diary. The best part of the trip was the least expected—those days when we had a free meal on our own. I ate creamed corn pie in Ohio, a big fat sausage with German potato salad in Missouri, one of the best cheeseburgers I'd ever had in a Colorado farm town, and my own weight in onion rings. I just couldn't get enough of anything coming out of the wire cages in the thousands of deep-fat fryers between New York City and Phoenix.

I made discoveries too. There were the big, bready Czech dumplings called knedlíky, which tasted delicious with meatloaf and gravy in a Kansas gas-station café, and later, smoky pinto beans cooked in a clay pot by an old Navajo lady in New Mexico. Best of all, everywhere we went in the West there was Mexican food, which I immediately loved.

We crossed the Rio Grande, which looked more like a muddy stream than a river, in Eagle Pass, Texas, on a rattling old bridge with metal girders, and then we were in Piedras Negras, Mexico. I'd been to Canada once, but that didn't count as an eye-opening visit to an unfamiliar land, since one of the first things I'd seen after we drove into Quebec was a Sears, Roebuck. The people there spoke French, but otherwise everything looked pretty much like the United States.

Mexico felt more like a real foreign country. We had to change money, and one of the peso coins I got had an eagle on it, like Montezuma's. It was hot and everyone else in the car slept, except for the counselors in the front seat. Mexico smelled different, like burning sugar, charred rubber, and sweat. Cactuses grew along the side of the road, children waved, and skinny dogs chased our cars. We got a flat tire and sat in the car by the side of the road for a long time until Mr. Shaw came back with the repaired tire. We wouldn't get to the campground by night, so we slept in an abandoned gas station and ate canned beef stew heated in the embers of a fire made from sticks and thorny brush. In the night, dogs barked and something howled, and every once in a while I'd hear metal hitting stone when Mr. Shaw threw a beer can into the fire.

One of the boys had an uncle in Mexico City, a dentist, and he arranged for us to spend a night sleeping on wrestling mats on the floor of the gym at the Mexico City Hebrew Center. It was the first time in over a month that I'd slept inside, and I surprised myself by missing the stars and preferring the cold night air to the warm, chlorine-scented gym. But in the morning there was a delicious breakfast in the cafeteria, fried eggs with salsa and tortillas, and thick, gently bitter hot chocolate. Mr. Shaw told us to eat quickly because we were going somewhere. I was surprised when we packed up completely and then went downstairs. There were taxis waiting for us.

"Boys, you're going to Acapulco!"

This was the special surprise that was part of every Camp Adventure season. We flew on a shiny aluminum Mexicana plane, and I could see the Pacific Ocean out my window as we were landing.

At the motel, we had three rooms—two for the boys and one for the counselors. Mr. Shaw said, "You're on your own today, boys, until dinner. Enjoy the beach! Be back here by 6 p.m., and don't forget, the sun here is very strong, so lots of suntan lotion, and whatever you do, no ice, no raw vegetables, and no ice cream. Eat only cooked food here, please. And don't leave anything valuable on the beach when you go swimming."

Soon I lay alone on my thin white motel towel, which was too short for me, and listened to the Spanish on my Zenith transistor radio. I didn't have any suntan lotion, so when I started feeling hot, I went for a swim in the big, warm, foamy waves that came smashing onto the sand. I zipped my beaded change purse, filled with folded dollars and peso coins, into a pocket in my billowing plaid bathing trunks and wallowed for an hour. The surf was strong, and I got egg-beatered a few times. When I'd had enough, I went back to my towel, lay down, and promptly fell asleep.

When I woke up, my radio was gone, and I went to a Denny's for lunch. I sat at the counter and ordered a chicken-salad sandwich and an iced tea. The air conditioning was so cold, it made me shake, and I'd just paid the bill when Mr. Shaw found me.

"Oh, Jesus Christ, Alec. You've got one helluva sunburn." He put me in a bathtub of cold water, and after about an hour, I had to use the toilet every couple of minutes. Mr. Shaw gave me some pills and told me to get out of the tub. He toweled me off and lathered me with a thick, white cream, and then I slept until the next morning, when we flew back to Mexico City. I had missed the divers jumping off the cliffs with torches and the restaurant with the brass band and the real Mexican food.

In Mexico City a doctor covered me with ointment and wrapped me in a sheet, and I spent the afternoon lying on a wrestling mat while everyone else went to a museum. We got mail that night, and I received a letter from my father, who wrote, "I hear that you're not being very friendly. If you want to have friends, you have to make an effort. They don't just show up like birds." I wondered how he knew that I hadn't been making an effort and concluded that Mr. Shaw must have written to him.

One day in a market in Oaxaca, something funny happened. I realized I liked being alone. No, I loved being alone. I wandered through the market and saw amazing things, like the smoldering skull of an animal being sold to eat and the bloody, glistening, dark red ropes of something hanging on a hook. Indigenous women with thick black braids were plucking chickens, and there was food everywhere. Something smelled really good, so I stopped at one stall where a man was grilling pieces of meat. "*Cabrito!*" he said, and smiled, showing a gold front tooth. He filled a tortilla with the meat, added some chopped tomato, lettuce, and sauce, and handed it to me. I hesitated, because of the raw vegetables.

"Is gift! No pay!"

I couldn't refuse and knew Mr. Shaw still had some of the upset-stomach pills I'd taken in Acapulco. The meat was pungent, chewy, and smoky. I couldn't wait to look up *cabrito* in my

Spanish-English dictionary and find out what it was. Back in the car, I did so, and I could barely believe my eyes. On a half dozen postcards I wrote, "I ate a goat today!"

It was a letdown when we crossed the border back into Texas. Everything was too neat and quiet, and people didn't smile as much as they did in Mexico. I missed the loud, happy music, the bright colors, and most of all the food. I liked the Mexicans a lot too, so I was surprised when everybody else in the car cheered after the bulging man in the pale-brown uniform, big pinched gray hat, and green sunglasses waved us through the tollbooth, and we were back in the United States. Near Galveston, we slept on a beach and got eaten alive by sand flies. In Houston we went to an amusement park and visited a space museum. When we crossed into Louisiana, Mr. Shaw told everyone that I had a great-great-grandfather who'd been a pirate in the Gulf of Mexico and lived in New Orleans. It was true, and a good story, but I could see the other boys looking doubtfully at me, searching for some trace of this buccaneer. We ate delicious spicy shrimp gumbo in New Orleans, where, through a pair of swinging doors, I saw some ladies dancing on a bar, shiny tassels on the tips of their breasts.

Our Pennsylvania license plates drew a cool response from the families at a campground in rural Georgia, and the Civil War battlefields we visited bored me; it was so hot and they were so sad. With every day that passed I was getting more and more worried. Despite doubts, I was still nursing some small hope that I had changed, that maybe I'd toughened up and become more like the boys I'd just traveled with for two months.

When we pulled into the school parking lot in Wayne, I saw my mother standing in the sun with my tow-headed sister, next to a car I didn't recognize. They'd gotten a new station wagon, a forest-green Ford Country Squire. My father was still in this car with my brothers. Once the cars filled with campers had parked, all the parents came and clustered around us, and there was a lot of handshaking and hugging. The counselors unloaded our packs and our duffle bags and put them on the lawn.

My father walked up to me. "How was the trip, Alec?"

"It was good. I learned a lot."

He picked up the duffle bag, I took the pack, and we walked to the car. I opened the door and was about to get in when my father pulled me by the shoulder.

"Aren't you going to say thank you to Mr. Shaw and goodbye to the boys?" Mr. Shaw was surrounded by a bunch of parents, but he broke away when he saw me.

"Thank you, Joe. It was a very interesting trip, and I learned a lot."

"I think he grew five inches this summer," Mr. Shaw said to my father. "Just shot up like a weed." The two men stood there smiling at each other for what seemed like an eternity.

"It would be great if you wanted to join us again, Alec. Next summer I'm thinking we'll head up through the Dakotas and the Pacific Northwest. You let me know, and it would be really nice to hear from you during the year in the meantime."

Dad shook hands with Mr. Shaw, who turned away to speak with another family group. We stood there for a minute, watching the crowd, and Dad jingled the change in the pocket of his madras shorts.

"Can we go now, Dad?"

He looked at me and shook his head.

"See ya, Alec."

I turned around. Tiny was standing there, with a man who had fuzzy red hair.

"Hello, I'm Paul Roth," the man said to my father, "and this is my wife, Rose."

Mrs. Roth smiled. "Tiny tells me you spent the whole summer scribbling away in your diaries," she said to me. "What a nice studious boy," she said to my father.

"Have a safe trip home," said Mr. Roth, and Tiny added, "Adios."

We continued to stand in the parking lot for another minute. "Is that all?" my father asked me. I didn't really have anything to say to anyone else, so I turned and walked quickly toward the car.

In an Amish restaurant, we ate flaky biscuits, meatloaf with onion gravy, string beans dressed with vinegar, and buttery mashed potatoes served by older waitresses wearing lacy white bonnets and long gray dresses.

"You sure sent us some dopey postcards while you were away," my father said. "All you ever wrote about was what you'd eaten—"

My mother interrupted. "Tell us about Mexico."

I tried, but there was no way to describe the serenity of the jade-green agave plantations in the early morning mist or why the charred smell of a fresh tortilla made me happy. So I talked about Acapulco and how the Pacific Ocean had been as warm as a baby's bath. I added that we'd been in an earthquake in Mexico City.

"Nonsense," said my father.

But it was true. There had been an earthquake, and I had saved the front page of a newspaper to prove it. I kept coming back to what I'd eaten — candied cactus paddles in Mexico and an alligator burger in Louisiana.

For dessert, the nice older waitress with steel-framed glasses brought a shoofly pie to the table, with a bowl of whipped cream. My mother cut and served it, and all of sudden, my sister piped up. "Alec, your voice has changed!" I wasn't aware of it, but my voice had changed that summer, and in more ways than one.

That night, I couldn't sleep in the soft bed of the air-conditioned motel room I shared with my brothers and sister. I didn't want to be part of a family anymore. I wanted to be alone. I wanted to be outside. I wanted to be back in Mexico. I wanted to just keep going, and this made me cautiously happy.

I couldn't have explained this flicker of joy, but I dimly sensed that maybe the trip had been a success after all. Oh, certainly not in the intended way. I hadn't ended up wanting to toss a Frisbee or join the boys skinny-dipping at night in the Gulf of Mexico. Instead, I'd learned how to travel. All I really wanted to do was to go to different places and eat, and then write it all down.

6

A MAP OF MY PALATE

When I was growing up, the foods I loved most had either been brought north from the South by the African American domestic servants who worked for my paternal grandmother or to the United States by immigrants from villages in Italy, Poland, and Greece.

We ate Southern cooking when we went to Sunday lunch at Grandmother Jean's. Emma, the African American woman from South Carolina who cooked for her, made the world's best fried chicken (she put flour and her "secret" seasonings, including Lawry's Seasoned Salt, in a brown paper bag and shook the cut-up pieces of fowl in it) and also country captain, a Low Country chicken stew cooked in a tomato sauce spiced with curry powder, served on white rice, and garnished with raisins and sliced almonds. At friends' houses I discovered other foods I loved, such as the rugelach made by an Austrian grandmother or the dill-brightened stuffed cabbage rolls cooked by a Romanian-born mother.

In the kitchen of my elementary school, with its tiled floor and walls the color of vanilla, hardworking women wearing white aprons, orthopedic shoes, and hairnets cooked some of the most delicious things I've ever eaten — spaghetti with homemade marinara sauce and meatballs, handmade pierogi filled with potato puree or cheese and topped with crisp fried onions, and moussaka slathered with béchamel sauce. They made everything from scratch, and many years later, when I ran into one of these cooks in a local discount store and thanked her, she was startled. She blushed and said, "Oh, you're very welcome, but I did nothing special—it was a holy honor to cook for you children."

At home, the food that ginned my appetite was summer fare because it had the most flavor. I loved barbecues and the produce found at the two farm stands in Westport. Rippe's, on the Post Road at the corner of Turkey Hill Road, was a simple wooden shed with roll-up garage doors. Old Mr. Rippe, a dour Yankee, had a soft spot for my mother, so when we stopped there, she'd come away with a pungent nosegay of fresh basil or a couple of extra ears of sweet corn. Wakeman's, the other stand, had better corn but didn't offer the variety of Rippe's, where bunches of gold, vermillion, and mauve zinnias bound in hairy twine stood in galvanized zinc buckets, and shiny eggplants, yellow squash and zucchini, green onions, and other vegetables were displayed in wooden crates on sawhorse counters. By August, though, the main reason people pulled off the road there was the tomatoes, improbably plump and juicy, coaxed from the thin, stony New England soil that nourished the rows of plants neatly staked up in the fields behind the stand.

In the back of the shop was a very old cider press, a massive cast-iron thing garlanded with cobwebs most of the year. The caramel-colored cider, sold in big, heavy glass jugs, was the one consolation when summer ended. Old Ma Rippe, Mr. Rippe's mother, used to make crispy cinnamon-sugar doughnuts spiked with cider. Though packaged in waxed paper bags, they still attracted swarms of yellow jackets mad with desire for their sugar coating.

Summer started with Memorial Day and the melancholy parade downtown, past the bank of Stars and Stripes in front of the lugubrious 1908 stone town hall. Men wearing creased army caps and stoic expressions marched along, accompanied by fire trucks and a few brass bands. That night, my father would barbecue the chicken my mother had marinated in bottled Italian salad dressing, and we'd have mayonnaise-slicked potato salad, slightly sulfurous from the hard-boiled eggs it contained, and strawberry shortcake. Mom made the cake from Jiffy mix.

The Fourth of July was always spent at Burial Hill Beach, named for the seaside prominence that was, I learned in elementary school, believed to be a midden created by the shellfish-loving Pequot Indians, who may have also have buried their dead there. We'd sit on old bedspreads on the edge of the hill to get a better view of the town fireworks, but when the night was clear, we could also see distant starbursts in the sky across the sound, above the beaches of Long Island.

The Birkbys would come up from Stamford in their yellow Plymouth convertible to picnic with us and watch the fireworks. Natty Mr. Birkby, the first man I ever saw wearing a pink shirt, was a textile designer in New York, and Mrs. Birkby, whom Mom had grown up with in Boston, had a passion for tennis, classical music, and gardening. Her voice was deeper than her husband's, and she had a taut, sinewy body. The couple's only child was named Dana. We'd eat parallel picnics and then share the devil's-food sheet cake, topped with an American flag made from red, white, and blue frosting, that Mrs. Birkby made every year.

The cake was good, but what I really wanted was in the Birkbys' picnic basket. The contents were intriguingly foreign. They brought gazpacho, "a chilled tomato-pepper-and-cucumber soup from Andalucía," as Mrs. Birkby described it. They poured it from a thermos and drank it from stubby glasses. They ate fat, fleshy green olives from Sicily; chorizo, a slightly withered-looking dark-red sausage they got in an "ethnic" grocery store; ratatouille; cracked wheat salad with chopped roasted peppers and fresh mint; and cold roast veal with tuna sauce spooned from a little Tupperware container. Why, I wondered, did they eat such interesting things, while my family made do with potato chips, dip made from onion soup mix, fried chicken, and potato salad?

When I asked, my mother answered tartly, "Mrs. Birkby doesn't have four children to feed." That made me feel guilty.

"And the Birkbys also have, shall we say, a taste for the exotic," added my father with a chuckle. The couple's gentle gender-bending was an irresistible target for his frat-boy sense of humor.

"That's enough of that, Sandy," my mother said schoolmarmishly, but I knew she too was amused by the Birkbys. She and Mrs. Birkby had known each other since they were nine years old and had a lot in common, including the disdain many New England women felt for members of their own sex who attached too much importance to their appearance. To them, there was something suspect and a little vulgar about obvious feminine wiles. They also shared liberal politics, a deep interest in art, and a buried sense of their own superiority. Me, I liked the Birkbys for their sense of style, her delicious cooking, his seersucker shorts, and the way their relationship suggested that nature could mischievously and inscrutably break its own norms.

Summer was also the season of restaurants, a rare pleasure I looked forward to ardently. We had many of these meals en route to vacations in Maine and on Cape Cod or Nantucket, where we'd stay in tidy, slightly austere middle-class inns. I was the only member of the family who didn't eat fried clams when we stopped at Howard Johnson's, which we all loved for its terrazzo floors, turquoise vinyl banquettes, and peppermint-stick ice cream. I'd have a patty melt while everyone else dredged thickly breaded clam bellies in tiny pleated paper cups of tartar sauce. The only flaw was HoJo cola, which was too sweet and not carbonated enough. Inevitably, my mother would mention that Aunt Bette, her older sister, had dated Howard Johnson Jr. and make a joke about how their marriage would have created a gastronomic dynasty, since my mother's family, the Drakes, had founded the Drake's Cake Company, which sold Devil Dogs, Ring Dings, and other snack foods and cakes throughout the East Coast.

Once we reached our destination, most of our dining was bracketed by "the American plan," meaning that our lodgings included breakfast and dinner in the price. The food issuing from these New England hotel kitchens was plain, made mostly by middle-aged Irish American ladies or cooks who came south from Canada's maritime provinces for the season. I loved the eggy-tasting popovers, the little glasses of tomato or cranberry juice on paper-doily-lined saucers, the shredded iceberg lettuce lashed with Thousand Island dressing, and the chicken à la king in frozen-puff-pastry cases. Once a week, there was fresh fish, which unfortunately was most often strongly flavored bluefish. I'd ask for an omelette instead, which always came with an orange pennant of melting American cheese.

Though the food at these hotels was plain, its dullness sharpened my appreciation of my mother's cooking. Her English and Scottish ancestors had left her with a meager gastronomic legacy—her totemic foods included B & M Boston baked beans and canned brown bread, frozen codfish cakes, and Christmas puddings—but she inflected our meals with her curiosity about the world. My father often teasingly disparaged her culinary daring, but I loved it.

Her medium was hamburger, which could quickly and economically be conjured into a dish that dispatched us from suburban Connecticut to Cuba, China, or Italy. Sautéed with chopped onions, canned tomato sauce, sliced green cocktail olives, pimientos, and paprika, it became Latin picadillo. Simmered with a small can of La Choy water chestnuts and canned bean sprouts, plus chopped onion, celery, and soy sauce, it ferried us down the Yang-Tse to dinner. Another day, we'd have hamburger "pizza," with the meat patted into a square baking tin and topped with spaghetti sauce, a can of mushrooms, grated Romano, and oregano.

Profoundly Protestant without being explicitly religious, my mother believed waste was wrong and thrift was virtuous. Even though she liked to eat, she chafed at gastronomic pretension, which meant anything too fancy or expensive. Restaurants were optional fripperies—theaters for good manners—and she didn't love them. But I did.

Especially the trips I made to the Apizza Center, because it was foreign territory. In the disjointed sociological geography of Fairfield County, a bunch of colonial farm towns strung along the New Haven railroad had become expensive suburbs of New York City. But they were interspersed with small indus- trial cities, like Stamford, Norwalk, and Bridgeport, which were, in those days, places where people made things—everything from toasters and guns to helicopters and sewing machines— in brick factories with tall, gaunt windows.

The Apizza Center was just down the block from factories where copper and zinc were smelted into brass for bead chains. Inside, there was a bar and plywood booths with red Formica tables, and leatherette seats lined both side walls. Up front it smelled of beer and cigarettes, but deeper into the room, it was warmer, and the yeasty smell of baking dough was punctuated by the sharper notes of tomato sauce. The pies, as they were called, were baked by wisecracking tattooed pizza makers wear- ing white T-shirts and peaked paper caps. They manned burn- scarred paddles at the coal-fired ovens in the back.

The pizzas were rarely ready when we arrived to pick them up, so we'd mill around in the front. I'd sit on a chair by the ciga- rette machine, and my father watched whatever sports program was on the television on the shelf behind the bar. I loved watch- ing the customers, and I envied them because they shared an easy conviviality that was unknown in my world.

They were from multigenerational Italian American families. Despite my family name, I'm only one-sixteenth Italian,
the genetic legacy of my paternal great-great-grandfather who
arrived in New Orleans from Italy sometime between 1780 and
1790.

What really fascinated me, though, were the couples. The
handsome dark-haired boys with slicked-back hair and black
leather jackets who were called "greasers" and the girls with
fuzzy sweaters, turquoise eye shadow, and pink frosted lips.
These young women looked "fast," which meant they were
thought to be having sex. I longed to go out on a date with one
of the greasers in a Camaro or a Dodge Charger, their favorite
cars.

One rainy Sunday in December when I was fourteen, I experienced another romantic inspiration. My mother asked me
to go with her to see the film *Jules et Jim,* directed by François
Truffaut, at the art cinema downtown. The story of the film,
about the friendship between a Frenchman and an Austrian
man in love with same woman, didn't interest me much, but
the city in the background had me on the edge of my seat. Paris
in black and white was almost painfully beautiful, moody, and
mysterious.

The following year, I visited Paris for the first time. I went
with my family. Waiting in the lobby of our hotel for a taxi to
take us to a bistro in the Latin Quarter, my mother would inspect us. Stopping in front of me, she'd straighten the maroon
Rooster knit tie I was wearing with a blue oxford shirt and the
madras jacket I loathed. After only two days in Paris, I knew
that its weave of pastel colors — lime, peach, sand, and strawberry — would look ludicrous to French eyes. These country-
club tones had nothing to do with the blasé chic of a city where
even the sandwiches were elegant. At the pâtisserie near our hotel, each one was wrapped on the spot in a four-sided pyramid of

shiny raspberry-colored paper, which neatly encased a gold ribbon that was tied into a loop at the peak, so you could slip your finger through to carry it.

The bistro, recommended by the hotel concierge, would have a name like Le Petit Chien. We'd arrive to discover it was hot, airless, and crowded. We were very overdressed compared to everyone else in the smoky room. When he came to the table with menus, our waiter spoke English.

"Well, that's a relief!" said my father.

"*Merci, monsieur,*" said my mother, accepting the menu from the server, who dipped his head and smiled at her. My mother translated it for us, stalling at the starter of pâté de tête. "Yuck," she said. "Head cheese."

"What's head cheese?" my younger brother asked.

"Something ghastly and very French," my mother replied. "It's a pâté made with the meat found inside of a calf's head." We thought she was kidding, but she assured us she wasn't. "The French eat absolutely everything," she explained.

In the end, we all ordered the same thing — frisée aux lardons (curly endive salad with a poached egg and chunks of bacon) and boeuf bourguignon.

While we waited for our food, I watched the woman at the table diagonally across from ours as she cradled her heavy bosoms while rearranging her bra straps under the thin fabric of her sleeveless blouse. When she noticed my gaze, she smiled and winked, and a flutter went directly to the pit of my stomach.

What I liked best about my salad was how, when I pricked the egg yolk, a bright yellow rivulet flowed into the greens, thickening the winey vinaigrette into a glossy sauce that clung to the frilly pale-green fronds of endive.

"What a great idea to put bacon in a salad," said my father. And then, to my mother: "Maybe you could try this at home."

She nodded vaguely.

The boeuf bourguignon had such a slamming viniferous but

potently bovine depth that it made me realize I knew nothing about how flavor was created. I ate everything on my plate and then served myself more noodles as an excuse to lap up more of the lush mahogany sauce. This dish was a carnal pleasure I would want over and over again. It struck me it would never taste the same way anywhere else in the world but Paris. I'd been eating beef stew my whole life but had never had one like this before.

"This stew is very tasty," said my father.

A day later, the six of us arrived very early at the Gare du Nord for the train to Calais. After that, a ferry would take us to London. My father had been so anxious about being on time that we had a good hour and a half to kill before we could board, so my mother suggested we go across the street and have breakfast in a café.

Paris was still waking on this summer morning when we sat down at two wobbly tables and ordered from a tall, lean young waiter with a white apron and his sleeves rolled up to reveal his long bandy arms. Pigeons pecked at crumbs on the sidewalk around us, and then we were served—hot chocolate for my brothers and sister and café au lait for me and my parents. As the waiter leaned across the tables with our drinks, I caught a whiff of his frankly male sweat. With his musk in my nose, I pulled apart a croissant, and a shower of flaky golden crumbs shattered from it. I got a knot in my throat. Somehow or other I would have to find a way to come back to this city and stay because I belonged here.

7

AT MY TUTOR'S TABLE

Well, you're not going to spend the rest of your life writing about dresses, are you?" said Mr. Keyes. His question's deliberate malice made my cheeks bloom.

"I certainly hope not," I replied, and he chuckled at my ill-disguised irritation. I took a slug of Champagne to get my wits back. And then the whole situation struck me as so hilariously improbable that I chuckled along with him. I'd never pictured myself as the Sunday lunch guest of my landlady, who was a French countess, and her husband.

Just six weeks earlier I'd moved into the apartment on the ground floor of the elegant limestone building that Mr. and Mrs. Albert Keyes owned on the rue Monsieur, in the 7th arrondissement on the Left Bank of Paris. The couple lived on the next floor up.

The previous tenant of my apartment, a journalist who worked for Reuters, was a friend of the English reception-ist in the Fairchild office. She'd tipped me off about the place when her friend told her he was moving to Asia. I jumped at the chance because the place was affordable, available, and fur-nished, and I needed to move out of the hotel where I'd been living at the company's expense. Even to my untutored eyes, the neighborhood looked stuffy and the furniture dumpy, but this was an expedient solution, especially since I had no idea how my new life in Paris was going to work out.

My first home in Paris was odd but comfortable. Its private entryway, from the garden behind the building, accessed a long hall with boldly ugly bronze-and-orange floral wallpaper. In the kitchen, mounted on the wall, was a massive ancient Frigidaire refrigerator with chrome tridents. The living room was graced with a large couch upholstered with the salmon-colored prickly wool fabric once found in European train compartments, and an amateurish oil painting of the countess's grand family château —she really was a countess—hung on a cream-colored wall. The bathroom's fir-green tiling would have suited a Prussian military academy.

But despite its peculiar furnishings and air of transience, the apartment was spacious and quiet, a propitious place for incubating dreams. Most important, it made me feel settled in Paris.

"Are there other subjects you enjoy writing about, Alexandre?" Madame la Comtesse asked me.

"Well, yes, I've written book reviews and travel stories and profiles of people. I'm also very interested in food and cooking, but I'm not really qualified to write about them because I don't have the expertise. In fact, moving to France has meant I've had to learn how to eat all over again," I said.

The fragile, birdlike countess cocked her head, with its Champagne-colored chignon, and looked at me pensively. "Cooking is a great passion of mine as well," she said, as if seeing me for the first time. "But why do you say that coming here means that you've had to learn to eat again?"

"Well, for one thing, the foods are so different."

"Really? How?"

"There's so much knowledge that goes into buying food here. The most obvious example is the cheese shops, but it's not only that. Yesterday I went to buy potatoes, and the greengrocer had twelve different varieties. I didn't know which ones to buy, so I asked him. 'It depends on what you're cooking,' he replied. I told him I wanted to roast them with a chicken, and then he asked me what texture and taste I preferred in potatoes. The choices here are endless." I omitted the fact that I didn't have a clue as to how to answer the vegetable man's question.

In my life, there had been three potatoes: Idaho for baking, Maine for almost everything else, and, more recently, the small red-skinned ones used for the salads in New York City delicatessens. But I'd never thought about what a potato actually tasted like, much less paid much attention to its texture. Oh, to be sure, I did love the aluminum-foil-wrapped baked potatoes served at steakhouses because they were barges for other things I liked a lot, like melted butter, chive-flecked sour cream, and especially crumbled bacon. But other than that, I'd never given spuds a second thought.

"And there are fewer choices in America?"

I nodded, unable to even begin explaining the essentially generic diet of the country I'd grown up in—a place where rice was rice and carrots were carrots. Period. And the main reason for my incoherence was that the enormousness of this discovery had pretty much rendered me mute. I mean, why did we eat this way?

"How curious, and I thought the United States was a very rich country. I do hope the food in America is better than it is in England. English food is filthy!"

"That's enough, Adélaïde!" snapped Mr. Keyes.

"But it is, Albert! It is! It's just horrid, isn't it, Alexandre? Albert told me you've lived there. So I know you know. Isn't English food dreadful?"

Both of them were staring at me now. The countess gently twirled the opal-headed gold stickpin in the bow of the scarf that was loosely tied at her slender neck, and Mr. Keyes gaped, one eyebrow raised in a preemptive glare.

"It's interesting that most of the best restaurants in London are French or have French chefs, but I do like a good fish and chips and a Sunday roast with Yorkshire pudding, potatoes, and all the trimmings," I said, and disliked myself for being so temperate.

"You see, Adélaïde! Most sensible people prefer a proper roast to having their meat cut up into bits and pieces in some rich sauce!"

"You know, Albert, I think Alexandre may be the only diplomat in this room." This was a dig at him. Mr. Keyes had held some important job at the British embassy in Paris for many years before retiring.

Carmela, who worked for the Keyeses, stopped to offer me some warm cheese straws, presented on a perforated white paper doily on a small silver tray. I was used to seeing her in the faded floral housecoat and unraveling brown cardigan that she wore while watering the potted plants, mostly hydrangeas and geraniums, which she nursed like children in the stone-paved courtyard. Today she was wearing a white apron over a black dress. I sensed a solicitous intervention in her sudden appearance.

"But Alexandre, what exactly would you like to say about food?"

"Well, eventually I think I might like to write restaurant reviews, to be a critic"—my own words surprised me—was this really something I wanted, or was I just trying to be interesting? "But I'd have to learn a lot before I'd ever dare to do that, and I'm sure that acquiring such expertise would take years."

The countess nodded. "Humility is always the best point of departure," she said, and smiled. "The first thing you'll have to learn is how to decipher a cook's intentions. And then, with more experience, you can judge the success with which those intentions have been achieved."

"Stop talking such rubbish, Adélaïde! Alexander wrote a fine article about Egypt in the *International Herald Tribune* a few weeks ago. That's the sort of thing he should be doing," said Mr. Keyes. He was wearing a moss-green herringbone jacket with leather patches at the elbows.

When Carmela paused before him, he shook his head at the cheese straws, rattled the ice cubes in his empty glass, and put it on her tray.

"Albert, do you really think . . ."

"Oh, would you stop being so tiresome, Adélaïde! And I'm sure Alexander would like some more Champagne as well."

I ignored the question implied in his suggestion because I was so interested in what his wife had just said. I wanted to hear more, but I didn't know how to address her. Certainly not by her first name, this elegant woman with watery aquamarine-blue eyes. Madame la Comtesse? Even if she was a countess, that seemed a bit rich. I was not sure how to navigate this delicate situation.

"Alexandre, please call me Madame Keyes," she said, and I was startled by her perceptivity. She spoke to me mostly in French, slowly and generously enunciating to give me time to sift what she was saying through the sieve of my long-dormant college French, while her husband preferred our mutual English. When speaking to his wife, though, Mr. Keyes would start off in French and then, when his impatience with her got the better of him, which was often, he'd collapse into English, which she spoke perfectly, with a plummy British accent. The violence of their fights—muffled shouting, hard thumping on the floor, doors slamming—had already shocked me on several occasions; their living room was situated just above my bedroom in my ground-floor apartment.

"*Merci*, madame, but what do you mean by intentions?"

"What were your mother's intentions when she cooked for you?"

I paused. "Well, I think she mostly cooked to nourish us," I replied.

"As all mothers do," said the countess. "And did she cook for any other reasons?"

I drew a blank.

"Did she cook differently for the holidays, for example?"

"Yes, of course."

"So nourishment and special occasions are reasons to cook, and there are others."

"What nonsense!" said Mr. Keyes. "The only thing worth saying about food is whether it's good or bad. Otherwise, it's hardly a fit subject of conversation. No writers worth their salt would choose food as a theme — writing about it is just a lot of pretension and puffery!"

"How very English of you, Albert! There's history and poetry and science in cooking for those who are perceptive enough to find it," said the countess.

The doorbell rang, and Carmela ushered in a young woman with thick pink-framed glasses, a pleated plaid skirt, argyle knee socks, and heavy brogues with tassels, "Maman," she said, and kissed the countess on each cheek. Then "Papa," and another pair of kisses. Caroline was beetle-browed, with pale coloring and a breathy little girl's voice.

"Caroline, please meet Alexander, the young man who lives downstairs. He's American, but that's not his fault. Alexander writes about dresses for some fancy New York magazine, but that's not his fault either, unless, of course, he secretly likes frocks," said Mr. Keyes.

"I work for a fashion publisher," I explained to Caroline, my cheeks ablaze yet again. "I took the job because it enabled me to move to Paris."

"Welcome to Paris, Alexander," she said, taking after her gracious mother more than her obstreperous father. Caroline refused a glass of Champagne, and we sat in silence for a minute, until she said, "Oh, Maman, what beautiful peonies! They're so dark red, they're nearly black."

"Yes, aren't they lovely. Alexandre sent them to me yesterday morning." The countess nodded at me with a smile.

Caroline sipped a Perrier and then recounted a giddy volley of some apparently amusing mistakes her students had made on their recent exams. She taught ancient Greek and Latin, so her elaborate academic explanations of their errors left me time to muse. I knew no Greek, and after three torturous years of Latin I remembered only one word: *agricola,* or farmer.

Why on earth, I wondered, had the Keyeses invited me to lunch? And if nourishment and special occasions, like holidays and maybe dinner parties, were two of the most important reasons to cook, what were the others? I couldn't think of any. And how did you find the poetry, history, and science in cooking?

Now that I was in their elegant salon, where gilt-framed oil portraits of Madame Keyes's ancestors hung on walls covered with puce fabric, I felt a little unnerved. This room was the forum for their arguments, which I found so shocking. It seemed a trespass of intimacy to be entertained in this space.

At least I'd had the sense not to wear a tie. Three or four times that morning, I'd put one on and then yanked it off before finally deciding that the item of clothing I least liked wearing would be too absurdly formal for the unwanted invitation I couldn't refuse.

Just a week earlier, Carmela had rung my bell minutes after I'd gotten home from work on a Friday. She was delivering a sealed ivory-colored notecard on a small silver tray. "It's from Madame la Comtesse," she said, to my visible confusion. I carried the note into the kitchen and opened it. The Keyeses were inviting me to come for lunch the following Sunday. Aside from the two times Mr. Keyes had come by to collect the rent, in cash, I'd had little contact with them. The rent-paying wasn't a mere handover of bills in an envelope, however. He'd stood in the doorway chatting for such a long time, I finally thought I should ask him in for a drink. A couple of generous pours of Scotch at my kitchen table put him in a good mood very quickly.

Carmela came back the following morning to see if I would accept their invitation, and when I said yes, she told me she'd let them know. The Saturday before lunch, she showed up at my door again with a bouquet of peonies in a tent of cellophane and crisp white tissue paper, with a white satin bow. They were from Moulié Fleurs, the most elegant florist on the Left Bank.

"They're beautiful," I said, confused.

"They're from you, *niño perdido,*" she replied, handing me a small white card. "Please sign."

Lost boy. At least I had the sense to ask her what the flowers had cost and reimbursed Carmela right away, but sometimes a great kindness becomes legible only with the passage of time. The correct way to offer flowers to a Parisian hostess is to send them before you arrive, so that she'll have the time to arrange them at her leisure.

Carmela invited us into the dining room, where Madame and Monsieur took seats at opposite ends of the table. Caroline settled into the chair with its back to the window. The light was too strong for her; you could see from their pink rims that her eyes were tired.

The parquet creaked, and Carmela returned with a U-shaped white-porcelain basket lined with a celadon-colored napkin and filled with plump, ivory-colored spears of asparagus with purple tips.

"They come from my garden in the Loire," the countess told me, as she passed a sauceboat of sunny, almost gauzy yellow sauce, which I spooned over the four fat spears on my plate. Once everyone had been served, I picked up my knife and fork, but before I could use them, the countess stopped me.

"*Non, non, Alexandre. On les mange comme ça,*" she said, daintily picking up a spear by its blunt end with her fingers and biting off the tip. "Never use a knife and fork with asparagus—it's unnecessary, and it spoils the pleasure of eating with your hands!" She kindly omitted the fact that the French also find it uncouth. The faintly bitter, mineral-rich spears had a very gentle taste of clover, and the richness of the hollandaise sauce was tempered, I perceived, by orange zest and orange juice. It was the best asparagus I'd ever eaten.

"It's sauce maltaise, which is a hollandaise with little bit of blood-orange juice and zest," said the countess.

"It's delicious, and the citrus tempers the bitterness of the asparagus without masking it," I said.

"Exactly!" she replied. "And this is also why we always drink Sancerre with this dish. It has a bone-dry finish, and its flintiness stands up to the sauce and the asparagus."

Mr. Keyes cleared his throat and butted in. "Oh, God help us, Caroline! Your mother has decided Alexander should become the next Curnonsky!"

"Thank you for that reference, Albert. As you may know, Alexandre, the late Curnonsky was one of the greatest French gastronomic writers. He also said two very wise things, which will be of use to you. 'Great food is when things taste of what they are,' and 'And above all, keep it simple!' Never forget either of these dictums, because they are essential and eternal."

"He was a fairy, wasn't he, Adélaïde?"

This time Caroline intervened. "Alexander, did you know that Yves Saint Laurent lives just around the corner?"

I did, and I told them the story of how on a rainy night the week before, I'd gone into the little shop across the street from the cinema to buy some milk on my way home and ran into him. He was standing at the cash register, wearing purple silk pajamas, a Bordeaux cashmere bathrobe, and Hermès bedroom slippers, and he was buying a lot of cheap candy. The cashier had just rung up his purchases, but he'd slipped away from his minders without any money. He was frantic like a cornered animal, embarrassed, and obviously high on something.

I told the cashier I'd pay for the candy. The designer tried to give me the expensive fountain pen he'd found in the pocket of his robe.

"*Non, merci, monsieur. C'est vraiment pas nécessaire,*" I said, and smiled.

"*Merci de votre gentillesse, monsieur!*" he said, and dashed out with his Mars bars and Kinder eggs.

The Keyeses were intrigued. "Did you call round for the money the next day?" Mr. Keyes asked. I shook my head.

"It's not something you would understand, Albert, but sometimes kindness is its own reward," said the countess.

What I didn't say was that this incident had also augured the early demise of my career with the fashion publisher. I should have written up my encounter with Saint Laurent as a juicy item for "The Eye," the sharp-toothed gossip column in *Women's Wear Daily*. But I didn't because I knew I'd be haunted forever by the mortified look on the poor man's pale face.

Carmela came in with two tureens. One was filled with fluffy white rice, which the countess passed to me after she'd served herself, commenting, "It's the good rice from the Camargue." And then, reacting to my blank expression, "La Camargue is the delta of the Rhône just before it reaches the Mediterranean. I think the salts in the alluvial soil there give the rice a subtle flavor, and it has a nice bite, which makes it perfect for dishes with sauce."

Carmela passed the other tureen, which contained a succulent-looking meat stew in a satiny white sauce with intriguingly small button mushrooms, glossy pearl onions, and thin rectangles of carrot the size of small matches, which must have taken someone a lot of work with a knife.

"*Et voilà, la belle blanquette de veau, Alexandre!* Have you had it before?"

"Never."

"It is one of the great dishes of Gaul, and one I very much enjoy making," said the countess. "I like June veal because the calves are born to cows that have been pastured. It's probably my imagination, but I think this means the animals are happier when they're born, which makes their meat tender. The flavor is better as well."

I nodded.

"Blanquette de veau is a celebration of innocence," she added.

The countess was right. The tender chunks of veal were tucked into a sauce that was as soft and soothing as a baby's flannel blanket. "It's not all that difficult to make," boasted the countess, who went on to explain how the meat was simmered for an hour or two in stock, preferably veal, with a clove-piqued onion and a bouquet garni. Then the pearl onions, mushrooms, and carrots were prepared, and a roux, the mixture of flour cooked with butter that is the base of many French sauces, was made, to which several cups of the stock were added. And finally, egg yolks beaten with cream were folded into the sauce to create what she described as *"l'effet cachemire"* (the cashmere effect). The gentle sauce made the contrasting textures as winsomely exciting as being licked by a kitten.

She hadn't mentioned it, but I was sure I tasted a tiny bit of lemon in the sauce. This almost imperceptible dash of acidity was the only thing that challenged the chaste sensuousness of this dish.

"It's a good thing I thought to open a second bottle of wine if you're going to drone on this way, Adélaïde," said Mr. Keyes, refilling my glass with the lovely, brightly red-berry-tasting Fleurie from the Beaujolais, which the countess had selected.

When Caroline asked her father a question about something having to do with ancient Greek, the countess leaned toward me and continued. "You know, Alexandre, I think we all have our little eccentricities, *non?*"

I smiled, cautiously.

"Well, I wouldn't like it widely known, but I've just subjected you to one of mine." Her eyes sparkled. "My father was in the military." (He was, I later learned, a very famous general from a long line of them.) "We lived in Morocco for several years when I was a girl and it was a French protectorate. My mother was very unhappy there, so she'd return to France for long periods of time, staying at the château in the Loire or taking a cure in Vichy. I spent most of my time with my Moroccan nursemaid, who fed me the same food she cooked for her own children. This is why I love olives and spices like star anise, which were then almost unknown in France. My favorite dish was a tagine of chicken with purple olives and pickled lemons. The brined lemons infuse the chicken with sunshine. I tuck them into many of the French dishes I make, just a tiny bit, to tease," she said.

I liked the countess enormously.

With Carmela as her assistant, it was Madame Keyes, I later learned, who held forth in the kitchen. She also did what she described as the "important" shopping, which meant trips to the butcher, the fromagerie, or the fishmonger. She was a superb cook too, with an easy mastery of dishes like boeuf à la ficelle (beef poached in bouillon), quenelle de brochet (fluffy pike dumplings, a specialty of Lyon) in a sauce Nantua, a béchamel enriched with crayfish butter, and salmon en croûte with a vivacious green sauce of watercress, chives, chopped hard-boiled eggs, and the excellent fruity olive oil the Keyeses brought back from their holidays in Spain. This oil was kept in metal drums and stored in their cellar, along with an extraordinary collection of wines. These had been accumulated over the course of the Keyeses' marriage but also reached back farther. Many of the wines had been inherited from her parents, who had built this apartment house in the silk-stocking Faubourg Saint-Germain, an aristocratic part of the city with excruciatingly elaborate codes for living a respectable life. I knew absolutely nothing about this tapestry of appropriate behaviors, including all of the things one should never do under any circumstances.

Among the first of the many *ça ne se fait pas* (it's not done) lessons I'd learned was that you didn't sit outside in the beautiful gardens behind the building. One soft, winey-smelling Indian summer day, I'd carried a chair to the shade of a chestnut tree there and settled in to read my book. A few minutes later, I heard a sharp knuckle rapping on the window from behind a parted curtain on the third floor. An elderly woman looked down at me and shook her head emphatically. Eventually Mr. Keyes appeared and explained to me that the gardens were strictly ornamental and not intended to be inhabited. "To take some air, Alexander, you go to a park," he advised me gravely. This prohibition struck me as sad and senseless, but I did what I was told.

Lunch concluded with a clafoutis, a thick, golden, sugar-sprinkled custard studded with cherries in an oval porcelain baking dish. "It's a rather homely conclusion to our meal, Alexandre, but I'm afraid I find most pastries from pâtisseries quite vulgar," said the countess. "I hope it doesn't sound too rude, but since the war, *la pâtisserie* has become *terriblement* nouveau riche. For me, the best desserts are simple puddings and tarts."

"I've always liked a simple tart myself," said Mr. Keyes, with a wink at me.

Caroline asked me what plans I had for August, the month that Parisians leave the city en masse for their month-long vacations in the country, at the beach, or in the mountains. I explained that since I worked for an American company and was new in my job, I would have no holiday in August. "How awful!" she said. "You know, I think you'll probably be the only one in this building for a couple of weeks. I'm so sorry!" I reassured her that I would go away for long weekends and that I was looking forward to discovering France.

The countess, who was looking slightly flushed, stood up.

"Caroline," she said, and her daughter came to take her by the arm. "Please excuse me, Alexandre. It's time for me to rest. You have been a charming guest and are an eager student of the French kitchen," she said.

Mr. Keyes offered coffee, which I declined, and port, which I also refused. After thanking him, I headed for the front vestibule where I'd arrived, but my host hustled me through the kitchen and into the pantry, where he opened a door that led to the back stairs. "The door downstairs will lock behind you when you close it," he said. "Good afternoon, Alexander."

That airless night I tossed and turned as I tried to make sense of the four-hour lunch, which had been as strange and exhausting as it was exhilarating. Why had they invited me? I couldn't figure it out. But then I'd start thinking about some of the things Madame Keyes had said at lunch and the poignant succulence of the blanquette de veau she'd served. The last time I'd had food so sincere was Emma's fried chicken at Grandmother Jean's house. I loved being in the kitchen with Emma, a chuckling barrel of a woman from South Carolina. She sang little whistling songs under her breath, talked to herself, cursed, laughed out loud, and constantly fed me a tidbit or two of something tasty while I did simple chores for her, like scraping carrots or skinning onions.

"A really good cook knows how to feed all the different hungers, honey," Emma had once said to me as she spooned cornbread batter into cast-iron muffin molds in the shape of ears of corn. I missed Emma's sweetness, and her cooking, and in the dark of a hot summer night in Paris, I felt the sting of homesickness. It would be years before I understood the gift the countess had given me. What she knew and I didn't was that no one could understand the cooking in the restaurants of France without a deep experience of French home cooking. She offered me more lessons over the course of two dozen or so politely didactic lunches spanning the two years I was her tenant.

8

THE OLD LADY'S PLACE

Who is this?" she said.

I'd dialed the phone number of Chez La Vieille so many times, I was startled when someone finally answered. I told the gruff-sounding woman that I wanted to make a reservation for lunch on the following Wednesday.

"But who are you?" she snapped.

I told her she didn't know me and repeated my request for a reservation.

"OK," she said, and hung up.

I dialed again, five times, before she picked up.

"*Merde!* I'm trying to cook!" she shouted. I told her we'd just spoken and that I was calling back because she hadn't taken my name for the reservation.

"I'll know who you are," she said, and again hung up. For a couple of days, I worried. How, actually, would she know me? This meal was important, a business lunch with Barnaby Thomas, the features editor of the Sunday magazine of a London newspaper for which I'd done a lot of work when I lived there. Beyond giving me assignments, he'd never paid me much attention before, so I was surprised when his secretary called to tell me he'd be in Paris for a day and wanted to have lunch with me before he got his train back to London.

"He loves bistros," she said. "He doesn't want anything modern and fussy. He loves real French food."

I asked around among the small circle of French people I knew, and many of them gave me the same suggestion, Chez La Vieille, a tiny bistro in Les Halles, the old market district in the heart of Paris. It was when Madame Keyes made the recommendation that I decided to go there.

I'd run into her at the butcher. I took a place behind her in line and finally summoned up the courage to speak to her. She seemed not to recognize me at first, but then she gave me a taut smile. I apologized for disturbing her but wondered if she could give me some advice. I explained that I needed a restaurant recommendation.

"Go to Chez La Vieille. It's a place they liked at the British embassy when Albert still worked there," she said, and turned her back on me to speak to the butcher, who held out two small coiled, pale-pink lamb's brains on a piece of white butcher's paper for her to inspect. She leaned forward, poked one of them, and nodded.

I shuddered. Lamb's brains. After I'd bought my quarter pound of hamburger, I caught up with her on the sidewalk outside and offered to carry her shopping home.

"Thank you, Alexandre," she said, adding, "We don't go out very much, but Chez La Vieille is very good." She walked briskly, a half step ahead of me, which was an implicit reprimand; it had been presumptuous, possibly even rude of me, to suggest we had any kind of social relationship outside the one she had framed. In public, I was her tenant and a foreigner.

When we reached the entrance to her building, I held the heavy oak door for her while she stepped inside. The raindrops on the plastic scarf that protected her waved meringue-colored hair glittered in the light of the lamp hanging in the entryway.

"*Bonsoir, Alexandre,*" she said coolly, taking her shopping and turning to the door off the cobble-paved porte cochere.

"*Bonsoir,* Madame Keyes, and thank you very much for the recommendation, but may I ask why you suggested Chez La Vieille?"

With her key in the lock, she spoke without turning around. "Because the woman who cooks there serves the kind of food your grandmother would have made if you'd grown up in the French countryside," she said, and then the glass-paned door to the stairwell closed behind her. I'd been dismissed.

Her suggestion was exciting — I guessed she was referring to the food I loved most since I'd arrived in Paris, the cooking in the city's bistros. I was collecting these addresses too. A short walk from my apartment stood Joséphine Chez Dumonet, an intimate dining room, vintage belle epoque in style, where the boeuf bourguignon had the kind of succulence achieved only through hours of patient simmering. And D'Chez Eux, a slightly stuffy restaurant with cracked-tile floors, where suit-wearing politicians and diplomats with ovine silhouettes slid into the booths to feast on cassoulet. My attraction to bistro cooking was more primal than knowledgeable, but I'd become obsessed by this food and was determined to learn more about it.

On the day of the 12:30 lunch at Chez La Vieille, I arrived at noon to make sure I actually had a reservation. (Just in case, I'd also booked a table at Chez Denise, a bawdy, old-fashioned, red-checked-tablecloth place nearby, which I liked a lot for its cheap red wine from a barrel and its trencherman's menu of escargots, stuffed cabbage, and mutton with beans.) When I opened the door and stepped into the small, dim dining room, a woman with a strong nose, short brown hair, and an apron over a floral-print housedress came out of the kitchen, wiping her hands on a dishcloth.

"What do you want?"

I told her my name and explained I'd made a lunch reservation the week before.

She shook her head, and I panicked. "You look like a notary or a lawyer in that coat! No one would want to fuck you wearing a coat like that! Take it off! It makes you look like a fool!"

I removed the camel-hair polo coat, and she threw it on a chair. She stood there, looking at me and shaking her head.

"You know, you're right about that coat. I hate it too," I told her, my cheeks crimson.

"Then why are you wearing it?"

I explained it was the only one I had, a much-loathed garment my mother had bought for me before I left for college.

"Don't you have a credit card? Buy something else, for God's sake. Now sit down!" she snapped.

Then the door opened, and two middle-aged men came in and kissed her on both cheeks. "Should I let this American *pédé*, this fairy, stay for lunch?" she said, nodding toward me. They looked at me. One of them blushed, and the other shrugged. Then she slipped behind the bar, grabbed an open bottle, and poured me a glass of white wine.

"Don't come in here wearing that coat again!" she said as she filled my glass. "I don't want people thinking I run a tourist trap."

Within a few minutes, the dining room was full, and the single waitress—mousy, large-breasted, and wearing a cardigan—was suddenly ministering to a mostly male crowd, people she obviously knew well. They teased her, and she teased them back. There was a lot of laughter in the room. I sat there and sipped my wine. The editor was twenty minutes late.

The chef, whom everyone was calling Adrienne, came back into the dining room, greeted several clients with a kiss or a clap on the back, refilled my glass, and gave me a saucer of fat-studded, garnet-colored slices of sausage.

"Did you get stood up?" she said, smirking.

"No! Not at all. I'm having lunch with a newspaper editor from London whom I work for." I noticed my coat had disappeared, and I wondered where it was. Even though I hated it, I would need it on a wet chilly day.

"Oh, *putain!* Stop looking like a dog someone's hit between the eyes with a stick! Where's your sense of humor?" she said, and stalked away. The two men sitting next to me laughed, and I hated them.

A few minutes later, Barnaby Thomas, flushed, with fogged-up glasses, stumbled through the door, took off his trench coat, handed it to Adrienne without so much as a nod, and sat down at the table. His jowly cheeks had a fine filigree of red veins, and one of the arms of his plum-colored tweed jacket, which could no longer be buttoned over his barrel of a belly, had a black-edged cigarette burn.

"My meeting ran a bit late," he said, sweeping his damp, curly steel-gray hair off his forehead and blotting it with his handkerchief. He ordered a bottle of Sancerre. Two minutes later, when the wine hadn't arrived, he scolded, *"Mademoiselle! Le vin! Vite, vite, vite!"*

Then, wiping his glasses with his napkin, he asked, "How are you getting on in Paris, Alec?"

I spoke briefly about working and living in Paris, knowing that this was of no real interest to him. Not hearing a word, he nodded impatiently. He leaned forward and peered at me over the top of his glasses. "The French are perfectly filthy people, but their food is brilliant!" he said. "Let's eat!"

The waitress took our order — a selection of hors d'oeuvres served from a trolley, then the veal kidney in cream sauce for him and the rabbit stewed in gueuze, brown beer from the north of France, for me.

Suddenly, Adrienne was tableside. "I'm switching your orders around. You'll have the kidney, he'll eat the rabbit," she snapped. "Tell him. This is my restaurant, and I can decide what you'll eat." I nodded, figuring we'd just change plates once we were served.

Barnaby went into ecstasies when the cart of hors d'oeuvres arrived: a couple of terrines with knives stuck into them, marinated herring with carrots and bay leaves, lentil salad, chopped beets in a glossy vinaigrette, céleri rémoulade, marinated leeks, champignons à la grecque with coriander seeds, stuffed tomatoes, potato salad with sausage and gherkins, head cheese, oeufs mayonnaise, and more. He tucked his napkin into his shirt collar like a schoolboy, served himself generously, and ate greedily, stopping often to refill his wineglass.

"That's a truly brilliant terrine," he said. "Would you mind asking if I could bring a hunk of it back to London with me?"

I told him we'd see when we finished the meal, though I'd be surprised if any was left at the end of the lunch service.

"Il a une sacrée descente, celui-là!" — "He really puts it away!" said the waitress, pulling the cork from the bottle of Saint-Amour that followed the Sancerre.

"I do love a good Beaujolais," Barnaby said, after he sipped the taste that the waitress had poured for him. "Such underrated wines." Adrienne arrived with our main courses, plunking the kidney down in front of me and setting the rabbit before my editor.

"Looks lovely," he said, and promptly plowed into it, while I gingerly inspected the plump kidney. It sat in a pool of pearly cream sauce tinted by pink tendrils of the organ's bloody juices.

"Bon appétit, m'sieurs," Adrienne said, cocking her head to make sure I understood that she knew I didn't want the kidney.

"Yours looks awfully nice, Alec. Can we get some more wine?" said Barnaby.

Warily, I cut a piece of the kidney and was as surprised by the organ's slightly taut exterior and soft, alarmingly rosy interior as I was by its carnal taste. In the absence of the uric flavor I'd feared, it was pleasantly potent.

"I must say, Alec, I'm surprised. You didn't strike me as someone who'd like kidneys," said Barnaby, using a piece of baguette
to mop up the rabbit's rich brown beer sauce. Now he wanted an
Armagnac, and he insisted I have one too. Adrienne served us,
and I noticed the dining room was emptying out.

"Did you enjoy the kidney?" Adrienne asked me.

I told her I did, and she snorted derisively.

Barnaby took a big sip from his snifter and told me it had
done him some good to get away from London for a night because his wife was having an affair with the contractor who had
recently redone their kitchen, and she had asked him for a divorce. "Dreadful old tart she is — accused me of being useless in
bed when we haven't even had sex for at least five years. Serves
me right for marrying an Australian. My mother tried to warn
me it would all go wrong, and I didn't listen."

I nodded impassively but found myself quietly relieved for
his wife.

"That harlot won't get ten pence out of me!" he said, and
glowered. He mopped his brow again, took another belt, and
glanced at his watch. "Oh, fuck! I'm going to miss my train. I
must go." He gulped his glass, fished a 100-franc note out of his
pocket, and put it on the table. "Send me some more ideas, Alec,
anything about Paris and France and food. I must go. Wonderful
lunch. Lovely to see you. Sorry to leave you like this," he said,
and was gone.

The bill came to 445 francs, or about $130, and Adrienne
didn't accept credit cards. I told her that I had only 200 francs
but could go out to a cash machine.

She shook her head. "I want my soup and a nap. Bring me the
rest tomorrow, and don't come back here wearing this," she said,
tossing the camel-hair coat at me and rushing me to the entrance.

"Thank you for a delicious meal," I said, and she growled at
me before she slammed the door.

———

The temperature dropped ten degrees that night, so the following morning I wore a heavy sweater under my jean jacket, the only other coat I had, when I went to work. Around 11:30, I slipped out of the office and walked to Chez La Vieille. In the street, I wondered why I'd put up with the chef's abuse, but I came from a family in which affection was almost always turned inside-out and delivered as a slight or an insult. I wanted to be her student, even if she was rough with me.

When she opened the door, she was licking a wooden spoon.

"It's you!" she said, and rolled her eyes dramatically. *"Viens!"* I followed her into her tiny kitchen. Tall pots simmered on a small gas range, and there was a big pile of chopped onions on the counter.

"Sit." I perched on a stool at a table covered with oilcloth and watched while she ladled some smooth orange soup into a bowl. When she put it down in front of me, I could smell her perspiration. She read my wrinkled nose and grinned. "Listen, *mon petit pédé,* cooking is hard work!" She chopped up a piece of toast and threw the croutons into my bowl. "Eat! You're too thin."

I handed her the money I owed her, and she put it in her apron pocket. She leaned against her stove and watched me. "I said eat!"

The pumpkin soup was sweet autumn velvet, and the croutons were slightly garlicky. "It's so good," I said. "Thank you."

She shook her head. "I don't know why I like you," she said, and I smiled. "*If* I like you!" She paused, and when she spoke again, her voice had softened. "You're such a strange boy. *Quelqu'un a brisé votre confiance masculine, mais vous allez la réparer"* — "Somebody broke your male confidence, but you're going to fix it."

Then, once again, she held forth authoritatively. "This cooking wasn't invented just to make foreign fairies happy," she said. "I cook with blood and bones and meat and wine. My food is about thrift. Do you even know what that is? It's when you're hungry but you don't have any money. It's about taking cheap meat, maybe a piece of an old cow or a tough rooster, and some vegetables and turning them into something that makes people happy. Nothing is wasted, ever. All good cooking comes from the fear of hunger." She poured herself a glass of wine. "When men make this food, they call it bistro cooking. When women cook it, it's *cuisine ménagère*, housewives' cooking, but the women know better than the men, because we cook to nourish and please, not to show off our big hairy balls."

I continue to lap up my soup. "Are you Italian?" she asked. "You have an Italian name."

I explained that my great-great-grandfather was an Italian but had married a French woman.

"So you're a mongrel," she said, and smiled. "The Biasins, my father's family, were originally from Parma."

We sat in silence. "Come, look," she said, skimming a cap of gray foam from the top of a stockpot. "I'm making stock because you can't cook without stock."

I asked her what was in the pot, and she winced. "Your French is terrible. You'll need to get a Frenchman into your bed if you're ever going to speak our language. I have too much to do to waste my time with you! Go!"

I thanked her for the soup.

"Go, I said!"

She leered. I went.

That morning, Carmela stopped me in the entryway as I was leaving for work. "Mr. and Mrs. Keyes would like you to come to lunch on Sunday," she told me. Madame's recent chilliness made me hesitate, but I accepted, and when I arrived, we sat in their living room and ate hot gougères with flutes of Champagne. We talked about politics, and Mr. Keyes surprised me with a compliment on an article I'd written about a trip to Morocco, which had been published in the *Guardian*.

"We're only three today because Caroline has a cold, so lunch will be simple," the countess said as she stood up to lead us into the dining room. Carmela served us a sliced boned veal roast with girolles (chanterelles), tiny potatoes, and buttery spinach.

"Tell me, Alexandre, how did you like Chez La Vieille?"

I thanked the countess again for her recommendation and said the meal had been delicious.

"That woman is a wonderful cook, but she's coarse and rather vulgar," said Mrs. Keyes, with a wan smile that didn't entirely mask her malevolence. Mr. Keyes chuckled.

"She had a cooking show on television, and her best friend is that dreadful Michou," Mrs. Keyes continued. Michou, the flamboyant gay owner of a cabaret in Pigalle who dressed in blue and wore glasses with smoked lenses, was a fixture in the women's magazines you'd page through at the hairdresser.

I was surprised to hear about the cooking show and asked Mrs. Keyes more about it.

"To be fair, she was rather good on camera, but the show itself was more of an entertainment than anything to do with really learning to cook. I think people were fascinated by her roughness," she replied.

"Adrienne's a tough old bird, and she can be quite rude to people she doesn't know," said Mr. Keyes. "She does like her fairies, though." He paused. "How did you get on with her, Alec?"

"I liked her very much," I told them, and suddenly the room was silent.

9

SEDUCTIONS

How did you two meet?" asked Monsieur Dubosc, once he'd sunk into his armchair after dinner.

I stared at the soccer match on the television beside the smoldering fireplace. I wasn't going to respond to that question.

This is how Franck, my latest boyfriend, answered his father: "We met in a café, Dad. Alec was sitting at the table next to me, and I asked him for a light, and we started talking. He has a crazy sense of humor, so we decided to hang out together for a while, and we became friends." The story strained credulity.

What had really happened was that two months earlier, after dinner and a movie with Christa Worthington, who had become a good friend, I'd stopped off at Le Quetzal, a men's bar in the Marais, then Paris's gayest neighborhood. I wanted a drink, but of course there was always the hope I might meet someone too. On that rainy Sunday, the smoky room was crowded, so I sat on a stool at the end of the bar by the picture window and chatted intermittently with Nick, the cute English bartender.

Suddenly someone pushed his way through the crowd and up to the bar and spoke to me. *"Bonsoir,"* said the tall thirty-something man with thick caramel-colored hair, a square jaw, and startling green eyes. *"Je m'appelle Franck,"* he said with a grin, and held out his hand. We shook hands, which was strange, because no one ever shook hands in Paris's standoffish gay bars.

Franck had calluses, and from his big grin and muddy boots, I could see that he obviously wasn't from Paris.

He asked me my name. Then he said, "Alec, may I buy you a beer?"

I shrugged. He was very good-looking.

"There's only one problem," he said sheepishly. "Can you lend me fifty francs so that I can buy you the beer?"

I laughed. "No, but thanks," I told him. I was just leaving because I had to work the next day.

"No! No! Don't leave! Wait here! Wait!"

I watched Franck go up to one of the owners of Le Quetzal, who was standing at the other end of the bar. Franck gesticulated and smiled and clapped the man on the back. The owner rolled his eyes and shook his head. Franck kept talking, and finally the owner held up two fingers to Nick, who served us the beers.

When Franck came back, I asked him what he'd done.

"I told him I'd wash glasses for an hour after the bar closes if he gave me two beers." He picked up his glass and said, *"Santé!"* We sipped our beers. "I hope I don't smell like cow shit," he said, and I asked him why he would.

"Because I'm a farmer." I thought he was joking, so I told him I'd never seen any farms in Paris. He shook his head and grinned. "I live in Normandy. And you, what do you do, Alec? And your little accent, where's that from?"

I told him.

"A journalist! You must be smart!"

Not all the time, I told him, and he laughed.

"You know we like *les Amerloques* in Normandy," he said, teaching me a new French slang word for *American*. "We're grateful to you, to the GIs." Franck told me he loved Normandy and belonged in the country. *"C'est ma place,"* he said. An hour later our glasses were empty, and the bar staff stopped the music and turned on the lights. Unexpectedly, in the harsh glare he was even more handsome.

"The people in bars like this, most of them, they're fake. But not you. You're a nice guy, Alec — I can tell, and I like you," he said. "I can't give you my phone number right now, but I would like to see you when I come back to Paris in two weeks, so will you give me yours?"

I did, and Franck kissed me on both cheeks, ruffled my hair, slipped behind the bar, and pulled on a pair of thick yellow rubber gloves next to the deep sink full of glasses.

"A bientôt, Alec," he said. I walked home, speculating as to why he couldn't or wouldn't give me his phone number. It made me wary, but I was thrilled when he called me a week later to say he was coming to Paris and asked if could we go out. When he showed up at my place for the first time, he had a Camembert, a Livarot, and a Pont l'Eveque in his duffle bag as presents for me.

After we'd seen each other three times in Paris, Franck invited me to Normandy for the weekend. I was excited because we had such a good time together, it was the beginning of fall, and I liked Normandy. That Indian-summer morning, I'd tucked a bottle of Champagne under the boxer shorts and sweater in my overnight bag, and when the train from the Gare Saint-Lazare finally broke out of the suburbs, I noticed apple trees flecked with red fruit and half-timbered houses sitting in green meadows. I looked forward to walks in the orchards and good Norman food — maybe escalope de poulet à la normande, chicken cooked with apples and cider in cream sauce, a dish I loved at Pharamond, a restaurant in Les Halles specializing in Norman cooking. It would be romantic.

Franck picked me up at the station in Argentan, but when we reached his home, its appearance came as something of a shock. A few sheets of rusty corrugated iron covered parts of the balding thatched roof of the low stone farmhouse. Inside, Franck's father was sitting in the living room with a blanket over his legs, watching television.

"Papa, this is Alec."

"*Bonjour,*" said his father, looking up from the game show he was watching, but he said nothing more.

Franck put the groceries he'd bought in the refrigerator and handed me some rubber boots. "We need to clean the barn," he said.

When we got outside, I asked him why he hadn't told me he lived with his father.

"Because if I had, you wouldn't have come," he said with a chuckle.

"But who does he think I am?"

"A friend," he said, and handed me a heavy shovel. It took us an hour and a half to scrape the manure out of the stalls into the central aisle, push it to the end of the barn, and finally shovel the stinking muck into a metal wagon attached to an old tractor. Slipping around on the slick floor, we worked in silence, and the more I stewed on his omission — not telling me he lived with his father — the more angry I became.

Just as I was about to blow up, he looked up and grinned. "Thanks for helping, Alec. It's really nice for me that you're here," he said. "I'm not complaining, but my life is pretty lonely." I took him in my arms and hugged him, a little frightened by the fact he'd just become a real person instead of my fantasy of a farmer in Normandy.

After we'd finished cleaning the barn, we went for a walk because Franck thought we might find some mushrooms in the woods. Mostly, he did the talking and I listened. His mother had died of what he called a "woman's cancer" when he was seventeen, and he had no siblings. The only other gay man anywhere near his village was the music teacher at the local high school; on the weekends he wore a woman's blonde wig at home.

I asked Franck how he knew that.

"We sell him wood, and he was wearing the wig one Saturday when I made a delivery to him. I think he did it on purpose."

Franck told me that when he went to Paris, he usually stayed with an elderly cousin of his mother, who was always so happy to see him, she never said a word when he'd return from a night out at seven the next morning.

That night the three of us sat at the oilcloth-covered table in the kitchen and ate lukewarm tripes à la mode de Caen, tripe stewed with calves' feet, cider, carrots, onions, and spices. Franck served the dish with instant mashed potatoes, which he had not blended properly, so little clots of dried potato powder remained in it. The Duboscs ate in a hurry because they didn't want to miss the televised soccer game.

"This is not as good as the tripe your mother made," Monsieur Dubosc said to his son.

"*Bien sûr que non, Papa,* but I wanted Alec to taste something special, something Norman that he'd never forget," Franck replied, and winked at me.

I'd always loathed tripe, and this Norman version was no better than the chewy "fireman's apron" I'd once unwittingly ordered. Popular in Lyon, the aptly named dish of breaded fried tripe gets its name from the rubber-coated aprons once worn by firemen in that city. Now I managed half of my shallow bowl of greasy, gray snippets, which had the texture of latex gloves, by gulping them down with big slugs of wine, and then I stood up and cleared the plates.

"Alec, sit down, you're the guest," Franck said. I ignored him, scraped our plates, and turned on the taps at the kitchen sink. I was about to start washing the dishes when he got up, pushed me out of the away, and turned them off.

"We haven't had dessert," he said, shuffling three bowls onto the table and flinging spoons down alongside them as if he was dealing cards. "Sit down! I thought you were so polite, huh?" He pried the paper lid off a square aluminum pan that had come from the same prepared-food joint as the tripe. Inside, blazes of cinnamon streaked the teurgoule, a pallid Norman version of rice pudding, but the spice couldn't rescue the oversweetened, seriously mushy grains.

"Not as good as your mother's," Monsieur Dubosc again told Franck, helping himself to another portion.

Then we gathered around the television. "Alec, do you have a girlfriend?" Franck's father asked me. He had returned to his recliner and put on his gray felt cap. He leaned forward to wrap the blanket more tightly around his legs. The dying fire was no match for the cool, damp, drafty room.

"I have lots of girlfriends." It might sound like a fib, but it was technically true. I had many friends who were girls.

"Maybe you can introduce Franck to a nice girl, then."

"Maybe I could," I replied, and smiled at Monsieur Dubosc, whose German shepherd had settled at his feet.

"I don't know, though. Parisian girls are so fussy. I don't think they'd like living on a farm," he mused. "That's why I married Paulette, Franck's mother. She was a village girl who wasn't afraid of hard work." The three of us sat there quietly until Franck joined in the cheers erupting from the stadium crowd on the television. SM Caen, the soccer team from that Norman city, had scored a goal.

"Alec, did you grow up on a farm?" Monsieur Dubosc asked me.

I explained that I'd been raised in the country outside New York City, but not on a farm. There was a dairy farm down the road, though, and my siblings and I often went there on our bikes as children because the farmer would reward us with bottles of Pepsi-Cola for doing small chores.

"What kind of cows did they have on the farm?"

"Big brown-and-white ones" didn't seem like a good answer. I guessed they were Guernseys.

"Here we prefer Holsteins because they produce more milk."

"Papa, be quiet! I'm trying to watch the game," said Franck.

———

After two nights in one of the hard twin beds in Franck's chilly bedroom, some fast, fumbling early-morning sex, and a lot of farm chores, I went back to Paris with the bottle of Champagne I'd come with.

"It's too fancy for my father," Franck had said when I pulled it out of my bag.

Franck's father insisted on coming with us to the station when I went to catch my train back to Paris. The three of us stood waiting on the windy platform, and when the train came, Franck's father clapped me on the back and said, "Next time you come, Alec, you call me Dgibèrt, not Monsieur Dubosc. Remember, we like Americans in Normandy. You saved us and gave us 'Ershey bars!"

After boarding, I fell asleep almost immediately, with a faint smell of cow manure in my nose and the mantra of Monsieur Dubosc's beautiful name, Dgibèrt, in my ears.

When I spoke with Franck during the week, I told him I thought he was making a mistake to assume that his father wouldn't eventually figure out that we were more than just friends.

"It would never occur to him, Alec. It's just not in his thoughts, and since I'm his only son and only child, it would make him sad."

The next time I visited the farm, it was Dgibèrt's birthday, so I brought a pack of Hershey bars from Grande Epicerie, the grocery store of the Bon Marché department store, the only place I knew in Paris that would have them, along with the same bottle of Champagne. On Friday night, we ate the pizza we'd picked up on the way home from the station and watched French variety shows on television. When, at the takeout place, I'd expressed curiosity about the pizza normande — with crème fraîche, sliced apples, and Camembert — Franck had groaned. "No one should do that to a Camembert," he said. "That's perverse!"

On a misty Saturday morning, Franck and his father decided to go hunting for pheasants. I said I'd rather stay home.

"No! Come with us, Alec!" Franck said, but I refused, telling them I'd never held a gun in my life.

"But you grew up in the country," Dgibèrt said.

"It was a countryside without guns," I explained, thinking of the tidy lawns and salt marshes of Westport.

After they left, I cleaned up the kitchen and threw out all of the spoiled food in the refrigerator. I had just sat down by the fire with a cup of tea and my book when the kitchen door opened. The short woman who entered was as startled to see me as I was to see her. Wearing rain-streaked steel-framed glasses and a buttoned-up tweed coat, she held a plaid plastic shopping bag in one hand and a large wicker picnic basket in the other. She introduced herself as Berthe, a neighbor, and said she'd come to cook. "I promised Paulette when she got sick that I would always look after Dgibèrt and Franck, and today is Dgibèrt's birthday."

She removed the striped yellow dishcloth that covered her basket, gave it a snap, and tucked it into her belt. The contents of the basket were arranged as carefully as a Flemish still life. There were mottled red and green cooking apples, potatoes powdery with the dust of dried mud, half a braid of onions with shiny copper skins, an old jam jar filled with ivory-colored cream, a conical block of butter wrapped in wax paper — Berthe proudly told me she'd made the butter herself — a plump chicken that still had its head and feet, a head of frilly garnet-colored lettuce, garlic, and some just-snipped branches of thyme and bay leaves, which doubtless came from her garden. Finally, she carefully lifted a fluted white-porcelain dish from her shopping bag and untied the knot of the white napkin that had been gathered around it to keep it safe. Inside was a tart filled with blackberry jam, which she'd made.

She refused my offer of help, telling me she knew this kitchen just as well as her own and adding that the Duboscs ate canned food when they were left on their own.

"At least I can peel the onions," I suggested, and she shrugged. We worked quietly for a while. She peeled, cored, and cut up the apples and then the potatoes as I skinned the onions.

"For apple soup," she told me. "It was something we cooked during the war, just apples and potatoes cooked in water some days, and with onions and cream or butter on the better ones. We never ate meat, and there was very little cheese, but we could hide a few apples and potatoes from the Germans. But this soup doesn't taste like something poor. It's nice." After melting a knob of butter and sautéing the onions in a Dutch oven, she added the bay leaves, thyme, and a pour from the jar of pale-yellow broth she'd brought along.

"How do you know Franck?" she said, stirring the onions with a wooden spoon.

"We became friends in Paris. He likes to come into the city sometimes because he's a little isolated here."

"His father worries about him, but he likes you. He told me about you, the American friend. But Franck needs to get married."

I said nothing.

"Thank you for cleaning up the kitchen," she said. "Most men are so messy."

Once the soup was made and the chicken was in the oven, Berthe changed the sheets in the bedrooms and did the laundry. When she finally sat down in the chair next to mine, I said, "It's kind of you to take such good care of them."

"It's normal," she said. "That's how we are in the country. We take care of each other. They chop my wood and fix leaks in my roof."

When Franck and his father came home late in the afternoon with a brace of birds, we drank Champagne from old mustard-jar glasses and sat down at the table, which Berthe had covered with the perfectly ironed sand-colored damask cloth she'd brought. The smooth apple soup was redolent of rich chicken broth, thyme-scented, and gently tangy. These were the comforting ancestral tastes of Normandy. They dated at least as far back as the apple trees and fowl intricately stitched on the borders of medieval tapestries depicting the battles and conquests of the region. For all of the recurring tumult over who would possess their verdant pastures and long, flat beaches, the Normans had always loved good food.

"This is one of the most delicious things I've ever eaten," I said, smearing a hunk of the baguette Berthe had brought with some of her sea-salt-flecked butter, which had the sweet perfume of cream.

"*Ouf!* Alec, you exaggerate, like all Americans!" said Dgibèrt, embarrassing me, so I kept to myself my thoughts on the ecstatic goodness of the juicy roast chicken, with its crispy bronzed skin, and the tiny potatoes infused with its rich drippings. The blackberry jam tart with crème fraîche was spectacular too, and Dgibèrt guffawed when he unwrapped the Hershey bars.

The next day Franck went to use the bathroom at the train station while Dgibèrt and I waited on the platform. "Thank you for the chocolate, Alec," Dgibèrt said. "It was very strange to eat the 'Ershey again after so many years. Now it's too sweet for me."

I suggested that wartime privation had probably gunned his boyhood pleasure.

"*Eh, oui,* it was a long time ago," he said. After the announcement that the Paris train would be arriving on track 2, he said, "You know, you should watch out for my boy. He's a good boy, but he is a wolf, and Alec, you are a lamb." When the train hissed to a halt, I kissed him on each bristly cheek, and Franck and I exchanged a wooden hug. The two of them waved goodbye from the platform and, with a sinking feeling, I realized I was falling in love with Franck.

Two weeks later, I was waiting to cross the place de la Concorde and thought: Dgibèrt warned you. The night before, Franck had stood me up on my birthday. The two lobsters I'd cooked for the meal we never shared were sitting untouched in my fridge. I knew Franck was in Paris, though, because a friend had called to tell me he'd seen him at Le Quetzal.

It was a beautiful fall day, so I decided to walk to the restaurant just off the Champs-Elysées where Patrick Lacroix, the menswear designer at Lanvin, had invited me to lunch. I'd met Patrick, a very debonair man, only once before, at a cocktail party after his fashion show, but he had been gracious and also shrewd enough to do a little research on me, the newcomer in the Fairchild office. After we'd been introduced, he whispered, "I love London too, Alec, but I hope you'll be very happy in Paris."

I was hoping some exercise would soothe the sting of the previous evening, and as I hurt as I was, I was also excited, because I was headed for Taillevent, the famous Michelin three-star restaurant in a townhouse on the rue Lamennais in the 8th arrondissement. I'd never been to a restaurant that served haute cuisine. As I walked up the Champs-Elysées, the wind picked up and the sky filled with low, fat gray clouds.

While I mingled with the Parisian crowd, I pretended to myself that if it was over with Franck, the one I'd be sorriest to lose was his father. But I knew I'd miss Franck desperately. Just as I reached the corner of the Champs-Elysées and the rue Washington, the first cold raindrop splatted on my forehead, and within a minute, it was pouring.

I didn't have an umbrella, so by the time I got to Taillevent, I was soaked. I stood across the street, watching black sedans pull up to the front door of the restaurant. At each arrival, a doorman rushed out to shield the customers with his big black umbrella. What to do? I couldn't go into the elegant restaurant as drenched and disheveled as I was. Maybe I would ask the doorman to deliver a message to Patrick, saying that I was very sorry, but I wouldn't be able to join him for lunch after all.

The doors of the restaurant opened again, and a man wearing glasses and a dark-gray suit crossed the street toward me, under a large dark-green umbrella.

"*Bonjour, monsieur,* and don't worry. It's happened to all of us!" he said in English. "I think you're expected for lunch, so please come with me." Inside, he led me to a small room and said he'd be right back. He returned with a towel, a comb, a jacket, a shirt, and a pair of socks, plus several coat hangers. "Please leave your jacket and shirt on the hangers," he said, and withdrew.

When I stepped out in dry clothing, he said, "Ah, that's much better then, isn't it?" Then he led me, grateful but puzzled by his omniscient kindness, into the dining room.

Patrick waved away my apology for being late but added that he was surprised someone who had recently been living in London had been caught without an umbrella. The man in the dark-gray suit returned with a cup of hot beef bouillon. "To ward off a chill," he said, placing it in front of me on a saucer.

"*Merci, Monsieur Vrinat,*" said Patrick. Then, in a lowered voice, he said to me, "He is the most charming man in Paris. And one of the most elegant."

I couldn't help asking Patrick if he'd sent Monsieur Vrinat to get me. "Of course not. I didn't know you were out there," he replied. "I think Monsieur Vrinat's powers of solicitude are supernatural."

Over flutes of Champagne and hot gougères, Patrick asked if I knew who Taillevent was. I didn't.

"His real name was Guillaume Tirel, and he was the chef to three French kings. Tirel wrote *Le viandier,* one of the first great essays about French cooking. He was born around 1310 and died in 1385, which just goes to show that a love of good food leads to a long life."

I was engrossed in the sumptuous menu when Patrick spoke again. "Alexandre, would you mind if I ordered for us? I have been here many times, and there are several dishes I would like you to try."

I nodded, even though I'd much rather have ordered my own meal. I just hoped Patrick wouldn't choose the pigeon. I had never eaten it and couldn't imagine why anyone would when lobster was an option.

"The chef here is Claude Deligne, who has cooked here since 1970. He is one of the great masters of classical French haute cuisine, and he hasn't been pushed off course by la nouvelle cuisine, with its vegetables that belong in a doll's house and dreadful tropical fruits like kiwis—I can't really believe anyone wants kiwis or star fruit or any of those other silly garnishes on their plates," said Patrick. "You see, Alexandre, my hero is Auguste Escoffier, the greatest French chef to have ever lived."

The sommelier brought out a huge leather-bound tome, the wine list. I glanced around the room while he and Patrick discussed what we would drink, and my amazement at being here, in one of the most famous restaurants in the world, elated me. Standing across the room with his arms folded, Monsieur Vrinat caught my eye and smiled.

"We'll begin with a Mersault," said Patrick. "And then I thought a Condrieu or a white Hautes-Côtes de Beaune—do you have a preference?"

"I'm afraid I don't know enough to have a preference," I replied.

"Then we'll have the Condrieu as our second wine. It's a happy white wine from the Rhône Valley, made with Viognier grapes."

Patrick surprised me by asking questions about my life—most fashion designers saw journalists as useful if exasperating mirrors of their own glory—and he was great company. He told me about a recent trip to Tangier, a place I dreamed of going. "It's a city that seethes with sex," he teased, and amused me with recent bon mots from his social circles.

"Someone asked Claude Pompidou why she'd had a face lift," he said, referring to the French president's wife. "And she said, *'Parce que j'en avais marre de voire ma beauté tomber par terre.'*" Patrick laughed. It took me a minute to get the joke — "because I'd had enough of seeing my beauty falling on the floor" — and then I chuckled too.

Our first course arrived. "Le cervelas de fruits de mer," said the one of the two waiters who served us.

I looked at the alabaster sausage in a puddle of glossy cream sauce on my plate. "Pierce one of the nipples gently," Patrick said, with a gleam in his eye. "It will release the pressure inside the sausage."

I flinched when our knees touched briefly under the table. Someone at the office had told me that Patrick lived with a Brazilian boy half his age. After only three months in France, I regularly found myself in way over my head for the simple reason that I was hopelessly naive. I hoped his sexual teasing was only playful.

The usual cervelas is a plump pale-pink sausage from Alsace, but this one was, Patrick told me, a mixture of pike, salmon (smoked and fresh), lobster, scallop roe, pistachios, truffles, crème fraîche, and eggs, all blended together and stuffed into a small fine stocking of pig's intestine. Then it was poached in white wine and served with a cream sauce made with seafood bouillon.

Garnished with natty sprigs of chervil, the cervelas was almost deceptively angelic, with buttery notes of pistachio balanced by small chunks of black truffle, which landed on the palate like tiny earthy comets.

I didn't realize that my contemplation had stalled our conversation until Patrick chuckled. "It's good, isn't it, Alexandre?"

"Incredible," I murmured. When I started to tell him why I

loved the cervelas, he held his index finger to his lips. "Pleasure is silent, Alexandre," he said, which embarrassed and irritated me. How could you not want to share your delight in a dish that had required hours of work to produce? Giving words to the happiness induced by this dish seemed the greatest compliment one could offer to the person who'd made it.

Meanwhile, Patrick was tasting the Condrieu, which the sommelier had just poured. "It's subtler than the Mersault, which is a lush wine that is easy to like," he told me. "Despite its soft floral notes, which come from the Viognier grape, it has the lean, taut muscles of a marathoner. I think it will go well with the next dish."

I nodded, but I wondered why he had the right to expound on the wine when he'd just told me pleasure should remain muted. It occurred to me that for the first time in my life, I'd been cast in what was then the prevailing feminine role at a restaurant, the passive recipient of pleasure. This irritated me too, since I believed that pleasure was heightened when it was reciprocal.

The waiters served us our turban de homard et de ris de veau, lobster mousse garnished with medallions of sautéed veal sweetbreads. I'd never eaten sweetbreads before and asked Patrick what they were.

"*Ouf!*" he said. "In English, I don't know." He waved a finger at Monsieur Vrinat. "Can you tell Alexandre the word for 'ris de veau' in English?"

"The thymus or pancreas of a calf, I think," replied Monsieur Vrinat.

The words sprang a panic in me. I didn't know what a thymus or a pancreas was, but the dish looked beautiful, a just barely pink crown garnished with beautifully browned nuggets of some sort of meat. Still, it was apparently a gland, an idea that made me cringe. I sipped my Condrieu, which had immediately become a favorite wine.

"Don't be afraid of the ris de veau, Alexandre. It's delicious," said Patrick, which did nothing to ease my apprehension about eating a thymus. And yet this was why I was sitting at this table. I wanted to be challenged. I wanted to learn.

The sensuousness of the lush lobster mousse hushed me, and, sensing that Patrick was watching me, I forked a piece of the sweetbreads and popped it into my mouth. Registering as a chalky, earthy, butter-basted animal custard, it punched my palate with bracingly bestial joy.

"The lobster mousse with sweetbreads is usually served as a starter, but I asked if we could have it as a main course because I wanted you to try what I think are the two finest dishes at this restaurant," he said, and then he sipped his wine. "I am enjoying our lunch because it is a kind of seduction I've never known before. One that's chaste but passionate, no?"

I nodded, but having been scolded into silence earlier, I couldn't tell him that I was deeply grateful to discover a type of intimacy I'd never known before either, the shared happiness of a satiated palate.

We had some cheese, and then hazelnut ice cream with caramel sauce. After the table had been cleared, Patrick reached into his leather briefcase and pulled out a book of fabric samples and some sketches of his next menswear collection. "I was inspired by the soldiers of the Austro-Hungarian Empire," he said. As he explained his sketches, I noticed the bald dome of his head had acquired the waxy sheen of well-polished furniture, and I wondered what this lunch had been all about. His extravagance and generosity had befuddled me, and when he'd finished talking about the other inspirations for his next collection, in terms of fabrics, colors, and mood, including "A hunt in the English countryside" and "The docks of Hamburg," he stopped and looked me in the eye.

"It's not because you will write about my clothing that I am interested by you, Alexandre. It's because I think we may share some old wounds, ones that have made us sensitive and strong."

This made no sense to me, until it did. By telling me that he saw me for who I actually was, Patrick was inviting me to reciprocate, to be interested in him as a person, maybe because this would make me understand his clothing better or want to write about him. Who knew? But his invitation was as sincere as Franck's had been when he told me that he was lonely.

Coffee was served with petits fours and chocolates. Patrick sipped his coffee and paused. "Tell me, Alexandre, what are the best things you've eaten since you moved to Paris?"

I hesitated because I knew what he wanted to hear. And then I told him the truth, because if we were going to become friends, it would have to start with that.

"An apple-and-potato soup I ate on a farm in Normandy and a kidney in cream sauce at a bistro in Les Halles."

Patrick cocked his head. "So you prefer peasant food?" I could tell he felt slighted.

"I like food that's been cooked from the heart."

Because I had to change back into my own damp clothing, we parted in the vestibule. I thanked him for the magnificent lunch.

"You're welcome, Alexandre, but I fear that this meal went way over your head," he said coolly, and walked out into the rain.

It hadn't, though; it was just that I preferred sincerity in the kitchen to technical perfection. I hugely admired the dishes I'd eaten with Patrick, but they'd never move me the way Berthe's soup had. Maybe this was because, like Patrick, I was an admirer of the French chef, restaurateur, and culinary writer Auguste Escoffier, who said, "The greatest dishes are very simple."

It was well past 4 p.m. when I got back to my office on the rue Cambon. I had an article that had to be filed before 5 p.m. New York time, so I worked very late. When I got home, Franck was waiting for me by the front door of my building, with a bunch of blue-dyed chrysanthemums and his overnight bag.

"I'm really sorry, Alec," he said. "Last night, I went for a drink with a friend since you were still at work and the night got away from me."

"You could have called me."

"I know. I'm sorry. These are for you." He handed me the flowers.

He'd missed the last train to Normandy, so I told him he could sleep on my couch. I also told him that it wasn't going to work out between us. He hid who he was, and I didn't. He'd never leave his Norman farm, and I wasn't giving up Paris. And I needed to be able to trust the person I loved.

In the morning, I gave him a cup of coffee and a big hug, smelling the smoke of the fireplace in the living room of his Normandy farmhouse in his hair for the last time, and he left. Stung by the realization that if love has its reasons, they can sometimes be the wrong ones, I nevertheless missed him for a long time.

10

THE TALK OF THE TOWN

Alec dresses like a college librarian," I overheard one of my male colleagues say. I'd just come through the front door to the office after lunch. Almost everyone in the meeting, in a room around the corner, laughed.

"And he doesn't know anyone," sniped someone else. It was true—I didn't have the same baseball-card-like knowledge of Parisian socialites that the other editors did.

I gathered that Dennis Thim, the new bureau chief, had just told the staff that he'd given me a plum assignment: to write up the dinner that Madame la Baronne Marie-Hélène de Rothschild was giving that night, before the start of the couture fashion shows, for the gossip-driven "Eye" column of *Women's Wear Daily*. Dennis had replaced my friend Christa, who had been abruptly fired. Mr. Fairchild had given her the news in the elevator, on their way back from lunch at the Hotel Ritz. Dennis loved the gossip and social intrigue that Christa had found tedious. A former advertising sales rep for Fairchild, he had no journalistic experience, and he'd had a chilly reception from many in the office. Since I hadn't cold-shouldered him—even if I didn't trust him, I felt a bit sorry for him—he was hoping to groom me as an ally, which was why he'd given me the assignment everyone else wanted.

"I think it's good to throw a curveball to the society types every once in a while. That's why I want Alec to do it," Dennis had told his staff.

I went into my office and softly closed the door. A few minutes later, Dennis knocked and came in. "Are you looking forward to the party?"

"Sort of," I said with a shrug. I was curious about this rarefied world, but I doubted the evening would add up to a good time.

"Come on, Alec, this will be good for you. And you have to get to know Marie-Hélène because she's the center of the solar system in Paris," said Dennis. "All you have to do is drift around the room while they're having cocktails, see who's there and what they're wearing, snag some quotes, and get some dirt. Mr. Fairchild loves catfights. Make sure you have correctly identified all of the guests too, and then you can take off once they sit down for dinner."

Before leaving to go to the party, I read up on the hostess. Marie-Hélène de Rothschild was the wife of Baron Guy de Rothschild, a very wealthy banker, and the daughter of an Egyptian mother and Baron Egmont van Zuylen van Nyevelt, a Dutch aristocrat and diplomat. She'd been educated at Marymount College in New York City and was now best known for the extravagant balls she gave at her magnificent country house. Parisian society's grandest hostess, she was an avid racegoer and horse breeder, a serious fundraiser for medical research, and an important patron of artists, musicians, and couturiers. In Paris, she and her husband lived in the Hôtel Lambert on the Île Saint-Louis. Built in 1640 by the architect Louis Le Vau, it was considered one of the most elegant private mansions in France.

A few hours later I took the Métro to the station nearest the Île Saint-Louis, one of the three islands in the Seine in the heart of Paris, and crossed the bridge on foot. Leaning on the stone wall of the embankment in front of the Hôtel Lambert, I looked up at the golden light coming from the windows of the Rothschilds' sumptuous home and tried to tamp down an almost paralyzing shyness. My improbable debut as a social chronicler of Parisian high society lay before me.

It felt very far away from my Greenwich Village studio, which had been so small, I could almost lean out from my sofa bed and cook breakfast. It was my first apartment, a cozy place from which I'd embarked to begin my new life in Europe. Lying night after night in my lumpy foldout bed there, I'd watched the ceiling moldings by the honey-colored glow of the street-light outside and dreamed of jumping those boundaries for a life in Paris, something I never thought could really happen. Now that I was finally here, to my surprise I at times actually missed my pizza-by-the-slice life as a modestly paid book editor in New York City.

I wasn't homesick, but learning the caste systems of Europe had made me value American egalitarianism. It created more of a sociologically level playing field, animated by a reflexive use of humor. This is what made Americans nice. I took a deep breath, approached the big wooden doors in the stone wall on the other side of the street, and pressed down hard on the shiny brass nub set into a square of green marble.

The sleepy-looking butler with basset hound eyes who opened the door took my coat and led me up the curved ramp of the beautiful stone staircase. Madame la Baronne awaited me at the top.

"*Enfin, mon scribe arrive!*" She glanced at her watch, but I knew I wasn't late. "*Bonsoir, Alexandre,*" she said, and looked me over from head to toe. Her face appeared world weary but not unkind, as though she'd seen everything and decided to be amused by it. She was wearing a beautiful necklace of lapis la-zuli, which flattered her short, waved, caramel-colored bob, and her full-length Nile-green silk dress.

I took out my pencil and pad, and she fluttered a hand. "Put that notebook away and just enjoy yourself," said the baroness. "If anyone says something interesting or amusing, you won't forget it. And if they don't, you can always make it all up," she added with a wry smile.

I laughed and put my pad in my pocket.

"Just be a good boy, Alexandre. Nothing rude about any of my guests in the newspaper, please," she said. *"Venez avec moi, chéri."*

I followed her into a sumptuous salon lit by massive candelabras and scented by huge bouquets of sweet-smelling white flowers, including gardenias. A waiter offered me a flute of Champagne from a tray, and just after the baroness had told me she would give me a list of her guests so that I didn't have to worry about spelling their names correctly, a maid came and whispered in her ear.

Madame la Baronne excused herself, and as I watched her walk away in a rustle of silk, I found myself surprised—I liked her. I thought she'd be a dragon, but she was warm and seemingly unpretentious.

I stood by one of the huge windows of the vast salon and observed the other guests, who chatted in small groups under the stunning crystal chandelier that hung from the coffered ceiling, which was gilded and painted. Aware that I should be mingling, I was bracing myself for a first attempt at small talk when someone spoke to me over my shoulder.

"Hi there!" said a tall, friendly-looking blonde. Her unlined face had the kind of bland beauty that spoke of unexamined privilege and the skills of an excellent plastic surgeon. "Are you the new journalist from Fairchild?"

I introduced myself.

"I'm Nan Kempner," she said.

An hour earlier her name would have meant nothing to me, but Dennis Thim had mentioned she'd be at the party. "She's a total clotheshorse. Nan's probably Yves Saint Laurent's most significant couture client—she's filthy rich and one of the original ladies who lunch. She loves getting in the paper, but Mr.

Fairchild thinks she's a little too obvious, so just use her as a good source of information. She's nice and fun."

While she and I chatted about Paris and London, she kept her eyes on the room. She asked me when the Fairchild photographer would be coming, and I told her he'd arrive during dinner. Suddenly it occurred to me that she might be good for a quote, so I asked her exactly what she did.

She laughed. "Oh, darling, I don't do anything. I shop!" she said. "Now let's get you out of this corner because no good reporter should ever be a wallflower! Come!"

I followed her over to three people who were chatting on the other side of the room, and she introduced me. They offered tight smiles and looked at me skeptically.

"Oh! We don't know this one!" said a younger woman, speaking in English. She looked vaguely familiar. It was Princess Caroline of Monaco.

In a rattled attempt to make conversation by offering up the only thing we had in common, I told her that I had gone to Amherst College, the school her brother Albert had also attended. Ignoring that, she asked, "How do you like working for Fairchild?"

A waiter stopped with a tray of smoked salmon roses and little potatoes that had been hollowed out and filled with sour cream and caviar. We each took an hors d'oeuvre, a pause I hoped would allow me to duck the princess's question, but she, Nan Kempner, and the two men (who I later learned were Parisian high society's favorite lapdog aesthetes, an interior designer and a landscape architect) stood there in silence, waiting for my answer.

"It's rather challenging," I said finally, and they laughed.

The conversation turned to the French president, François Mitterand, and his plan to redesign the Tuileries Garden. They all fretted that the new design might be *vulgaire*, an accusation more feared in these circles than being called immoral or depraved.

Madame la Baronne reappeared at my elbow. "Alexandre, one of my guests tonight is feeling ill and cannot stay for dinner, so I will seat you at the table," she told me.

My heart sank, as if I'd heard a jail door slam behind me. I was already desperate for this evening to be over. Their fame and wealth notwithstanding, most of these pampered people were surprisingly dull. The baroness introduced me to another group chatting by the window, without telling me who they were. I recognized the ashen, vacant-eyed Yves Saint Laurent, who wore a black turtleneck and indigo velvet jacket. He was trembling slightly and trailing cigarette ash on the floor around him, oblivious to the butler who stood behind him with an ashtray. I'd seen one of the other men several times at Le Trap, a louche gay bar near the Café de Flore in Saint-Germain-des-Prés. In another corner, I thought I recognized a handsome young man as the owner of La Maison Blanche, a fashionable restaurant in the 15th arrondissement, and an older woman — I thought I'd heard someone say she was his mother. They were chatting about a feud between Karl Lagerfeld, the designer at Chanel, and Giorgio Armani.

"Oh, well, boys will be boys," said Nan Kempner, who'd sidled over.

"So, Alexandre, are you married?" taunted the man I'd seen at the gay bar.

I shook my head.

He needled me. "Still haven't found the right woman yet?"

Ignoring him, I turned to the stout older woman, who was wearing a girlish velvet headband to hold back her lank salt-and-pepper bob. "I love your son's restaurant," I said.

"I am his wife, sir, and he doesn't own a restaurant," she replied, and turned her back to me.

For the next twenty minutes or so, I fumbled my way from one conversation to the next, often only half understanding what was said because the talk was sprinkled with the first names of people I didn't know and my French was still wobbly.

"A table, s'il vous plaît," the baroness announced, and we filed into a dining room. On every wall huge mirrors, in ormolu frames, reflected dozens of lit tapers. The table was beautifully set with a coral linen tablecloth, heavy silver, and solid silver serving plates adorned with a family crest, which were promptly removed by the butler who'd let me in earlier. To my surprise, I was seated to the left of the baroness and, to my horror, directly facing the woman I'd just insulted. Yves Saint Laurent had disappeared.

The butler poured an excellent white Bordeaux, and we were served a thatch of baby lettuce leaves and herbs on gold-edged plates.

"Que c'est drôle, Marie-Hélène, d'avoir un journaliste à table avec nous!" — "How amusing it is to have a journalist sitting at the table with us!" — said the woman I'd offended. Her tone implied that my social standing was just beneath that of the servants. Several people at the table laughed, and I felt my cheeks burning.

I'd just taken a slug of my wine when I realized the man I'd seen at the gay bar was speaking to me. "Where in America are you from then, Alexandre?" he said, and the rest of the table went silent.

I told him I was from Connecticut, and his eyes glittered.

"New England is just barely acceptable. The rest of America ..." His voice trailed off. He was exhibiting the snobbish French idea that New England, and only New England, just barely merits a pass. *"Mais, mon Dieu, que les Américains sont incultes,"* he added. He found us uncouth.

A burst of adrenaline shot through my veins and broke the

dam of my manners. "Uncouth some of us may be, but at least we're generally very polite."

Nan Kempner winked at me, and the interior designer said, "Touché!" Everyone else at the table looked at me as though seeing me for the first time. The little spat had delighted them.

"Mon cher Alexandre," said the baroness with a pursed smile, "you will find that the Gauls are *très féroce.*" She picked up her knife and fork, signaling that the incident was over.

Not for me, though. My pulse was still pounding, and I felt a dizzy mixture of embarrassment at having lost my composure and a small, hard pearl of pride. To my astonishment, I'd just done something rare for me, especially in a daunting situation like this one. I'd managed to stick up for myself instead of avoiding confrontation.

In fact, I'd had enough of being cast as a figure of fun, something that seemed to occur every other day. The weekend before, I'd gone to the food hall of Le Bon Marché department store to buy chicken breasts for my first Paris dinner party. When I reached the counter, I asked the white-smocked butcher for *"quatre seins de poulet."* Four chicken breasts — or so I thought.

He'd stared at me with bug-eyed amusement. Then he said loudly, *"Eh, bah, bien, si les poulets en Amérique ont des seins, j'y vais demain!"* — "If the chickens in America have breasts, I'm leaving tomorrow!" Everyone in line guffawed.

I had no idea what I'd said incorrectly until an elderly lady behind me quietly explained it. "Monsieur, in French, the word *sein* is used only for a woman's bosom. What you want to order is *blancs de volailles,*" she added kindly.

And this was nothing on the day before, at the barber. When I asked him to shave my neck, he reared back in alarm. For an English speaker the treacherously similar French words for neck, posterior, and the male sex are difficult to master, so I could only assume I'd made a glaringly obscene mistake.

Now the only noise in the dining room was cutlery on porcelain. I prodded a leaf on my plate, and it fell away to reveal a tiny wizened claw. I quickly tucked this away under a larger leaf, thinking someone in the kitchen had made a ghastly mistake, but the baroness leaned forward and with a flick of her fork exposed the hideous little claw again.

"Mangez le! Ce sont les grives, Alexandre — un délice qui vient de ma maison à la campagne," she insisted, plucking a tiny leg from her own salad and nibbling it. I didn't know what a *grive* was, but it looked awful.

"The English word is *thrush*," said the man I'd seen in the gay bar, in English. "And it *is* a delicacy."

The other guests were twirling tiny drumsticks and nibbling at other pieces of their birds, except for Nan Kempner, who made a quick grimace when our eyes met. I laughed — grateful for an ally, and everyone looked at me again. I picked up a piece and bit some of its meager meat. It tasted like a wet dog smells, so, reacting as swiftly as a practiced pickpocket, under the table I tore a page from my little notebook, folded it around the miserable avian appendage, and stashed it in my blazer pocket.

While our plates were being cleared, the baroness spoke. "What a shame!" she said, shaking her head as my nearly untouched plate was removed. "It's very easy to see who the Americans are at my table tonight. Alexandre, why are Americans such fussy children at the table?"

"I think maybe it's because we like our songbirds in trees, not on our plates," I said, and Princess Caroline laughed.

Continuing the evening's gastronomic theme of *un dîner de chasse,* a hunt dinner, the next course was roasted pheasant, served with sautéed cèpes and boiled potatoes. I helped myself to three potatoes, a spoonful of mushrooms, and a small piece of the bird. Looking down the table, I saw two mushrooms on Nan Kempner's plate and nothing else.

The pheasant had been hung so long, its taste made me sweat

at the temples before it registered on my palate with a putrid shock. Next came a cheese course with salad, and we served ourselves from the tray that a butler held. The baroness proudly told me that the Brie was produced on the Rothschilds' farm outside Paris. I cut myself a small piece of it.

She put her gnarled hand on my arm and shook her head. "Alexandre, never cut the nose off a cheese," she said, a reprimand that was audible to everyone. I sensed this was a retort to my remark about Americans preferring their birds in trees.

What she was telling me, I later learned, was that the French consider it bad manners to cut a piece of cheese in a way that leaves it with a blunt end, as I'd done. Instead, with allowances made for the shape of the cheese, you should always cut from the side. It was useful information, but I knew nonetheless that the baroness had intentionally embarrassed me. At her table, I was meant to understand, she was the one who orchestrated the conversation.

Since all of the guests at dinner were on permanent diets, the meal concluded with petits fours and little cups of pear eau-de-vie sorbet. After the photographer from Fairchild had finished taking pictures of the guests, I waited until the baroness had said goodbye to Princess Caroline and a few of the others who'd stood up promptly after drinking their little porcelain cups of coffee.

"Thank you for a very memorable evening," I said to Marie-Hélène de Rothschild.

"You're quite welcome, Alexandre, and you've been a most unusual guest, which was amusing," she replied.

When the butler showed me out, and I was once again just another Parisian walking home in the middle of the night, I felt a huge relief. I decided the evening had been a success, but it wasn't something I wanted to repeat. When I got home, I ordered a sausage pizza.

The next day I wrote my story about the dinner, which I

titled, "Boys Will Be Boys," recounting the chatter about the feud between Lagerfeld and Armani and mentioning the precipitous and unexplained departure of Yves Saint Laurent. I left it on Dennis Thim's desk.

"Alec, this is so great!" said Dennis, when he found me in my office. "There's a cocktail party at Hubert de Givenchy's tonight I'd like you to cover."

I told him I didn't want to.

"Why? I talked to Marie-Hélène today, and she said she liked you and that you were clever and feisty."

"I'd like to write more for *W*," I told Dennis. "But not society stuff."

"It would be really good for your career. It will get you noticed," he said.

"I don't care." I'd made my decision. Since it left me with a sick feeling in the pit of my stomach, I'd never write gossip again.

11

MY TOUR DE FRANCE

knew it would be rude to cancel lunch with Noëlle Bobin, the press director of the French Menswear Association, for a third time.

I liked the husky-voiced, chain-smoking Noëlle because, when we'd first met, I learned she loved to eat. The problem was, I knew our conversation would inevitably turn to menswear, a subject I found excruciatingly dull. Fortunately, La Providence, the restaurant where we were meeting, was just a short walk from my office.

The dining room, painted white, had a ceiling of exposed wooden beams the color of caramel, and the warm air smelled of cinnamon. A gentle-looking middle-aged man with a chestnut-brown cowlick and the face of a sad boy was drying wineglasses behind the bar. I gave him Noëlle's name, and he suggested a table by the window. It was covered with the same cheerful beige-and-raspberry-plaid fabric as the café curtains in the front windows. The little restaurant felt snug on a cold, rainy day in December two weeks before Christmas.

"Welcome," he said as he bought me wine in a glass with a stubby green stem. "It's an Alsatian Riesling." I noticed his pretty blue eyes, his misbuttoned baggy plum cardigan, his scuffed brown brogues. He looked like a kid who was late for school.

Noëlle was never on time, so I took the newspaper from my briefcase and read, and a minute later the man timidly offered me a star-shaped cookie on a small plate. "We made these this morning," he said. "They're called Zimtsterne, a type of bredele, which is the name for Christmas cookies in Alsace."

I told him I'd never been to Alsace.

"You must go! I don't mean to boast, but we have the best food in France, and this is the season of the Christmas markets."

The soft glazed cinnamon cookie was delicious with a sip of Riesling. He grinned when I said so. "We make more than one hundred different kinds of bredele in Alsace. We love Christmas."

Noëlle arrived, and she and the cookie man kissed each other on both cheeks.

"*Ça va, mon Antoine?*" she said to him.

He smiled, poured her a glass of Riesling, and gave us menus. "I'm very busy today because Ginette is out sick with a cold," Antoine told Noëlle before he disappeared into the kitchen.

"He is one of the nicest men in Paris," she whispered. We looked at our menus, and I knew nothing about any of the dishes that were listed. "Have you eaten Alsatian food before, Alec?"

I hadn't.

"I'm sure you'll like it. I'm originally from La Lorraine, the sister province of Alsace, so I've been eating this food my whole life. I think it's one of France's greatest regional kitchens." This was the first I'd heard of French regional cooking. Noëlle must have noticed the blank look on my face.

"French cooking is sort of a big casserole of all the country's regional kitchens," she said. "Every province has contributed something to our gastronomy." She ordered an Alsatian salad — Bibb lettuce with Gruyère cheese and sliced cervelas sausage to start, and then the plat du jour, which was coq au Riesling. I said I'd have the same thing.

It was a disappointment when Noëlle began talking about

trends in neckties. She was telling me about a project to showcase the silk weavers of Lyon as part of a new French brand of
ties when Antoine saved me by setting a square tart down in the
middle of the table. "Since your guest has never eaten Alsatian
food before, I decided flammekueche would be the best place to
start."

"Antoine, you're trying to make me fat!" protested Noëlle.

"Not fat, Noëlle. Abundant," he said.

The tart had a thin crust of bread dough and was topped with
matchstick lardons and finely sliced onions, which had charred
here and there while baking on a base of white, creamy fromage blanc and crème fraîche. The gently soured taste of the fromage blanc was the perfect backdrop for the drama of onions
wilted to sweetness by the oven's heat and the salt and smoke
of the cured pork. It was like a Germanic version of pizza, and
I loved it.

The tender Bibb lettuce had trapped some of the grainy mustard vinaigrette in its tender folds and came with a thatch of
nutty grated Gruyère cheese over slices of pale-pink cervelas. As
I ate, I couldn't help but think that it was a much better version
of the bologna-and-cheese sandwiches in my lunch bag when I
was a kid. The cervelas had a skin that snapped when you bit in
and was finer, less fatty, and more delicate than bologna, with a
distant sweet floral taste of mace.

While we ate, Noëlle began to tell me about La Providence's
owner, Chef Schweitzer. He came, she said, from a famous military family in Alsace. His "ferocious" father had been a general in the French army, and his three brothers were also in the
armed forces. After serving in the army as the head of France's
military mission to Mali, Chef Schweitzer had gone to hotel
school and completed apprenticeships in several famous Michelin-starred restaurants in Alsace. He'd wanted to open his
own place in Strasbourg, but his father had told him that he
"couldn't abide the shame" of having a son who was a cook, so

Chef Schweitzer had moved to Paris. I was eager to meet this virile, food-loving soldier who'd stood up to his father to make a life of his own in the kitchen. I hoped he'd come into the dining room at the end of our meal.

The fowl braised in Riesling with brown mushrooms, bacon, shallots, parsley, and cream had the gentle sweet-and-sour tang of the Alsatian white wine and was falling-off-the-bone tender. Antoine brought it to the table in a poppy-colored enameled casserole, along with a blue-glazed bowl of buttered hand-rolled spaetzle.

"What I really admire is that he didn't come to Paris to do fancy cooking, but real Alsatian farmhouse food," Noëlle said, mopping up her plate with a piece of baguette. Even though neither of my grandmothers cooked, I knew what she meant—this was humble but deeply satisfying food that expressed a strong, proud sense of place and that was carefully prepared with a deep desire to make people happy.

We finished up with Muenster cheese, which came to the table with a shot glass of cumin seeds as a garnish, and airy slices of kougelhof, a raisin-flecked, almond-topped yeast cake. At the end of the meal, Noëlle wrote down the address of one of her other favorite restaurants, Chez Maître Paul, which specialized in the cooking of the Jura, in the east on the Swiss border.

When Antoine brought our coffee, he glanced at the little piece of paper with a perforated edge in the middle of the table. "Chez Maître Paul is very good," he said. "If you go there, you must have the poulet au vin jaune et aux morilles (chicken in yellow-wine sauce with morels). But you must also come back to me on Fridays for the baeckeoffe," he told me. "It's a dish of pork, mutton, and beef, with leeks, carrots, and sliced potatoes, that cooks in a hot oven with white wine and herbs. Its name means 'the baker's oven,' and it was a casserole that women made and brought to the baker to slow-cook in the embers of his wood-fired oven after the bread was done."

Suddenly it dawned on me that Antoine and Chef Schweitzer were the same person, and I felt like an idiot. But in his worn forest-green corduroy trousers, Antoine Schweitzer hardly looked like a soldier, much less a talented chef. I'd assumed he was the maître d'hôtel or the manager or something.

When I went to dinner at La Providence the following Friday, to taste the baeckeoffe, I brought Fiona, the only friend I had at work.

Mr. Schweitzer blushed shyly. *"B-b-bonsoir,"* he stuttered. The restaurant was busy, and we were served by Ginette, the wisecracking red-haired waitress who'd been out sick the day I'd gone to lunch with Noëlle.

"So you're the American Antoine was talking about," she said, after hearing my accent when I ordered. "He said you're very interested in food."

I told her I was.

"Then you're in the right place," she said with a little chuckle. She put her hand on her hip and cocked her head. "And what else are you interested in, *chéri?"*

The baeckeoffe came to the table in a pale-blue ceramic casserole, which had been sealed with baked bread dough. After placing the casserole on a trivet, Ginette cut the golden band of bread with a knife and opened the heavy lid with a potholder. The comforting shawl of steam that rose from the bubbling vault was scented by wine, bay leaves, and something resinous I couldn't immediately identify. Ginette insisted on serving us and pointed out the small black berries, which turned out to be the source of the elusive aroma. *"Baies de genièvre,"* she said, adding that Mr. Schweitzer had gathered the juniper berries himself on the farm he owned in Alsace. The berries embroidered the soothing casserole, a sort of French version of shepherd's pie, with invigorating gastronomic pointillism that gave the dish some dash.

When Mr. Schweitzer stopped by our table at the end of our meal, I thanked him.

"I'm glad you enjoyed it, because there's nothing more Alsatian," he said, adding, "You know, in France, our cooking is our history. It dates back to a time when our country was rural and people mostly ate only the foods they could grow themselves."

As I dined at La Providence with friends, one boyfriend after another, and sometimes on my own, it became my haven. I loved Mr. Schweitzer's food, and I felt comfortable there because, despite the polite awkwardness between us, there was an inchoate intimacy that I was in no hurry to verbalize. I sensed he probably wasn't either. We'd recognized something in each other and that was enough. So we talked mostly about food, and Antoine Schweitzer became my eager tutor.

I never left a meal there without a new restaurant address or a casual lesson in the cooking from a part of France I'd never been to. I learned about piperade, the Basque specialty of soft scrambled eggs with peppers and onions, and aligot, fresh Tomme cheese curds whipped into mashed potato and garlic from the Auvergne in central France. Other dishes, such as kig ha farz from Brittany, a pot-au-feu cooked in a fabric sleeve with a crumbly garnish of buckwheat-flour porridge, were less urgently enticing to me. But I was game for anything. Mr. Schweitzer's goal was to arouse my curiosity, and mine was to be his student.

Ginette thought we were crazy. "*C'est un peu trop!* Can't you talk about anything else but food?" she groused one night.

Almost a year after I'd first visited La Providence, I'd had to stay at work late, rewriting captions for photographs of a fashion shoot because the editor in New York wanted more description. I'd seen the show but couldn't remember the clothing fabrics or other important details, so I winged it as best I could. It was 10 p.m. by the time I finished, and I was the last one out of the office. Walking to the Métro, I was hungry, and glum about the prospect of a can of soup alone at my kitchen table. I turned around and ran up the rue Saint-Honoré to La Providence.

"How nice to see you, Alec," Mr. Schweitzer said when I came through the door. At this hour, only one other table was still occupied in the dining room. Mr. Schweitzer gestured toward my favorite spot by the window.

"My mother made this," Mr. Schweitzer said, serving me a thick mauve slab of compressed pieces of goose liver on a lettuce leaf, with little golden cubes of Riesling gelée and warm toasted brioche. "Foie gras is a specialty of Alsace. It's also the pride of southwestern France, but ours is better."

I thanked him with wan enthusiasm. I'd never eaten foie gras before and hadn't shaken my aversion to organ meats.

"Please try it."

I nodded dubiously. He put a hand on my shoulder. "You have so much culinary curiosity, Alec, but you're afraid of too many foods. There will always be things you don't like, but you should try everything at least once."

I stared at the goose liver, wishing it would turn into one of the appetizers on the menu that I really wanted, maybe a nice hot square slice of flammekueche. Mr. Schweitzer returned to his usual perch behind the bar, but I could feel his eyes on me from across the room. I gingerly cut a small piece of the foie gras, smeared it on a corner of brioche, and popped it into my mouth. Waxy at first and then melting, the terrine had a frank farmyard taste of damp straw, muddy puddles, and dried corn. It was sweet and funky up front, and it finished with a soft slash of bitterness. I loved its unguent texture, and the little cubes of Riesling jelly, which added gentle floral notes to the liver, created a very elegant and complex dish. The foie gras, which Mr. Schweitzer had served with a glass of Gewürztraminer, was absolutely delicious.

"So, you liked it," he said as he cleared my empty plate. When

I tried to compliment him, he waved his free hand to make me stop.

"Alec, from what you told me, I think you've used your love of food to set yourself free, but you always go back inside your cage. You don't have to."

I was as startled by the intimacy of his observations as I was by their accuracy, and I avoided his eyes. The party at the only other table had paid and left, and it was just the three of us in the dining room. Ginette poured me another glass of wine and invited me to join them.

I did, and after a few seconds, the awkwardness dissolved.

"You seem a little sad tonight, Alec," Mr. Schweitzer said gently. And yes, I was, because I was tired from working late so often and weary of the catfight atmosphere in the office and the daily challenges of trying to make a life for myself in the city I'd fantasized about for years. The fact that my boyfriend hadn't called me in several days didn't help either.

"It's just been a bad day," I told him, and served myself from the steaming platter of choucroute garnie in front of me. Eaten with dabs of nostril-stinging mustard and waxy boiled potatoes, the choucroute was as comforting as a heavy down quilt on a cold night and deeply satisfying, especially the cumin-seasoned smoked sausages. Mr. Schweitzer told me he had them sent directly from a charcutier in his village, near Colmar.

"How is your new life in Paris coming along?" he asked, dropping his eyes and pulling pills off from his gray sweater.

I insisted that everything was fine.

"*Bébé*, it's not easy, what you're doing," said Ginette. "You're a long way from home and everything's new and complicated, and — well, it takes time."

I changed the subject because I didn't want to be pitied. We chatted about the weather and our favorite singers — they were thrilled when I told them I'd discovered Dalida, the Italian Egyptian torch singer I'd heard on the radio.

"Are you meeting people?" Ginette asked.

"I am," I said, and launched into an account of my dinner with the Rothschilds. When I got to the part about my spat, I hesitated. Then I told them the story anyway, and they laughed.

Mr. Schweitzer took off his glasses and wiped them with his napkin. "You know, I think that argument at the dinner party may have been good for you," he said. "Because with the work you want to do—not the fashion, I'm thinking, but maybe something to do with your love of good food, you have to have the confidence to be critical, to take a stand. And that night you did. The next time, you'll say what you think with less emotion, which means you can be fair and honest."

Ginette brought another bottle of Riesling, and they eagerly asked me questions about where I was from, my family, and New York City. Both of them had dreamed of going to New York the way I'd once dreamed of Paris, and I could see they were spellbound as I told them I'd lived in a minuscule studio in a walk-up in Greenwich Village with a bunch of other oddballs.

They wanted to know more, so I told them about the old Hungarian man in the homburg hat who lived below me and was one of the world's experts on the stamps of the Austro-Hungarian Empire. I also mentioned Alice, the Argentine-born former Radio City Music Hall Rockette who'd retired after surviving breast cancer and lived up two flights with her merchant marine husband. She spent her days smoking joints, drinking blackberry brandy, painting faces on stones she found in parks, and sleeping with the Cuban superintendent when her husband was away. I told my Parisian friends that even though I'd had very little money, I'd been happy because I could still afford a warm, freshly made mozzarella from the cheese store on Bleecker Street, a croissant or two from the excellent bakery run by an Algerian-born Frenchman around the corner from my apartment, or a big glass of cold beer in the bar just across the street, where there was always good chat and sometimes the prospect of sex. I told them about spending hours reading in a beach chair on my fire escape, where I grew basil, parsley, and chives in pots, and walking to end of a rotting pier on the Hudson on the Fourth of July to see the fireworks exploding over New York Harbor.

Mr. Schweitzer asked me when I'd eaten French food for the first time, and I described the lunch that my mother, brother, and I had eaten in New York City, at a restaurant called Charles V, which was stuffy and expensive. I added that in those days, most Americans reflexively associated all French restaurants with those two adjectives, which made the two of them laugh. My onion soup there had been delicious, but what stayed with me the most was a curt conversation I'd had with the waiter. I'd wanted to know why my soup was so good, and he'd tersely replied that it was because it had been made with a stock from veal bones and meat trimmings.

"Why did you find that interesting?" Mr. Schweitzer asked. I explained I'd never thought about where flavor came from before, and the idea fascinated me. I became obsessed by the flavor of bones, because what was the flavor of bones?

"You were a strange boy, weren't you?" Ginette said with a laugh.

We were still sipping chilled snifters of Alsatian pear eau-de-vie at 1 a.m. when we started talking about where we would go for our summer vacations. Mr. Schweitzer would spend his holiday taking care of the garden and orchard at his house in Alsace. Ginette was going camping in Brittany with a friend, and I planned to travel to Biarritz for a few days and eat my way through Basque Country, after which I would spend the rest of August in Paris.

"Why? It's hot in Paris in August, and everything closes," said Ginette.

I explained that I'd dreamed of living in the city for such a long time, I wanted to know it during every season.

"Well, now you have your dream, Alec. So I suppose you should make the best of it," said Ginette, who got up and cleared our glasses.

"Dreams are like seeds from an unknown plant," said Mr. Schweitzer. "You never know what will grow from them until they've been sown."

Ginette insisted on giving me a ride home in her beat-up red Renault, and I kissed Mr. Schweitzer on each soft, fleshy cheek before we left. "Thank you for the little trip to New York City, Alec. I enjoyed it," he said.

Mr. Schweitzer was the first real friend I'd had with whom I could talk about food. He was the one who taught me that the essence of French cooking was found in its countryside. By feeding me the foods of Alsace, then by sending me to other great provincial kitchens in the city, he set me up for my own gastronomic Tour de France.

12

THE GAME OF FAME

was startled when the phone rang while I was shaving. It was
7 a.m. The press attaché for Giorgio Armani called me in my
Milan hotel room to tell me the designer wanted to have dinner with me that night. It was more a summons than an invitation. Mr. Armani was the sacred cow, the designer Mr. Fairchild was enthralled with, which is why almost all of his senior
editors in New York City wore only Armani's clothing — pur-
chased with generous press discounts supplemented by the occasional, ostensibly forbidden unreported gift. Most of Fairchild's
Europe-based editors found this designer too corporate and decidedly uncool, but they held their tongues. I reminded the attaché that I already had an 11 a.m. appointment to preview the
next season's fashions with Mr. Armani, whom I'd met briefly
several times before. She briskly told me she'd canceled it. We
could discuss next season's trends at dinner. Then she gave me
the address of La Briciola, the restaurant where we'd meet,
stated that Mr. Armani was looking forward to seeing me, said
"Ciao, ciao, caro," and hung up.

Her arrogance was still bothering me when I got to Fairchild's
Milan office, in the Piazza Cavour, where I worked during my
trips to the city. When I told Nadine, the Milan bureau chief,
what had happened, she confirmed my suspicions. "He wants
to size you up," she said, adding, "He does this only when he

thinks someone might become important. And of course he'll tell Mr. Fairchild exactly what he thinks of you." Musing about the situation during the day, I decided Mr. Armani was probably reacting to the stir I'd caused the season before, when I'd slammed a Gianni Versace show called "Diamonds Are a Man's Best Friend." It had been little more than an excuse to send a succession of almost obscenely handsome bare-chested male models down the runway in slinky black-wool-crepe suits ornamented with rhinestone buttons, beading, zippers, and other frippery. The clothing was gigolo-wear defined, and I said as much. This had gotten me banned from Versace's upcoming shows. Being publicly shunned had made people notice me.

Before I left the office to go to dinner, I had an idea. I called Dennis Thim in the Paris office and suggested I do a little story about my intimate tête-à-tête dinner with Mr. Armani. That way, he'd be reporting on me, and I'd be reporting on him. Dennis agreed but said it needed to be meaty. There was no point in running yet another puff piece on the exalted designer. "Do something with some bite, but be careful, Alec, because, well, you know . . ."

I arrived at the restaurant early, and without giving Mr. Armani's name, I was shown to a corner table under a huge cascading flower arrangement. How did they know who I was, I wondered. Did I look that American? The maître d' poured me a complimentary flute of very good Franciacorta sparkling wine but refused my request for a menu. "Mr. Armani always orders for his guests," he said, which irritated me.

Speaking to the maître d' in Italian, I asked him how he'd known that I was Mr. Armani's guest.

He explained that the Armani press office had described me. "Your Italian's pretty good," he said in English.

I knew Mr. Armani had arrived even before I saw him. A brief lull in the chatter of the dining room made me look up from my magazine. The elegant white-haired designer had paused at the door just long enough to be noticed, and then his hat, scarf, and coat were whisked away. I stood to shake hands, and once seated, we awkwardly exchanged overlapping greetings and questions in French — Mr. Armani always pretended he didn't know English. His ice-blue eyes had a cruel beauty, and his nostrils and smile were taut. Knowing he had a house at Lake Como, I mentioned that I hoped to visit the lake in the spring; I'd never been there before. I hoped this might provide us with a neutral subject of conversation.

Ignoring my remark, he asked me where I was from, where I'd gone to school, and where I lived in Paris. When I told him I lived in the rue Monsieur, he raised his eyebrows and gave me an approving nod. He clearly knew this chic little street in the 7th arrondissement. He was polite but cool, so I understood it had been presumptuous of me to think we might have a real conversation. He clearly expected me to submit to his blunt interrogation like a vassal.

Our meal began with grilled porcini mushrooms, which had been flattened into small, round chewy steaks under a weight on a very hot grill, then sliced. The dish was presented with a sauceboat of oil, parsley, and finely chopped garlic. I accepted the waiter's offer of the sauce.

"Garlic is so vulgar," Mr. Armani said as the waiter spooned the sauce onto my mushrooms.

"Oh, I love garlic," I replied. He wrinkled his nose and shook his head.

With their shaggy taste of leaf mold and earth, the succulent mushrooms reminded me of an autumn walk in the woods. When the waiter cleared our plates, I told him how much I'd enjoyed the porcini.

"You're very familiar with the waiters, Alexander," Mr. Armani said with pursed lips.

I laughed because I found his censorious remark absurd. "That's probably because anyone who's ever worked in a restaurant knows how hard it is." It occurred to me that my summer jobs had actually given me a useful perspective very different from that of someone who'd never done such work. I knew how restaurants operated and what went on in the kitchen.

"You worked in a restaurant?" Mr. Armani looked horrified.

I explained that in the summer during college I'd worked as a waiter at several seaside hotels in New England to earn money for the coming school year. I had started out as a busboy.

"What's a busboy?"

This too I explained.

"Very lowly work," he said, shaking his head. He was obviously wondering how someone blighted by such menial labor could possibly have become a journalist.

I couldn't resist mentioning another college summer job. "I also worked as a salad chef. Americans eat a lot of salad, especially during the summer — green salad, but also potato salad, cucumber salad, pasta salad . . ."

"Pasta *salad?*"

I nodded. His expression suggested he was now certain I was a barbarian. I was starting to have a good time. "Yes, in America we make pasta salad with macaroni and mayonnaise and celery, with olives and other things in it."

"What a horrible idea," he said, wide-eyed. "So in America, you've not only ruined pizza, you've ruined pasta too?"

I couldn't resist the bait. "There's some very good pizza in America. In New Haven, a city in Connecticut where I grew up, they put clams on pizzas, and they're absolutely delicious."

"Who would do such a thing!"

"Well, the Italian immigrants who settled there."

"Ah!" he scoffed. *"Gli immigrati . . ."*

I was learning that Europeans often looked down on those had immigrated.

Our main course arrived, riso al salto, a golden-crusted cake of rice presented in a heavy cast-iron pan. The designer explained that it was made from leftover saffron risotto. Served in slices, it was crunchy on the exterior but still creamy inside, and it confirmed an important thing that I'd noticed about food. Dishes made with leftovers are unfailingly among the best in any kitchen.

"Alexander, are you Italian?" the designer asked me while we were eating.

"Not really. I'm probably three-quarters English and Scottish, with a good chunk of Rhineland German, some Irish, and a great-grandmother from Antwerp who was probably Jewish. Plus some French and Italian."

Then, sounding like a child, he asked me, "Then how do you know who you are?"

I laughed. "That's never been a problem for me."

We said good night under a streetlight. "You are strange, Alexander, but I appreciate you," Mr. Armani said when we shook hands, and then I watched him walk down the street, the A-line of his loden-green overcoat, a classic of the male bourgeois Milanese wardrobe, swaying behind him.

"Alec, this Giorgio Armani story is so real and intense," Dennis said. In my take on our dinner, I ignored the fact that Mr. Armani was a world-famous designer and sketched the evening in terms of the man I'd had dinner with. With no press attaché to groom our conversation, I'd discovered him to be a cautious, intensely disciplined, and fiercely private aesthete. His reserved earth-tone clothing, with clean architectural lines, made sense because it was as austere as he was. Knowing he'd studied medicine before becoming a window dresser — a bold defection in 1960s Italy — and then a menswear salesman at La Rinascente, a big department store in Milan, I admired him for creating a new definition of elegance with global resonance, even if it was mostly ignored by the bourgeoisie in a city as conservative and class-bound as Milan. In the end, I felt sort of sorry for him because he seemed to have little aptitude for pleasure.

"What I really loved was the whole thing about how freaked out Armani was that you'd worked in restaurant kitchens," Dennis said. "But I doubt they'll run this story in New York because Armani is Mr. Fairchild's pet. I'll send it in, though." The story never saw the light of day, but Dennis told me some of the editors in New York had been impressed by my audacity. I didn't know if that meant I'd be feted or fired. I was already possibly risking my position with Fairchild by doing some freelancing on the weekends for other newspapers and magazines, to build a collection of writing samples useful to my future. These assignments had nothing to do with fashion, the bread-and-butter of Fairchild Publications. But Dennis had hinted that the New York office might not look favorably upon these efforts.

But clearly he still wanted me on board. Two weeks later, he marched into my office and said, "I'd like you to go to Switzerland and profile Patricia Highsmith. Do you know who she is?"

"The mystery writer."

"Exactly. She's a crazy alcoholic lesbian. So, you'd be perfect for this story," he said with a smirk. "I want you to do something like the profile of Julian Barnes you did for *European Travel & Life*. Let me get in touch with her and see if she'll agree to an interview."

I loved the idea of meeting Patricia Highsmith and eagerly accepted the assignment.

A couple of weeks later, after a 5 a.m. ring of the alarm clock, two flights, and a drive lasting an hour and a half, the photographer and I found ourselves in front of a heavy wooden door with a big metal bell and chain on a muggy summer morning in the Ticino, the Italian-speaking southern part of Switzerland. The woman who opened the door had a fierce look on her flushed face and was wearing a white oxford shirt, a scarlet felt vest, jeans, and penny loafers.

"I've changed my mind. Go away!" she said, and slammed the door in our faces.

I rang the bell again, and again, and again. Finally, in a rage, she opened it. "I told you to fuck off, didn't I?"

She started to close the door again, but I held up my arm and pushed back. "Miss Highsmith, we've been traveling since 5:30 this morning. This interview has been planned for weeks and was reconfirmed with you twice yesterday. We're going into the village to have the coffee you should have offered us, and we'll be back in an hour to do the interview." I was furious — damned if I'd go back to Paris empty-handed.

When we returned an hour later, she opened the door on the first ring. "I'll give you fifteen minutes, but not more." She glowered.

We sat in her garden, where she took a long swig from the thick brown bottle of beer she'd just opened by knocking the cap off on the edge of a stone table. "Before I answer your questions, I have one for you," she said to me. "I want you to tell me the maddest thing you've ever done in your life. And don't lie, because I'll know if you do."

I immediately knew what that thing would be, and it made me shiver. Still, I stalled — but then I spoke in a rush.

"When I was a freshman at Amherst, I fell in love with a handsome senior," I began, then paused to ask the photographer to go for a walk in the garden.

"No!" Miss Highsmith said, knowing he spoke good English. "I want him here." She leered at me, and I felt a sickly admiration for her talent for humiliation.

"His name was Armand Eisen, he was from Kansas, and he was the captain of the college wrestling team. He also had a very pretty blonde girlfriend at Smith, which did nothing to dent my passion for him."

Miss Highsmith was listening intently. Here's the rest of the story I told her.

On a snowy afternoon when I was back in Connecticut for Christmas vacation, I went to the local drugstore and bought a tacky greeting card that said "I'm thinking of you." I knew Armand was staying on campus in January to work on his thesis, which was about Sir Arthur Conan Doyle. Knowing that the mail was sorted by box number, not name, I typed Armand's name but penciled in my own box number in the campus address.

I mailed the letter and told my parents I had to return to school early to work on a special project, which was only partially true. When I got there, the greeting card, in which I'd typed the signature "A secret admirer," was in my postbox as planned. I erased my own box number, typed in Armand's, and waited. That night, when I saw the lights go on in his dormitory room down the hill, I went to call on him. Armand seemed pleased to see me when he opened his door. I explained I'd come back early to work on a research project and had found this letter in my mail.

"I didn't know you'd be around during interterm," he said. "Want a beer?"

I sat there sipping it as he opened the envelope.

"Gosh, that's weird," he said, and handed me the card.

"Sort of flattering, I suppose," I replied.

"I hope it's not from one of the women who work in the cafeteria," he said with a snort.

We chatted, and he asked if I wanted to go for a pizza. Suddenly I was terrified that he'd check the postmark. While he was in the bathroom, I fished the envelope out of his wastebasket and put it in my coat pocket.

For the next two weeks, nearly alone on the empty snowbound campus, we saw each other almost every day. Armand's girlfriend was away. We talked about all kinds of things: his thesis; what it was like for him to grow up Jewish in a small city on the Great Plains, where his father was a surgeon; his fascination with Sherlock Holmes; and school. Once or twice we went to a movie in Northampton. We were becoming good friends.

Our idyll ended one night when, armed with a bottle of cold white wine, I knocked on Armand's door, and his girlfriend answered. Armand invited me to go out for a pizza with them, and once I got home, I felt despondent. We saw each other much less often when the new term began, and I missed him terribly. One day while studying in the library, I stopped at a campus-calls-only phone and dialed his number. The sound of his voice made me weak in the knees, and I hung up. By late May, I was calling him and hanging up three or four times a day.

Armand confided to me that he was having a serious problem with a phone crank, which was driving him crazy. I offered to help him sleuth out who it might be, and he finally focused his suspicions on a student who lived on the same floor I did, someone who was also on the wrestling team. One night I knocked on this guy's door and asked if I could use his phone because something was wrong with mine.

The following morning, Armand phoned to say that the college had called the town police, who were coming to question this classmate. My pulse jumped and my ears began ringing.

I cleared my throat. "Phone the dean immediately, and tell him to call off the police."

"Why? They traced the call."

"It's really important! The police must not come! I'll be there in a minute."

A few moments later my phone rang, and the dean's secretary summoned me to see him in an hour.

After I'd confessed my actions to Armand, he held his head in his hands. "This is so fucking crazy," he said. "You know I'm not homosexual. Why did you do it?"

"I don't know, but I'm very sorry."

"Just go, Alec."

Soon I went to see the dean, a handsome, soft-spoken Englishman with green eyes and long, thick eyelashes. He was sitting at his desk when his deliberately dour secretary showed me in.

I cleared my throat. "Sir, I'd like to apologize for the terrible embarrassment and inconvenience I've caused the college."

"Would you like to tell me what this was all about?" he said, avoiding my eyes.

I mentioned the psychological distress caused by my parents' decaying marriage and noticed that he then started fidgeting. Suddenly it occurred to me that my situation might have struck a nerve related to his past. This idea fed the fib that followed.

"Of course, sir, but before I do, I want you to know I realize I have some very serious issues, and I've already made arrangements to see a psychiatrist this summer."

He stared at his desk, rubbing his thumb against his index finger.

"This was something I did before this incident," I added. "I'll give you the psychiatrist's number, so that you can speak with her during the summer, if you need to."

We sat in silence.

"That won't be necessary, Alexander."

Oh God, was I going to be expelled?

"I assume you realize the great seriousness of this situation," he said.

I nodded.

"You've put me in a very awkward situation."

"I apologize again, sir. I'm very ashamed and truly very sorry."

"I've spoken with your professors. Your grades are excellent, and they think very highly of you."

Once again we sat in excruciating silence.

"Very well, Alexander. Against my better judgment, I'm going to give you the benefit of the doubt, since I respect the fact that you are planning to address your problems this summer."

I had my hand on the doorknob when he spoke again. "Alexander, I think that Sir Arthur Conan Doyle might have agreed with me that the great disappointment of committing a successful crime is having to keep it to yourself. What you did was fiendish and perverse. You humiliated Armand Eisen, and I fervently hope that you'll put your powerful but currently disturbed imagination to better use in the future."

I walked down the corridor, went into the men's room, and threw up.

When I finished this story, Patricia Highsmith was cackling. "Now that was excellent," she said, her eyes gleaming. "You really are mad, but I don't think you're dangerous, although you might be if deprived of sex. What you need is a beer." She uncapped a bottle and handed it to me.

"Your story was good, but it wasn't at all original. Love is the only thing that's nearly driven me mad too." She paused. "You know, you remind of Ginnie, but with a dick," she said, referring to Virginia Kent Catherwood, the horse-loving Philadelphia heiress who'd been one of her greatest passions. "I think we could fuck if we got drunk enough," she said. "But who would fuck whom?"

I accepted the drink and spent the next three hours, and many beers, interviewing Miss Highsmith.

"Do you feel better now?" she demanded as she escorted us to the gate. I had no idea what she meant. "I did you a favor, didn't I? No crime is complete without the confession. You tortured someone at college, and now that I made you tell me your story, I've set you free, you idiot," she said with a beery grin as she slammed the gate behind us.

As the plane took off for Paris, I turned to the photographer. "You know that story wasn't true, right?"

"*Bien sûr, Alec*," he said tonelessly, without looking up from his magazine.

The Highsmith profile was a success, and I promptly got another plum assignment, this time to interview the French television anchor Anne Sinclair, who was then the Barbara Walters of France. It took a month of torturous phone calls to get an appointment, and her secretary told me she had twenty minutes for me, no more.

Anne Sinclair and I ended up speaking for almost an hour, about media, politics, her family, and our favorite restaurants. I wrote the story and sent it to New York. At the office the next morning, just as I was turning on my computer, Kevin, the newly arrived European editor who'd been sent from New York to oversee the French office, marched over to my desk. He was a sallow, humorless man with a predictable penchant for double-breasted Armani suits. He asked, "Why did you send the Sinclair story to New York without showing it to me first?"

"Dennis Thim read it before it was sent in," I said, adding that I didn't know that this was the new protocol.

"From now on, I read everything before it leaves this office. There are some big problems with this story, so you'll have to go back and interview Anne Sinclair again."

I explained that this would be impossible, but based on my notes I could fix whatever problems he had found.

"I insist you see her again, and I want the revision by Monday," he snapped, and walked off.

At lunchtime, I went for a long walk along the banks of the Seine. When the church bells chimed two o'clock, I hesitated at the entrance to the Métro and decided not to go back to the office. Instead, I went to a movie, and after that, to dinner alone at what was then one of my favorite brasseries, Le Balzar, in the Latin Quarter. The simple Gallic meal—lamb's-ear lettuce

and roasted beets, roast chicken, and a big runny hunk of Camembert with a bottle of good Bordeaux—made me happy and
cleared my head. Though perhaps an edit or two might improve
it, I knew that the Anne Sinclair story was actually very good.
I walked home, took a hot shower, and went to bed. The next
morning, I went to the office and quit my job at Fairchild. It was
time to move on.

13

BECOMING A PARISIAN

The first thing to do was find another apartment during the two weeks that I still could get a reference showing I had a full-time job. My place on the floor below the Keyeses' was now too expensive in the face of my uncertain future as a freelance writer. Finding an apartment is a miserable task in any large city, but in Paris it was complicated by the general reluctance to rent to foreigners and the prevailing assumption that Americans are rich, which was decidedly not true in my case. I pored over ads in the papers and visited some shockingly gloomy places, including one with a shared toilet in the stairwell and another where the kitchen was a single-ring hotplate on a shelf. As the days ticked by, I was getting desperate.

Then one morning I saw a classified ad in *Le figaro*. It described the apartment as *"très charmant,"* which I doubted, but the long, narrow floor plan described in the ad included three rooms plus a tiny kitchen, and the place overlooked a courtyard garden. It was furnished too, and most important, I could afford it. The rental agent would be on the premises for first-come, first-serve visits from 10 a.m. to noon on Tuesday.

That morning, when I turned the corner onto the rue du Bac, my heart sank. A long line of people extended around the corner; they were all waiting to visit the same apartment. After I took my place at the end of the queue, I panicked. Everyone

else was clutching thick folders of bank statements and refer-
ences. All I'd brought was my work reference, checkbook, and
passport. We gave one another furtive, appraising glances and
avoided eye contact.

Fifteen minutes passed, and then, out of the corner of my
eye, I saw a red Austin Mini park on the other side of the street.
Its well-coiffed blonde driver struggled to open the dented-in
driver's-side door. She leaned into it hard several times, but it
didn't budge. I crossed the street, wondering if I'd be allowed
to retrieve my place in line, and opened the stuck door for her.

"You're very kind, monsieur," she said as she got out of the
car. She was holding a thick cardboard file.

"My pleasure, madame," I said, and smiled at her.

"Are you American?"

I nodded.

"And what do you do?"

Her question surprised me, but I told her I was a journalist.

"Are you here to visit the apartment at 134 rue du Bac?"

I said I was, and told her that I already lived in the neighborhood, in the rue Monsieur. She looked me up and down.

"Come with me," she said, and led me into the bakery between the café and the apartment building's heavy front doors,
to the back. Through a side door, we passed into a cobbled
courtyard with a single birch tree and an ivy-bordered garden
of patchy grass. We reentered the building through the courtyard. I followed her up two flights of glossy wooden stairs that
smelled of beeswax.

The apartment was painted white, with exposed wooden ceiling beams. There was a heavy, dark wood dining room table with
several rush-bottomed chairs and a tiny kitchen with a fold-
down table and a stool, moss-green tiled walls, and a window
with a lace curtain overlooking the courtyard. The main room
was furnished with a secretary desk, a couch, and an armchair.
Beyond them, a double bed was tucked into a window alcove.

The bathroom had mint-green tiled walls and pink plumbing fixtures. All of the rooms were small but flooded with light.

"It's very nice," I told her. "I'll take it."

"That was fast!" she said with a smile. "OK, I'll need a check for two months' rent, and it better not bounce, because it's being deposited today. There's no second chance with a place like this —everyone wants to live in the rue du Bac." She watched me as I wrote the check and filled out several forms.

"I hope you're religious," she said.

I must have looked puzzled.

"There's a famous church and a convent on the other side of the garden wall," she said.

"Well, at least the neighbors won't be having loud parties," I said, and she laughed.

"You'd better not be either, because this is a very conservative building. Your landlady is an old woman who lives in Burgundy, and she expects her rent on time too. Don't ask her to do anything here either, like fix the broken oven or paint the place, because she won't. My advice to you is to be her good little grandson, and this will all work out just fine." She gave me her card. "In case you want to send me some flowers," she said. "Which you should. I like camellias."

When we went downstairs, she said, "You'd better leave through the bakery." Then she handed me the keys to my new place. I watched from the corner when she exited through the front door of the building and announced, to loud groans, that the apartment had already been rented.

When I arrived carrying boxes the following weekend, a woman was using a snaking hose to water the potted plants on the cobblestone entryway. "Who are you?" she asked, with a glare.

I explained that I had rented Madame Model's apartment in the old stables at the back of the garden.

"But no one told me! They should have told me. This is not

normal. This is very bad," she said in French, with a heavy Portuguese accent.

I suggested she call Madame Model.

"I will need a letter."

I said I'd ask her to write one.

"You cannot move into the apartment until I have received the letter."

I apologized but said I had no choice. I'd told my present landlord I'd be gone by Monday morning.

"Why are you moving? I hope you are not a thief or a criminal!"

I was slack-jawed. I improvised: "No, my landlord decided he wanted the apartment where I'd been living for his daughter."

"This is a respectable building, monsieur. I hope you will not be inviting riffraff to your home." Then the barrage of questions began: Where I was from? What did I do for work? Was I married? Why wasn't I married? Was I Catholic? She concluded by saying she hoped I didn't have any diseases.

Finally, I excused myself, explaining that the box I was holding was very heavy. As I walked away, a jet of icy water soaked the back of my trouser legs.

"Oh, *pardon*," she said without looking up when I turned.

This is how I met Madame Rosa, my concierge. She would work ceaselessly to make me miserable for the ten years that I lived in two different apartments at this address.

The day I started moving out of my old apartment, Carmela knocked on my door.

"*Bonjour*, Monsieur Lobrano. Madame Keyes wanted you to have this. She hopes it will encourage you to learn to cook good food," she said, handing me a small cardboard box and an envelope that Mr. Keyes had left with her before the couple had driven south for a holiday in Spain. "We all wish you well, Monsieur Lobrano."

Inside the box was a heavy dark-green enameled casserole. It was accompanied by a pair of index cards on which Mrs. Keyes had written a recipe for poulet basquaise, Basque-style chicken in a sauce of tomatoes, peppers, onions, garlic, and white wine. It ended with these words in her spidery handwriting: "Very easy! And very good!"

The envelope from Mr. Keyes contained a check refunding my deposit and a note:

Dear Alec,

We're very sorry to see you go, but I understand your prudence as you start a new chapter in your life. No more writing about dresses then! Good luck with your writing and warm regards,

Albert Keyes

Their kindness made me sad, and I realized how protected I'd felt during the two years I'd been their tenant.

I rented a car for my move and enlisted a friend, Christophe, to help me hoist boxes out from my old apartment and into the new one. After everything had been unloaded, I took Christophe out for some oysters and a good bottle of Menetou-Salon, one of my favorite Loire Valley whites. Then I stayed, for the last night, on the rue Monsieur.

The next day, I unlocked the door to my new apartment early in the morning and got to work. The vase of dried-out flowers on the dining room table told me no one had lived here recently. The place also needed to be painted and scrubbed. In the kitchen, the four gas jets worked, and the waist-high fridge was serviceable if tiny. But the electric oven was ancient, filthy, and broken, and I doubted it could be repaired. I'd get rid of it and buy a new one that could fit into the same niche.

Taking stock of the dented aluminum pans and the single dull knife in the cutlery drawer, I made a list of things I would need in order to cook properly in this tiny kitchen. Some purchases could wait, but I had to have at least one large good-quality pot, a salad spinner, and some knives.

After the drudgery of cleaning all morning, it was a relief to arrive at E. Dehillerin, the famous cookware store in Les Halles that I'd read about in a Paris guidebook. It was a hive of pots, pans, and tools, many of which I couldn't even imagine a use for.

I explained to a patient older man that I wanted to buy some knives. He asked me a few questions and then said, "So you are a beginner cook. Congratulations! What you need are three knives —a chef's knife, a bread knife, and a paring knife. When you've made some progress, you can come back and buy more, maybe a boning knife and a smaller chef's knife." It was extravagant, but I bought the three knives as well as a stainless-steel pot and the salad spinner.

"Tonight you should roast a chicken. It always brings good luck to roast one the first time you cook in a new kitchen," said the man when he handed me the shopping bag filled with my purchases.

I told him my oven was broken.

"Then you will make a boeuf aux carottes (beef braised with carrots). It's easy, and you can use your new knives." He wrote down the recipe on a piece of torn brown wrapping paper and told me to wait a minute. He returned with a vegetable peeler, which he dropped into my bag. "A good cook always thinks ahead."

In the Métro with my new knives, I felt more Parisian than I had at any time since I'd moved to the city two years earlier. I was so eager to use them that when I got home, I decided unpacking my suitcases could wait. Instead, I shopped for the ingredients for the beef stew, which I would make in the casserole Madame Keyes had given me.

I was chopping an onion when the doorbell surprised me. "Hello," said a smiling woman in a white oxford shirt and jeans colorfully spattered with paint. "I'm Françoise Meynard, your neighbor from across the hall. I wanted to welcome you to the building. It's always a lot of work getting settled into a new place, so my partner, Horatio, and I wanted to invite you over for dinner tomorrow night if you're free."

After I'd finished making the casserole, I spent the rest of the afternoon washing windows, fixing two leaky faucets, and unpacking clothing. Meanwhile the apartment filled with the rich smell of beef simmering in wine with garlic, herbs, onions, and carrots. By the end of the day, I was exhausted, but I peeled a few potatoes with my new peeler and finally sat down to dinner around 9 p.m., on the hard wooden stool at the table in my tiny kitchen. It was lit with a single candle. The blunt bovine deliciousness of the dish I'd cooked made me happy but also a little lonely. Something this good was meant to be shared. Still, in the space of a day I'd made this new apartment my home, and I'd done it by cooking.

"Nice to meet you, Alejandro," said Horatio when he opened the door the following night. He was Argentine and had studied as an architect. Françoise was a painter who spoke perfect English because she'd been born in Australia and spent part of her childhood there. They were both charming and very attractive. As we drank the bottle of Champagne that I'd brought, I told them how I'd come to leave my old job.

"Bravo!" said Françoise when I finished. "Everyone eventually has to decide when they're going to stop putting up with the crap they think they should do and begin living their own life. For me, it was after dropping out of law school, where I'd gone to please my father. I hated it, and he knew I'd hate it, because I'd been drawing and painting ever since I was a child. But he pushed and pushed, so I went. When I quit, he didn't speak to me for more than a year, but eventually he came around."

Horatio's story was more complicated. He'd grown up in a small country town on the Pampas with a widowed mother who was a seamstress. His brother, an engineer with a big American industrial group in Hartford, lent Horatio the money to study architecture in Spain, which he did, but then he failed his certification exam. He didn't know what he was going to do next until he met Françoise in a gallery at the Prado. He eventually followed her to Paris, where he was working as a private Spanish tutor.

They briefed me about life in the building. "Madame Rosa is a terrible gossip, and she can make your life hell if she decides to, so you should tip her," Françoise advised. "It's customary when you move into a new building with a concierge."

I hated the idea. "How much?" I asked.

"Five hundred francs." This was roughly $100, a fortune for me.

"She's a witch, but you should do it, Alec," said Horatio firmly.

Since it was a warm summer night, when I got home I opened all the windows in my apartment and made up my bed. It had a new mattress, which had been delivered that morning. The nightcap of fiery Argentine brandy that Horatio had insisted on pouring had knocked me out.

I was awakened by singing so ethereal, it frightened me, and in the twilight fuzz of a hangover, I put my hand on my heart to make sure I hadn't died during the night. Then I remembered the nuns. Soon I would learn to tell time by the bells of their church.

Occasionally when it was hot, the nuns left their windows wide open, and one night I was astonished to see one of the sisters with a tent of aluminum foil over the slick black dye on her hair. Evidently their vows didn't preclude every form of vanity. Walking by the garbage bins on the sidewalk outside their dormitory early in the morning, I spied big empty cassoulet cans, which surprised me, because it seemed sort of hearty for them. There were also soup and orange juice cartons, plastic milk bottles, cheese wrappers, and the occasional empty Doritos bag. It seemed that the nuns were just as wantonly hungry as I was.

The next day, my appetite sharpened by the buttery smells wafting from the bakery, I dressed and knocked on the door of Madame Rosa's tiny loge.

"What do you want?" she barked as she opened the door.

"This is for you," I said. I smiled and handed her an envelope containing a 500-franc note. She snatched it and slammed the door without another word.

The move had left me with a badly dented bank account, and as I wandered the stalls of the Sunday morning market on the boulevard Raspail, I decided I wouldn't be bullied by Madame Rosa again. I would be polite to her, but no more.

On the cusp between summer and fall, the market made me giddy with its temptations. Since I'd previously traveled so much and usually had eaten in restaurants, I'd never shopped at an outdoor Paris food market before, and the stalls elated me with their edible possibilities. I'd gone out to buy a few tomatoes, maybe some squash, and salad, and returned home with plump blueberries from the Basque Country, a melon, some country ham from the Aveyron, chorizo, and ivory-colored crème fraîche ladled on the spot into a glass jar.

I also succumbed to some cèpes from the Auvergne — a what-the-hell extravagance, a Saint-Marcellin cheese in a little terra-cotta cup, a hunk of Abondance from the village of the same name in the hills behind Lake Geneva, and, daring myself, a small sole, because I'd decided I would teach myself to cook. How could I write about food if I didn't cook?

In New York, I had lived for seven years with a food-loving lawyer named Tom. We had been avid fans of Pierre Franey's "Sixty-Minute Gourmet" column in the *New York Times*, but in the kitchen Tom was the more experienced maestro, and I was the onion chopper and potato peeler. Later, living alone in my tiny studio in Greenwich Village, I found inspiration in M.F.K. Fisher's *How to Cook a Wolf.* Using her appealingly off-the-cuff recipes, I learned to make minestrone, steak with a sauce of pan juices deglazed with bottled oyster sauce, and a frittata with tomatoes, zucchini, and cheese. My ardor for cooking wasn't dampened by having so little money. If I shopped carefully, I could indulge myself and buy my meat at the Jefferson Market, a grocery store over on Sixth Avenue, where the white-jacketed butchers were as amiably attentive to my purchase of dollhouse rations as they were to another customer's order of a standing rib roast that probably cost half my weekly salary. When they weighed my chopped steak, the butchers often added a pinch more after they'd taken it off the scale. "You're too skinny," one of them often told me.

One rainy Saturday morning, a bald, ovoid man in a gray suit with a tight vest took a place behind me in the line. He smiled at me, and I smiled back. When I placed my order, this man interrupted and said, "Mario, make that four lamb chops, a steak, and four Italian sausages, two hot, two sweet, and put it on my bill."

When I protested, the man said, "Don't be a silly boy. Take that meat and invite a friend over for dinner." The butchers went along with him because James Beard, whom I didn't recognize, was a very good customer.

Now that I was living in Paris, the rotation of simple dishes I cooked in New York seemed too lowly for the amazing French produce. I would learn to cook French food.

The following weekend I invited Françoise and Horatio to dinner and made them poulet basquaise from Madame Keyes's recipe. I burned the accompanying rice, but the chicken was so good, they had seconds, which deprived me of the leftovers I'd been counting on.

Aside from the market in the boulevard Raspail, my other compulsive destination was the expensive Grande Epicerie, the luxury supermarket annex of Le Bon Marché department store, at the end of my block. It was the best food hall in Paris, and I could browse its counters and shelves for hours, occasionally giving in to delicacies like a pot of Corsican clementine jam, some green-tea-flavored dark chocolates, a caramel éclair, or several links of Alsatian sausage.

Recipes were my means of getting to know my new neighborhood, since people frequently offered them. And when someone didn't, I'd ask, which always made the person happy. The woman who'd sold me a bunch of golden turnips in the market told me to braise them in a small cup of water with a little pour of xérès (sherry) vinegar and a teaspoon of sugar, and the barrel-chested butcher on the rue du Cherche-Midi regularly jotted down suggestions on the corner of the paper he wrapped my meat in. "This is what I make when my wife goes to visit her sister," he explained. "You sear a ham steak in a hot pan, a couple of minutes on each side, then take it out and keep it warm. Add a knob of butter and some chopped shallots and a minute later deglaze the pan with a good pour of Madeira. With egg noodles and a green salad, you've got a good meal in no time." I ponied up for the Madeira, and he was right—the simple wine sauce made the ham succulent and special.

Living alone, I also became obsessed by bread, which had a place at every meal, toasted at breakfast, with an omelette or soup or a salad at noon, and with some cheese after dinner. At first, I bought a demi-baguette every day, but that was too much for me, and since I couldn't bring myself to waste anything, I quickly ended up with a huge canister of breadcrumbs. I made them in the ancient blender I found at the back of a kitchen cabinet.

One day Françoise knocked on my door and asked if I wanted to come over for a quick lunch. "It gets boring to eat lunch alone, doesn't it, Alec?" she said. I followed her back across the hall to her kitchen, where I watched her toast four pieces of bread from a sliced loaf that had a brown crust; it looked craggy, like a stone. When the slices jumped from the toaster, she took them out, rubbed them with a garlic clove, drizzled them with olive oil, and sprinkled them with salt and thyme. Then she placed creamy rounds of goat cheese in the middle of each slice and slid them under the broiler until they were runny. We ate the toasts of creamy cheese with a green salad. It was one of the best lunches I'd had.

"Poilâne and Rocamadour," she replied, when I asked her about the incredible bread, which had a firm crumb and a bracing tanginess, and the cheese. "Rocamadour is a type of Cabécou, a goat's milk cheese from the department of the Lot, in the southwest."

To combat the monotony of making the same dishes at noon, Françoise and I agreed to swap recipes when either of us found something simple and good. After lunch, I walked to the Poilâne bakery in the rue du Cherche-Midi. The big, brown flour-dusted rounds of the bread I'd fallen for were displayed upright in a wooden rack, etched with a swirling P. I bought a quarter loaf of what had instantly become my favorite bread, and the bakery became a permanent fixture of my life in this new neighborhood.

For the first time I was cooking for myself every day, usually both lunch and dinner, since I was working at home and couldn't afford to heedlessly go out almost every night, as I'd done when working late hours at Fairchild. Eventually, I developed a routine. After a quick coffee at home in the morning, I'd go out to buy the paper from the kiosk at the corner, sometimes stopping for a second coffee on the terrace of Le Nemrod, my neighborhood café, and do my daily shopping. Soon I was being greeted by name or, in the case of Etienne the butcher, as *"mon ami américain,"* while the saleswomen at the Quatrehomme cheese shop preferred the more formal "Monsieur Alexandre." My love of French food was slowly but surely making me a Parisian.

I also started collecting cookbooks, since the only ones I had were the three paperbacks I'd thrown into my suitcase when I moved to Europe — Marcella Hazan's two *Classic Italian* volumes and *James Beard's American Cookery*. I'd gotten a copy of the ponderous *Larousse gastronomique* at a flea market in Burgundy while visiting a friend for the weekend, but what I needed was a good primer for French cooking. Françoise told me that she liked *La véritable cuisine de famille par Tante Marie,* so I bought that too, and *L'art culinaire moderne* by Henri-Paul Pellapart, which her grandmother had given her; I hunted down a copy at a secondhand bookseller. *Tante Marie* was fun to read and glean for ideas, but it wasn't quite right, so one afternoon I walked over to W. H. Smith, the English-language bookstore, and bought a copy of Julia Child's *Mastering the Art of French Cooking*.

Two days later, I came home from doing errands and found a message from Gregory Usher, an American who ran the cooking school at the Ritz Hotel, saying he had admired a piece I wrote and inviting me to dinner. When I called him back, he explained he was hosting some friends at his favorite bistro, Chez Georges, and hoped I could come. I said I'd be delighted.

"Wonderful, 8:30 p.m. then, 1 rue du Mail in the 2nd, it's just off the place des Victoires."

The day of the dinner, I agonized over whether to wear a suit and wondered who else might be there. Finally, I put on a jacket and jeans, yanked off my tie, and decided I'd walk to the restaurant to get some air. When I arrived at Chez Georges, I immediately liked the long, softly lit dining room with its sconces and framed mirrors. The maître d' led me to a table where an older woman with short, curly brown hair was seated on the banquette, sipping a glass of white wine.

"Hello, I'm Julia," she said. She looked very much like my paternal grandmother Jean. "You're the one Gregory said went to Amherst, is that right?"

I nodded.

"I went to Smith, but back in the days when there were still dinosaurs roving the Connecticut River Valley. I hated it," she said, and in French asked the waiter to pour me a glass of wine.

"I was unhappy at Amherst too."

"Good, then we have something in common," she said brightly. Her eyes narrowed. "Why didn't you like Amherst?"

"It was too smug and preppy for me."

"That's exactly why I hated Smith," she said.

As we chatted, I noticed that people at other tables were staring. Julia buttered a red-and-white radish with a long whisker at its tip and chomped on it. "The radish is one of nature's most underrated creations," she said. "A nicely buttered radish is just the thing to remind any cook to stay simple in the kitchen. Most foods don't really want improving."

There was a sudden dull thud in my head. With an avalanche of awe, I realized I was speaking to Julia Child.

"So what are you doing in Paris, Alec?"

"I'm a freelance journalist."

"Who do you write for?"

I explained that I'd done a few pieces for the *International Herald Tribune* and was just starting out.

"What is your subject?"

"I've written travel and food stories, and I'd like to write more about food."

"And what do you have to say about food?"

"Not much yet, but I hope to learn."

"That's a good boy. But you don't want to get too big for your britches. You know, I think we could do with some more wine."

I spoke to the waiter and then asked her how she became involved with food.

She seemed surprised. "I wanted to make my husband happy, and I think cooking made me like myself better," she said, and snorted. "But let's not get all Freud-y here. The best reason to lie down on a couch that I've ever found is for sex, and we're here for dinner."

Gregory Usher and his handsome French boyfriend, Patrice, arrived, together with a French food writer, a wine merchant, and an American woman from Fort Worth who was taking classes at the cooking school at the Ritz. The Texan, who'd gone to Mount Holyoke College near Amherst, was charming.

Gregory ordered a succession of dishes, which we shared: a soft, creamy chicken-liver terrine that was as earthy and satisfying as sex in a barn, and marinated herring with boiled potatoes, a muscular comfort food that recalled the wet wharves of northern European ports. After that, the meal tacked in a more elegant direction, with homemade goose foie gras served with warm toast points and a tart rhubarb compote. For main courses, we had salmon in sorrel sauce — thrilling, because I loved the sour copper-penny taste of this vegetable I'd never had before, seared scallops in a beurre blanc sauce, and grilled turbot with a sunny yellow béarnaise sauce flecked with finely chopped vinegar-pickled tarragon. Dessert was a mountain of profiteroles filled with vanilla ice cream and served with silver sauceboats of hot dark chocolate sauce as thick as tar.

It was a spectacular meal, and afterward, when we were waiting for taxis on the sidewalk, Julia nudged me. "What did you think of the food?" she said.

"It was very, very good," I replied.

"What did you like best?"

"The grilled turbot with béarnaise sauce."

"Anyone who likes béarnaise sauce will turn out just fine," she said, and shook my hand firmly before getting into her cab.

When I opened my eyes the next morning, the first thing I thought of was one of Julia's comments: "I think cooking made me like myself better." Its guileless honesty thrilled me because I knew it was true for me too.

14

EARNING MY WAY WITH A FORK AND PEN

A lec, I'm going to be blunt. You to have to get off your ass and learn to hustle," said my friend John, a jack-of-all-trades expat Texan who made his rent doing everything from decorative painting to antique hunting and modeling. "Just sending people letters isn't going to work. You have to meet them in person and push. I know you're talented, but nobody else does," he insisted over a glass of wine after a movie on a rainy Sunday night. I hated hearing this advice but knew he was right. I'd sent a dozen editors résumés with cover letters suggesting story ideas, and I hadn't heard back from any of them.

My daily fascination with what I ate and cooked was the axis of my new life as a fledgling freelance writer in Paris, but a month had quickly passed since I'd left my job at Fairchild Publications. Aside from doing a little story on all-night restaurants for a British food magazine, I hadn't earned a cent. I had enough savings to hang on for another month or two. But what would happen after that? I had no idea, and surges of anxiety often yanked me from my sleep.

I'd also written several pieces for the English-language city magazine *Paris Passion*, so I stopped by their offices the next day in the hopes of drumming up more work. Drawing on a pool of talented expat writers, *Passion* was an exceptionally good magazine and had a staff of excellent editors, including an Englishman known for penning memorable subheads, including one for a recipe for coq au vin: "What Could Be Better? This Wonderful Dish Combines Two of Our Favorite Things, Cock and Wine." But during my visit, I learned the magazine had just been bought by *Time Out,* which was planning to expand to Paris and keep most of *Paris Passion*'s staff.

Karen Albrecht, the American publisher, explained that the staff would be doing a weekly insert in English in the back of *Pariscope,* a popular weekly entertainment magazine. "Maybe you'd like to do the food column for our section, Alec?"

As we hashed out the details, we determined that this task would include writing reviews of two new restaurants every week, along with a seasonally appropriate themed box with six to eight much shorter write-ups—restaurants with the best terrace dining during the summer, where to eat a great choucroute garnie in the fall, and so on. My monthly fee would be 2,000 francs, about $400.

I asked Karen if I'd have a budget for testing restaurants.

"No, I'm afraid not," she replied, leaving me wondering how I would manage to cover eight new restaurants a month without spending my entire fee. "Hopefully, you'll be covering some of these new places for other publications you write for," she suggested, and then had to take a phone call.

"Hey, Alec, let's go get a coffee," said another editor I knew in that office, so we went to the café at the corner. When we sat down, she congratulated me on the new column.

I thanked her but said I was worried about how I could afford to do it.

"Let's keep this between us, but dozens of invitations to new restaurants come into the office every month. *Time Out*'s policy is not to accept free meals, but you and I both know that's not practical, so I'll send the invites along to you and give people your phone number when they call to tell us about their new opening. My advice is that if you have a good meal on an invitation, write it up, but if you have a bad meal, just don't cover the place."

I told her that this arrangement made me uncomfortable.

"Alec, don't be ridiculous. If you eat eight meals a month at an average price of 120 francs, that's almost half of your fee."

I sighed. "You're right, I guess, but I'm disappointed."

"We're not the *New York Times* or *Gourmet* magazine, Alec. You're going to have to learn to tightrope-walk like every other freelance journalist," she added with a chuckle.

Still, I began my column with the intention of avoiding invitations. There was no way to write a restaurant review if I wasn't free to tell the truth.

The first furor over one of my reviews came after I visited La Coupole, the famous brasserie in Montparnasse. It had recently been renovated after becoming part of Jean-Paul Bucher's restaurant group, which he launched by buying Brasserie Flo, known for its beautiful art nouveau interior, in 1968.

I'd been in love with the nonchalant, louche allure of Parisian brasseries ever since I'd first visited a very famous one, Au Pied de Cochon, in Les Halles years before. These restaurants have a special and much-loved place in the city's restaurant landscape. The first ones were opened by Alsatians fleeing their eastern French province at the end of the Franco-Prussian War, when the region was annexed by Germany. *Brasserie* means "brewery," and because these restaurants were originally simple taverns that served sausages and stews with freshly brewed beer, they were given that name.

By the end of the nineteenth century in rapidly growing Paris, brasseries had evolved into something different—big, busy, egalitarian restaurants where you went for a fast feed at a fair price and enjoyed the intriguing spectacle offered by a large urban dining room. Their business boomed when the

Universal Exposition of 1900 drew almost fifty million people to Paris and coined the French capital's enduring reputation as the world's most glamorous city. Many brasseries spiffed up for these crowds, setting up oyster stands out front and redecorating boldly within.

If bistros were the home of Paris's hungry id, its brasseries were its ego on display, with no lack of vanity. These restaurants were also a stage, an act, where the contagiously happy atmosphere of other people's good times was the racy garnish to a diner's experience. Brasserie menus mostly offered a dressier Gallic equivalent of American short-order cooking: salads, tartares, and grilled dishes that didn't require hours in the kitchen.

I'd always liked La Coupole. The food was only, as the French would say, *correcte,* but you could get a better-than-average meal if you knew your way around the menu. My friends and I came here mostly for the beauty of the paintings, individually rendered by twenty-seven different artists, including Matisse and Léger, on the capitals of the pillars that held up the high ceiling. I loved it that Albert Camus had celebrated his Nobel Prize here with friends and fellow writers, and I reveled in the banter of the theatrically world-weary waiters. They perfectly understood the role they played in the experience of a meal here, as they teased, flirted, and shot off one-liners. But most of all we came here for the pleasure of just being in Paris and having a good time.

When I moved to Paris, the risqué reputation that La Coupole had earned during the 1920s, when it was frequented by everyone from Man Ray and Josephine Baker to Hemingway and F. Scott Fitzgerald, had already entered a twilight senescence. But the vast room, with its perfect sight lines and gentle lighting, still drew a Left Bank crowd of book editors and fashion designers, most of all on Sundays, when other restaurants were closed. When I met friends for a Sunday blues–beating dinner there, I ate a rotation of the same dishes — some oysters, smoked salmon, or onion soup to start, and then steak tartare, grilled sole, or a steak with, as the waiters always reassured you, freshly made béarnaise sauce and an amber avalanche of hot, crispy, slender frites, which were so good dredged in the sauce meant for the steak.

My brasserie-going habit waned as the prices rose at these establishments and they were bought up by one of two local chains, the Frères Blanc or Jean-Paul Bucher's Brasserie Groupe Flo. So I was curious the night I spun through the doors into the room I knew so well, with my friend Michèle, to experience the new iteration. After I'd refused a table in one of the distant ice-floe corners of the dining room, we settled in at a deuce within a respectable distance of the stained-glass cupola that defined the social axis of the room.

Michèle looked around at the groups of Japanese tourists and tables of traveling salesmen and shook her head. *"C'est une catastrophe!"* she said. The restaurant both of us had known and loved had disappeared.

The next day I wrote my review:

All it took was many yards of mud brown upholstery and the sharp pencil of a penny-pinching accountant or two to snuff out the famously giddy atmosphere of one of the best-loved brasseries in Paris . . . Aside from the incomprehensible ugliness of the reupholstered seating, the capitals on the forest of pillars in the restaurant have also been cartoonishly over-restored, but what's really banished the restaurant's charm since it became part of Jean-Paul Bucher Groupe Flo restaurant chain is that most of the veteran staff is gone . . . A starter of mushy smoked salmon was served with a plastic interleaving sheet still in place, a browning sprig of curly escarole, and a single pat of foil-wrapped butter . . . The famous onion soup was tepid, flavorless, greasy, and gray, like dishwater in a blocked sink.

I went on in that vein. My editor was skittish about what she called my idol-smashing review, but I finally persuaded her to publish it, because *Time Out*'s reputation was built on truth telling.

A day after it ran, she called me in a panic. "Jean-Paul Bucher is absolutely furious. He's threatening to pull all of his advertising from the magazine, in both the French and the English pages. He also said he might sue you, as an individual, for defamation." She paused to let that sink in. I was almost immediately drenched with cold sweat. "He'll decide after you come to explain your review to him in person. I'm sure you don't want to do this, Alec, but you have no choice," she said.

Mr. Bucher's secretary brusquely told me he'd meet me at Brasserie Flo at 11:30 two days later. In the meantime I had a constant sick feeling in the pit of my stomach. I had no idea that reviewing restaurants could be so dangerous.

When I arrived, I found the meaty, balding restaurateur sitting with his back to the room at a corner banquette beneath beautiful murals of the forests of Alsace.

"Will you join me in a glass of Champagne, Alexander?" he said.

I wasn't feeling especially festive, but nodded.

"Now, I want you to tell me why you, an American, felt qualified to write such a rude review of my restaurant, one of the most famous in Paris."

I explained that I'd had a passion for French food for most of my life and added that my nationality had nothing to do with being qualified to criticize the restaurant's cooking. My taste buds told the truth.

"La Coupole is about more than just food, Alexander. It's about the history of Paris and all of the artists who ate there in the past and eat there today," said Mr. Bucher.

"La Coupole's history is fascinating, Monsieur Bucher, but

what's far more important for me when I go to a restaurant is the quality of the cooking. I want people who read my reviews to have the best meals possible when they visit Paris, and on this basis, there was a discrepancy between La Coupole's fame and the quality of its cooking, especially relative to the prices charged," I told him.

"But what do you know about French food?" he demanded. He signaled to a waiter, who arrived at the table with four ramekins of nearly identical yellow sauce. I understood they represented some kind of a test, and I panicked, worried about the possible legal ramifications of failing.

"Taste these and tell me what they are," he said.

I couldn't refuse. But I was frankly terrified. Would I be led away in handcuffs if my palate didn't perform? I identified them as two béarnaise sauces, one freshly made, the other from a mix or an industrial kitchen, and two hollandaise sauces of the same provenance. He nodded and sipped his Champagne, then steepled his thick fingers and surveyed me thoughtfully

"You're an arrogant bastard, Alexander, but you do have a palate," he said. "Now we'll have lunch." He ordered a big tray of oysters, langoustines, and lobster halves, and as we ate, he told me that he'd begun his career as an apprentice in the kitchens of l'Hôtel du Parc de Mulhouse, when he was fourteen. "When did you start working, Alexander?"

"When I was sixteen."

He was surprised. "And what was the worst job you ever had?"

I told him I'd worked at the glove counter at Filene's department store in Boston for a few weeks as a Christmas extra — a total nightmare. But my worst job had been my month-long summer stint as a salesman at the Big & Tall Men's Shop in a suburban strip mall.

"What was difficult about that?"

"I tried to help the men when I could, but they avoided me because they were so embarrassed by their own bodies."

Mr. Bucher told me that he'd bought Brasserie Flo when he was only thirty with the intent of saving the brasseries of Paris from extinction by modernizing them. I listened, and I liked him, but I wasn't entirely convinced.

It was well after 3 p.m. when we finished our meal. I was surprised that I had, guardedly, enjoyed it.

"So what would you say about the meal we just shared?" he asked.

"That I learned a lot and enjoyed it very much."

"I did too, Alexander. But my advice to you is to go forward with respect and humility. You must always remember your words can do a lot of harm — to waiters, to kitchen workers, to cooks, to everyone who works in a restaurant that you criticize publicly. So be very careful — be sure of your judgments because you could get into trouble, a lot of trouble," he said. "You'll always be welcome in my restaurants, Alexander. Just be fair." Then he shook my hand and left.

Karen Albrecht called me the next morning. "I don't know what you did, but Jean-Paul Bucher has lifted his threat to cancel all his advertising, so good job. Maybe in the future, though, you can be just a little less exigent?"

I told her I couldn't do that.

"That's what I thought you'd say." She laughed. "And to be honest, that's why I asked you to do this column to begin with — you're so serious about it, and that's good."

The next person I reached out to in my hunt for work was Judy Fayard, an Alabama native who was working in Paris as the European editor of *European Travel & Life*, an excellent travel magazine published in New York. Judy suggested we meet for dinner at Coconnas, a restaurant in the place des Vosges, and at the end of a long, wonderful, garrulous meal there, she suggested I go down to Lyon and spend a day with Paul Bocuse, the most famous chef in France, as the basis of a profile.

Two weeks later, I frantically raced through the streets to Les

Halles de Lyon, the city's main food market. A wildcat strike had shut down the city's buses and subway, making it impossible to find a cab. I arrived forty minutes late for my meeting with the most famous chef in France. I was sweat-soaked and my lungs were burning when I spotted him, dressed all in black and calmly sipping a coffee at the bar where he'd told me to meet him before he showed me his favorite stalls.

I sputtered apologies until he put his heavy hand on my shoulder and shook his head. "It's OK! Relax, my friend!" he said, and led me to another counter, where he ordered a dozen freshly shucked oysters and two glasses of white wine. "I think you need a little snack."

There are few better breakfasts than oysters and a glass of white wine, and I was surprised by his friendliness. We sampled our way through the market, eating a runny Saint-Marcellin cheese from La Mère Richard, his favorite cheesemonger, and at Charcuterie Sibilia, a thick slice of pâté en croûte, a pork terrine in multiple shades of pink. It was studded with green pistachios, wrapped around a lobe of foie gras, topped with amber aspic, and encased in a crumbly pastry. The chef proceeded to give me a tutorial on the charcuterie of Lyon, introducing me to sabodet — a fat sausage made from pork belly, snout, and ear, and simmered in water — as well as a variety of dry sausages, including Jésus de Lyon and rosette.

At the neighboring *volailler* (poultry merchant), Mr. Bocuse pointed out Bresse chickens, with their red cockscombs and dark-blue feet. "This is the best fowl in the world, because the birds are free-ranged for four months and then fattened on a diet of milk and grain. Their meat is firm and full of flavor, so you should eat it whenever you get the chance," he said, and clapped me on the back. "I think you're like me, Alexander," he said. "We love good food and good wine, and we love to fuck, no?"

Blushing, I nodded vigorously, and he laughed.

We took a cab to visit another of his favorite places, the open-air market on the Quai Saint-Antoine, the embankment of the Saône. On the way, Mr. Bocuse said, "You know, Alexander, you have an aptitude for pleasure, and no one should write about food without it."

When we arrived at the market, the tall, bald chef was recognized immediately. "Ahhhh, the smell of cèpes always makes me want sex," he said, sniffing at one of the fleshy bronze-capped mushrooms, its thick, dirty stem flecked with peaty soil, that he picked up from a stall. "I'm right, no?"

"You are," I admitted, overriding the prudish manners I'd been taught, which were always at odds with an appreciation for sensuality more natural to me. I was amazed at how comfortable I'd become with this jolly old satyr in the space of a few hours.

"Nature is such a tease because so many of the best foods smell like sex, every kind of sex," he said, stopping to plant a kiss on the cheek of an awestruck woman who came out from behind her counter to offer him a little wooden box of wild raspberries from the Ardèche. "*Pour vous, Monsieur Paul!*" she trilled.

"*Merci,*" he said, and then he picked up a berry and offered it to her. She dropped her eyes. "Taste!" he ordered her. After she'd opened her mouth to receive the ruby-colored fruit from his fat index finger and thumb, her shoulders slumped in a sort of beatitude I'd never seen. On this soft Indian-summer day we stopped by a low stone wall on the edge of the Saône and ate the berries, which smelled of roses and pine needles.

"Alexander, what did you like to eat when you were a boy? What foods excited you?" he asked, as we continued our stroll through the market. It was a wonderful question, and a disarmingly intimate one too. I'd never met anyone who was so overt about the relationship between gastronomic and sexual pleasure as this giant of a man with a sharp nose and large, round, dark eyes.

"Cheese, bacon, pasta, pizza, mushrooms, garlic, onions, sausage, shrimp, asparagus . . ."

"Asparagus?"

I nodded.

"Not bad!" Mr. Bocuse said. "And your mother's cooking?"

"I liked her meatloaf, barbecued chicken, and boeuf bourguignon." Calling it boeuf bourguignon was, however, rather generous, since the dish was made with Holland House red wine, canned mushrooms, and frozen onions.

"Did your grandmothers cook?"

I shook my head. "Not really."

"What a shame!" He stroked his chin. "What I'm wondering is where you got your randy appetite. It's a gift to be a little wild when you eat," he said. Delivered by Paul Bocuse, the man with the most incisive palate I'd ever encountered, this compliment was as humbling as it was puzzling. I'd never really thought about the origins of my palate before. And though I didn't dare tell him, what he'd said was only partially true.

What would he have thought of me, I wondered, if I'd confessed that until I was twenty, I'd refused the lobsters my grandmother served at her summerhouse in Rhode Island because I was alarmed by their crimson color and hated all the cracking and spattering involved in extracting the quivering claw meat from the shell.

The following day, when I went to eat at Monsieur Paul's famous restaurant in Collonges, just outside Lyon, I blurted out that I'd avoided lobster for many years.

He guffawed. "You have the right to not like a food, or to be frightened by one. The important thing is you eventually tried it. What really surprised me yesterday was that you liked savory foods over sweet ones when you were a child. That's uncommon," he said kindly. Though I felt absolved of my idiotic dislike of lobster, my similarly misplaced aversion to the excellent fried clams served at Howard Johnson's—I always ordered a patty melt while everyone else in my family ate clams—was a secret I'd planned to take to my grave.

The meal that night was spectacular. It began when an individual white-porcelain soup tureen came to the table with a domed cap of flaky, dark-blonde pastry. When I pierced it with my spoon, the vapor rising from the pool of mink-colored soup topped with thick matchsticks of black truffle was so potent with the musk of beef, bones, and tubers that it made me want to physically wallow in a bath of this liquid for hours. The next course, omble chevalier, a delicate fish from Lake Geneva, layered with thin slices of potato to mimic its scales, was also magnificent, as was what followed: breast of Bresse chicken napped with cream and flavored with morels. Even the fluffy white rice that accompanied the fowl was full of flavor, which I decided came from a ladle of almost caramelized chicken stock and a very faint whiff of coal smoke from the stove it had been cooked on.

When the great chef appeared at my table again at the end of my meal, I fell into a fit of superlatives, trying to tell him how much I'd loved the soup I knew he'd invented for the former French president Valéry Giscard d'Estaing in 1975, and the Bresse chicken too.

"The meal seems to have made you very aroused," he teased. "It's a lot of hard work, but it's not very complicated, Alexander. Sincerity and simplicity are the essence of all good cooking."

"I was lucky to have learned to cook from a woman," he continued, referring to Eugénie Brazier, one of the great Mères Lyonnaises, those female chefs whose cooking won the city its gastronomic renown during the early twentieth century. "Women cook to offer love through pleasure. Men preen in the kitchen to impress," he told me. "Remember the women who cooked for you when you were a child because you'll never know food so honest and kind. Always let their cooking be your compass."

Judy Fayard called me a few days after I'd turned in my profile of Paul Bocuse. "Alec, this is a wonderful story, and I think it will make people notice you," she said. And it did.

15

THE NEW BISTRO IS BORN

S uddenly I found myself on the front lines of a French revolution. It would be waged with knives and forks and pots and
pans and leave the Paris restaurant scene changed forever.

I had just returned from New York City, where I met a group
of smart magazine editors with whom I'd work for many years.
They included William Sertl, who was at America's largest
travel magazine, *Travel & Leisure;* Gary Walther at *Departures;*
and, at *Food & Wine*, editor in chief Mary Simon, Catherine
Bigwood, and Malachy Duffy. I'd also spoken with Barbara Fairchild and Karen Kaplan at *Bon Appétit.* To my disappointment,
I didn't get in to see anyone at *Gourmet*, the eminent publication to which I most aspired but had thus far eluded me. Shortly
thereafter, I accepted *Travel & Leisure*'s offer to become its Paris
correspondent, reporting on culture, hotels, and new restaurant
openings. Bill Sertl had a keen nose for news and a madcap wit
that camouflaged his seriousness and sensitivity. I was to send
him a monthly memo that detailed the latest news from Paris,
which we would discuss by phone and decide what should be
written up for the magazine.

One morning during a dreaded trip to the post office in the
rue Dupin, where the lines were always interminable, I got a
hot tip from a counter clerk, a friendly blonde who'd first deduced something about my life from the packages I received.

"Your little accent is so cute. Where are you from?" she'd asked me a few months earlier. I told her and then asked her the same thing, because she spoke with a pretty, lilting accent of somewhere in the south. She was from Béziers, in the Languedoc. Our "cute little accents" became our shared joke, and after I told her I was a food writer, she started offering me advice about new restaurants. Many of her recommendations were really good too, since her hobby was eating well on the cheap.

So I was very curious when my friend waved to me frantically from behind the counter, indicating I should step to one side and wait until she could serve me. This took a while, but when I got up to the counter, she jotted something down on a small piece of paper and handed it to me. It was the name of a restaurant: La Régalade, 49 avenue Jean Moulin.

"You have to go! It just opened, and the food is amazing. Go as soon as you can!" she said.

When I got home, I called La Régalade and made a reservation for the following night. The restaurant, about which I knew nothing, was inconveniently located in a quiet residential neighborhood of the 14th arrondissement, on the distant southern edge of the city. "This place had better be good," I thought during the very long walk from the Métro station to meet Guillaume, the food-loving lawyer I'd met on a train on the way home from a long weekend in Brittany. I'd been seeing him for two months.

When I arrived, he was already seated in the small, dim dining room with the heavy rustic decor of a 1950s provincial auberge — dark wood, wrought-iron wall sconces, and cracked tile floors. "I think this going to be great, Alec. The plates I've seen going by look really good," he said when I sat down. The waitress brought us the white wine we ordered and propped the chalkboard menu on a chair next to the table. We read it together, and it was nearly impossible to make a choice because everything on the 150-euro three-course menu sounded so appealing. After the waitress removed the chalkboard, she reappeared with a basket of bread, a terrine of pâté de campagne, and a crock of cornichons, to be plucked from their bath of vinegar with a pair of wooden tongs.

"We didn't order this," said Guillaume.

"It's part of every meal here, and it's complimentary," she replied. The dense brown-crusted pork loaf, emollient with richly flavored fat, became my permanent benchmark as the ultimate expression of the French charcutier's ancient craft, which originated in medieval times when few people had ovens of their own.

For a first course, I ordered ravioli stuffed with foie gras and was astonished when the waitress shaved a few fine slices of black truffle onto the tender pillows of pasta at no extra charge. The seared foie gras inside the featherweight pasta parcels had the texture of just-set custard. This was one of the best dishes I'd ever eaten in Paris. The bouillon teased the ruddy flavor of the liver by offering a richer, more potent rendition of the flavors of the duck as a backdrop. Guillaume's tiny bay scallops, cooked in their shells with salted butter and garnished with a mixture of finely chopped fresh herbs and tiny crunchy fried croutons, were stunningly sweet and pure. The croutons added a contrasting texture to the tender shellfish, which were flattered by the bright vegetal punctuation of chopped chives, parsley, and tarragon.

Our main courses were superb. My grilled red mullet fillets came with a garnish of cèpes and roasted chestnuts, a dish with an unexpected yin-and-yang balance between the iodine-stoked flavors of the sea and the earthy ones of the forest. Guillaume had chosen a pomme macaire de boudin noir béarnais —a baked stuffed potato that included crumbled blood pudding

—and that was spectacular too. "Somehow this chef has managed to take something that's really homey and rustic and make it elegant," he said.

I'd never eaten food like this in Paris. The vivid and nimbly creative cooking was something completely new. It ripped the corsets off the traditional idioms of French cuisine by mixing classic bistro cooking with regional food—the waitress had told us that Yves Camdeborde, the chef, was a native of Pau in southwestern France—and then refining it with the technical perfection of haute cuisine and the spare but provocative use of expensive luxury ingredients like truffles and foie gras.

When it was time to order dessert, I finished with a slice of Ossau-Iraty, the sheep's milk cheese from the Basque Country, which was served with black cherry jam. But Guillaume threw me for a loop by ordering rice pudding. Rice pudding? It was probably the most avowedly unsensual dessert I could think of, and it cast him in an alarming new light. I remarked that what people like to eat often reveals a lot about their personality.

He looked confused, so I told him about the time I'd met an FBI agent in a bar in New York City. He was good-looking, and I was titillated by his work, so I accepted his invitation to dinner at his apartment the following Saturday night. He served me baked pork chops topped with a spoonful of apricot jam, instant mashed potatoes, canned peas, and a glass of milk. Then he asked me if I'd like some vanilla ice cream with butterscotch sauce as a "special treat." The question was meant to sound suggestive, but it caused my erotic curiosity about him to go limp. But I nodded, and he went into the kitchen.

I was still sitting at the dining room table, which was covered with a lace cloth, when I heard scuffing sounds. Then a door opened, and an old woman in a pink housecoat walked into the room just at the moment when the agent returned with the ice cream.

"Mom, Alec. Alec, Mom. Would you like some ice cream, Mom?"

She shook her head. "Just a glass of water," she said, serving herself from the pitcher on the table and then disappearing behind the door she'd come through. I'd had no idea this man lived with his mother.

"Don't you just love butterscotch sauce?" the agent said with a smile as we finished our ice cream. He cleared the table, kissed me on the forehead, and said there was a good movie on in about ten minutes. "Let me just check on my mom before we cozy up on the couch," he said with a wink.

After he left the room, I bolted down the hall, grabbed my coat, and fled. Sex with anyone whose idea of seduction was the meal I'd just eaten would never work.

The following night when I got home from the office, I almost had a stroke when I saw the agent sitting on the steps of the brownstone where I lived, on the Upper West Side. This was in the days before the internet, and I hadn't given him my address or phone number. Still, he found me.

"I just came to tell you that you'd better watch your step, Alec, because you could get yourself into some very serious trouble," he said. Then he got up and walked away, leaving me to live the next couple of months in terror.

Guillaume gave me a strange look. "I like canned peas," he said, sealing his fate. And then our desserts arrived. Dribbled with salted-butter caramel sauce, his rice pudding was fluffy, creamy, redolent of vanilla, and filled with chopped dried fruit and pistachios. It was so good, it forced me to reconsider the possibilities of rice pudding. In fact, everything about this dinner was so intensely satisfying that thinking about it today, twenty-seven years later, still makes me ravenous.

After dinner, I wanted to meet the chef. The waitress told me to wait by the door while she went to see if he was free to come out for a minute. Five minutes later, a stout man with a strong jaw line, hard dark eyes, and thick, wavy espresso-brown hair emerged. He stood with his arms folded while I thanked him for an excellent meal and then asked him a question or two about his background. Where had he cooked in the past?

"Here and there," Camdeborde said, with obvious impatience.

"Would you describe your cooking as sort of a hybrid between traditional bistro dishes, regional recipes, and French haute cuisine? It seems to me that you've invented an original style that mixes all of these things together," I said.

He shrugged. "I'm too busy for this right now," he said, but before he could walk away, I asked if I could stop by the following day to interview him.

He shrugged.

I insisted. "What time would be convenient for you?"

"I don't know. You can come by tomorrow at 10 a.m., and I'll talk to you if I'm not too busy," he said, and left.

Guillaume looked at me with raised his eyebrows. "That was rude."

"It was, but it doesn't matter to me when he cooks so well," I replied.

All night long I thought about the dinner I'd just had. Camdeborde's food was fascinating because he was thumbing his nose at many of the established rules of French gastronomy. In 1992, for example, you'd almost never have found red mullet on a menu anywhere north of the Riviera because this sweet, succulent little fish with fine bones was considered too lowly to be served by any ambitious restaurant. Then there was the culinary wit of applying the precision of French haute cuisine technique to homely, rustic regional dishes and the very modern absence of cream-enriched sauces.

The next day, I went back to La Régalade and waited for half an hour before Camdeborde came out of the kitchen. "So what do you want to know?" he said.

I asked him about his background, and he told me his father was a charcutier, which explained the amazing terrine. Like father, like son, except that it had been made by his brother Philippe, also a charcutier in the southwestern French city of Pau. Camdeborde had dropped out of school at fourteen, started cooking at seventeen, worked at the Ritz Hotel, Maxim's, and La Tour d'Argent, all in Paris, and most recently with chef Christian Constant at Les Ambassadeurs at the Hôtel de Crillon. "Constant taught me so much," he said.

"Like what?" I asked.

"To skip sauces and use fresh bouillon instead, to go with shorter cooking times, to use fresh herbs and citrus for flavor, to stay simple. He also taught me to mix it up and to break down the barriers between different types of French cooking."

I asked for an example.

"Doing bistro cooking like it was haute cuisine and haute cuisine like it was bistro food," he said. After ten minutes, he stood up. "I have to get back to work," he said, and walked away.

I was stewing in the Métro on the way home when Madame Keyes's phrase came back to me: "What is the intention of the chef?" I decided Camdeborde's brusqueness was deliberate because he had no use for the established conventions of running a restaurant in Paris. Instead, his goal was simple—he'd cook the way he wanted to, and if people liked his food, which he was confident they would, he'd be successful. But being judged a critical success by the French food establishment, or anyone else for that matter, was of no interest to him. He was a gifted iconoclast who was going his own way, and Paris would be a much better and more interesting place for eating because of it.

That afternoon I called Bill Sertl in New York and told him we had to get a story about La Régalade into the pages of *Travel & Leisure* as quickly as possible.

"Can I have it tomorrow?" he said, and I made sure he did. In the short piece, I announced that La Régalade was the most important new opening in Paris in a very long time because its young chef, Yves Camdeborde, had invented a new type of restaurant, the modern bistro, which was serving a style of French cooking that had never existed before. Camdeborde's cooking was spectacularly good too, especially for the amazingly reasonable price of the prix-fixe menu, roughly $30 for three courses. With more and more press coverage on both sides of the Atlantic, La Régalade quickly became such a hit, it was nearly impossible to book a table.

Camdeborde wasn't the only young chef in Paris who had decided to throw a brick through the windows of the ossified French gastronomic establishment. Eric Fréchon and Thierry Breton, two other young chefs who had also trained with Christian Constant at Les Ambassadeurs, opened modern French bistros of their own in just as unlikely off-the-beaten-track neighborhoods. Breton had bought a 1950s vintage auberge named Chez Michel near the busy Gare du Nord, and when I went there for dinner, the dining room's traditional stolid decor, with half-timbered walls and ceiling, made his fresh and impressively light take on the sturdy cooking of Brittany even more surprising. His rich terra-cotta-colored fish soup was puckishly garnished with chorizo and Parmesan, foreign ingredients not then common in Paris restaurants, and his quietly elegant terrine of marinated pheasant came with lentils in a fresh tarragon vinaigrette that tamed the frank flavors of the wild bird.

The main courses my friend John and I had that night also showed off the intriguingly earthy but improbably refined style of the Brittany-born chef. Boned roasted pigeon was stuffed with foie gras and came with side of wilted cabbage to offer a whole jazzman's keyboard of suave bass notes in the same dish, while the chaste sensuality of a thick-crusted slice of pan-roasted cod was awakened by a brightly herbaceous vinegar-spiked salsa verde. This vivid-green condiment told me Breton had renounced the dairy-rich French sauces he'd learned to make during his haute cuisine apprenticeships. Instead, he was looking to dress up the plainness of his region's traditional cooking with fresh herbs, reduced stocks, and umami-rich garnishes that often came from beyond the borders of France.

Chef Eric Fréchon's cooking at La Verrière, his restaurant in the remote 19th arrondissement on the northern edge of the city, likewise amplified the culinary insurrection of a new generation of Paris chefs. His soup of white beans from Soissons, a town in Picardy in the north of France, came to the table with slivers of Spanish pata negra ham, freshly toasted croutons, and a dark green curlicue of grassy olive oil that made this classic farmhouse dish urbane. Langoustines were wrapped in brik, the fragile pastry leaves used in North African cooking, and fried, which gave them a crunchy crust that contrasted with their tender meat. The accompanying salad of lamb's ear lettuce, dressed in a gently musky honey vinaigrette, enhanced the natural sweetness of the crustaceans. Both dishes had a shy elegance that fell completely outside the rote categories of French cooking, since they rejected all of the sauces that had signaled serious cooking in France for more than a century and prized the natural flavors of food instead. Camdeborde, Breton, Fréchon, and others had dared to set themselves free from the Gallic recipes they'd learned as hardworking apprentices in Michelin-starred kitchens. Instead, they were doing French cooking their own way. Their polite but powerful revolt was as fascinating as their cooking was delectable.

In a country that follows chefs with the excitement accorded to its star athletes, this gastronomic insurgency was often scolded by established restaurant critics but quickly embraced by a younger generation of food writers, who rejoiced in the unbridled culinary creativity of these chefs. One of the writers, Sébastien Demorand, coined a term to describe this new cooking: *la bistronomie.*

But this heady story of the reinvention of French cooking was abruptly pushed off the page by the erupting fame of Ferran Adrià, a Catalan who was getting rapturous reviews as the world's best chef for the cooking he did at El Bulli, a restaurant in Roses, a small town on the Mediterranean north of Barcelona. The esteemed Michelin three-star French cook Joël Robuchon called Adrià "the best chef on the planet, a genius capable of giving life to a cuisine that's never existed before," and dozens of other food writers seconded this euphoric praise.

After brutal staff changes at *Travel & Leisure* that came with the arrival of a new editor in chief, I had become the European editor for *Departures* magazine, and so I suggested a story on Adrià's restaurant to my new boss, editor in chief Gary Walther. He signed off on it immediately. I booked three successive meals at El Bulli under an assumed name and made an appointment to interview Adrià.

My friend Judy Fayard agreed to join me on this trip, and our first meal at El Bulli began with the solemn presentation of a "virtual olive," a small oval slip of gel filled with liquefied black olive. It was gastronomically clever and an apt preview of the meal to come. It was followed by pistachios in tempura batter and a candy-bar-sized portion of bone marrow topped with caviar. Adrià's food induced the giddy wonderment of a children's magic show, but throughout the meal, I also found myself thinking of the Catalan surrealist artist Salvador Dalí. Adrià pushed flavors so hard and performed so many complicated hat tricks in the kitchen that our dinner felt more like a participatory performance-art experience than it did a meal. After a dish of preserved cèpes with a salad of potatoes, black truffles, lamb's lettuce, and rabbit kidneys, I concluded that this meal was almost more about theater than food. Many of Adrià's dishes were brilliant and often amusing, but by the time the medallions of monkfish with eucalyptus oil, baby onions, and cubes of black currant aspic arrived, Judy and I were both desperate for this long and very strange meal to end.

After three $400 meals at El Bulli, I interviewed Adrià, a warm but agitated man who drew dozens of Venn diagrams as he explained the way he conceived his dishes. He said that he thought of cooking like a science, with predictable outcomes that basically follow the same inevitable logic as chemistry. After two hours of listening to his fascinating rapid-fire monologue in French, the language we shared, I returned to my hotel, where it was a relief to eat a dish as effortlessly legible as a seafood paella.

On the way home the following day, I stared out the window of the plane at the snow-capped peaks of the Pyrenees and thought about my meals at El Bulli. Newspapers and magazines around the world styled this Iberian awakening as signaling the gastronomic fall of Gaul, provoking a lot of schadenfreude. The subtlety of French food struck many as staid when compared to Hispanic theatrics in the kitchen, but I knew it would prevail long after the novelty of Adrià's molecular cooking had faded. The reason was simple. I could happily eat at La Régalade every day but had permanently satisfied my curiosity about El Bulli after three meals.

Despite all the attention that the Spanish chef Ferran Adrià was receiving, it was both thrilling and fascinating to be living in the midst of a French revolution that would ultimately leave a much more lasting imprint on the way the world cooks and eats today than anything that was happening south of the Pyrenees.

16

THE NAKED TRUTH

met Leoš, a doctor, during a four-day trip to Prague to write about the fledgling revival of the Czech capital's restaurants after the recent end of Communism. We'd started chatting in a café and had fallen in love during an overnight trip to Karlovy Vary (Carlsbad), the Czech spa town where he'd invited me for a holiday weekend on a rare day off from the hospital where he worked. Now, for over a year, we'd been traveling back and forth between Prague and Paris as often as our time and money allowed.

When we woke early on a scorching Sunday morning in Prague, Leoš asked me if I wanted to go for a swim in the country. I did, and I assumed this would mean a quiet day alone together on a riverbank or at the edge of a lake. I asked him if we should make sandwiches. "No, we'll find something to eat when we get there," he said with an oddly furtive smile.

We drove for an hour, descended a long gravel road, and parked under some linden trees near a grassy embankment. On the other side of the berm, we slid down the sandy slope to a path along the edge of an old quarry's huge water-filled dredging pit. At the far end of the frigid-looking dark-green waters was a beach dotted with striped umbrellas.

When we got there, I saw that everyone was naked. A tall

woman with heavy breasts and gray hair in two tight braids over her shoulders walked toward us, wearing nothing but a pair of sunglasses and red-rubber swimming sandals. Leoš kissed her on both cheeks. "Mom, this is Alec," he said, in both Czech and English, for our mutual benefit.

"You're just in time for lunch," she said with a big smile, and Leoš translated. "I hope you're hungry!" she added, and kissed me on the cheeks. I smiled and nodded. Leoš walked next to his mother and I lagged behind, which allowed me time to recover from the shock of meeting his naked mother.

I followed Leoš and his mother to a large group of naked people sitting on towels and bedspreads at one corner of the narrow strand. They stood up when we arrived, and I met Leoš's grandparents, father, sister and brother-in-law and their two children, and his aunt. None wore a stitch of clothing. Leoš promptly stripped off too and nodded at me to do the same. It took me a minute to find my nerve.

Leoš's grandparents both spoke French, so I sat with them, chatting about Paris and the Prague Spring and my work. I immediately liked his grandmother, who had kind blue eyes and thick, honey-colored hair. She told me about the year she'd spent working in Africa as a young doctor, taking part in a Czechoslovakian aid project.

I noticed she'd been reading *A Bend in the River* by V. S. Naipaul. We talked about the book and its author. "In the end, he belonged nowhere, did he? He hated Trinidad, his birthplace, and he never felt completely comfortable in England. He was also disdainful of India, the land of his ancestors. I think his bitterness eventually damaged his talent. He never learned that you can't run away from pain," she said, and paused.

"So, Alexander," she asked, "where do you belong?" I noticed there were two small pieces of potato chip stuck to her breastbone below a pretty necklace of amber beads, the only thing she was wearing.

"I feel comfortable everywhere," I said, satisfied by the truth of what I'd said.

"Yes, I believe you do, because you're curious and open-minded, but where is it that you belong?"

"I'm not sure that I belong anywhere, really. I know that I'm happy in New York City, London, and Paris, three places where I've lived, and sometimes when I step off the train at the station in the small coastal town in Connecticut where I grew up and smell the salt marshes on a hot day, I know I'm home, if that means the place that I carry in my imagination."

"So that's where you belong?"

"Not anymore, because I could never afford to live in that town, and I went away because I wanted to."

"Everyone who leaves their home, their country, does so for a reason," she said. "Do you know your reason?"

This European incomprehension of the essential wick of American identity, choosing to leave your homeland in the hopes of a better life in the New World, was familiar to me after living abroad for five years. I gave what seemed to me the simple answer to her question: "I wanted to see the world, and I fell in love with France a long time ago."

"But I think there must have been a reason you wanted to go away."

I smiled and shrugged.

"I'm sorry," she said. "Perhaps I am insisting too much, but I think maybe I am as curious as you are." I felt no malice from her, but what she said had unsettled me. "Well, anyway," she said, "where you belong right now is at this picnic, and I'm very happy that you're here."

Leoš pulled me up from the blanket. "Let's go for a swim!" he said, so we waded into the icy waters of the quarry. I asked him why he hadn't told me we were going to meet his family, and he said he didn't want to make me nervous beforehand. I told him it had been a shock, in more ways than one, and he interrupted me. "They all like you, Alec. So soon I think I will tell them that we are more than just friends."

"I think they may know that already," I replied.

"Why?" He sounded alarmed. "What makes you think that?"

"They're very intelligent and observant people, and they see what's in front of them," I said, which made Leoš sulk all afternoon. He had not yet told his family he was gay. After our swim, we had lunch, fat sausages his father grilled over wood collected from the surrounding forest, and salads of cabbage, beets, and potatoes that his mother had made. Then we all dozed a bit, until I noticed Leoš's brother-in-law setting up a volleyball net. Here I drew the line: I was not going to play nude volleyball. My nakedness was enough of a concession without having to put my athletic clumsiness and dangling parts on display at the same time.

At the end of the day, we said goodbye to Leoš's family because he needed to take me back to Prague to get my bus. Our farewells were warm, and then we were in the car, stuck in traffic, with the heat cooking my full-body sunburn. Leoš asked me if I'd had a good time, and I told him I had, but that it had been a jolt to meet his buck-naked family and be expected to strip as well. "Why didn't you tell me that the family picnic would be naked?" I asked him.

He looked surprised. "You don't have naked picnics in America? It's very healthy," he said.

I thought of my mother in her skirted one-piece bathing suit printed with forget-me-nots and my father in his boxy plaid trunks, and I laughed out loud. "Maybe some people do, but we never did," I said, laughing harder. The idea of my parents at a naked picnic at Burying Hill Beach in Greens Farms, Connecticut, was hilarious.

For once, though, I felt relief along with the sadness of parting when the bus, in a cloud of sweet-smelling diesel fumes, backed out of its bay at the Florenc Central Bus Station in Prague. It had been an intense day, and I was glad to be alone. Leoš stood and waved until the bus turned at the corner and began the tail-bone-torturing fourteen-hour trip back to Paris. In 1994, these buses had no air conditioning, so it was sweltering inside on a summer evening.

My friends in Paris thought I was crazy to undertake these epic bus journeys, but aside from the fact that flying was too expensive for me on the every-other-week rotation imposed by love, I liked being lost in transit. The long hours were a time to think, an anonymous pause during which I felt free because I was nowhere and no one knew me.

Around 4 a.m., when the bus pulled into a rest stop some-where in Germany so we could stretch our legs, use the bath-room, smoke, and, most important to many of us, grab a tall, cold beer in the gas-station cafeteria, the naked picnic was start-ing to strike me as more poignant than embarrassing. Noth-ing — a scar, appendages that were flaccid or drooping, or parts too large or too small — seemed flawed when everything was exposed. Shorn of shame, shared nakedness became quite or-dinary.

That night, with the sweet smell of linden flowers gusting through the windows of the bus, I was pensive. The new life I'd dared when I'd quit Fairchild was now rooted, and I'd learned a lot during these five years. When I thought about it, I real-ized that writing a good restaurant review was similar to plot-ting a short story, with the vital difference that it was tethered more strictly to reality. These essays also needed a point of view, and I was finally finding my voice. I'd also learned that gastro-nomic expertise per se is dull and can be irritating unless it's leavened by humility, humor, and emotion. As I drifted off into a sleep that would leave me sore and stiff in the morning, with the pleasantly bitter taste of German hops on my tongue, I felt content with my life. Still, something about the conversation I'd had with Leoš's grandmother whined around me like a mosquito in the dark.

When I opened my eyes very early the following morning, I felt a flush of pleasure at seeing a florist arrange his buckets of flowers on a tiered sidewalk stand outside his shop with a meticulousness that was profoundly Parisian. Two or three times he stood back from the stand, and then moved a bucket to make the display more appealing. As I watched, I felt that I belonged in this city, which had become my home. I knew many reasons why I'd made the choice to live in Paris. Most of them were obvious—its food, its beauty, and its sensuality among them.

Sorting my mail after I got back to my apartment, I was surprised to find a note from my aunt in New York City, written on her monogrammed stationery:

Dear Alec,
    I just wanted to let you know that I've given your phone number to an old family friend, Joe McCrindle, whom you may recall from Quogue summers many years ago. I think he may look you up the next time he's in Paris. Hope all's well with you.

                                            Love,
                                        Aunt Dottie

Joe McCrindle did look me up. A few weeks later, he wrote to say that he'd soon be in Paris and that it would be nice to see me again. He wasn't sure if I'd remember him, but he'd been a frequent houseguest at my paternal grandmother's summerhouse in Quogue on Long Island. He suggested a date for dinner in a bistro near his hotel, just off the place du Marché Saint Honoré. Strangely, I had no memory of him on Long Island, but I wrote back and agreed to meet for dinner.

When I mentioned Joe to my mother during a phone call, she sounded flustered.

"Joe McCrindle?"

"Yes."

"Well . . . how did he find you?"

"Aunt Dottie gave him my address."

"Why on earth would she have done that?" she blurted out. "Do you remember him?"

I told her I didn't. Joe and Dottie had dated, she reminded me, even though everyone knew that Joe, who was an independently wealthy art collector and literary magazine editor, was a homosexual.

"What happened?" I asked her.

"Well, Dottie eventually broke it off." She paused. "Sweetheart, I don't know that you really need to see Joe. He's by way of being a bit of a bore, and I'm sure you have better things to do."

I said nothing.

"I don't think that it's a good idea at all. I really don't. In fact, I would strongly suggest that you don't see him. Or speak to him. Ever."

This made me even more curious to meet Joe, who turned out to be a heavy man with gout, thinning ash-gray hair combed in the style of the preppy schoolboy he'd once been, smudged glasses in heavy black frames, and a patch or two of whiskers his razor had missed on his rosy, meaty face. Our dinner began amiably enough, although he was irritated that I was five minutes late. We conversed about travel, France, books, and food. He loved French food as much as I did.

While the waitress was opening the second bottle of Bordeaux, Joe sopped up the sauce on his plate with a piece of bread and popped it into his mouth. "Ah, is there anything nature has produced that is more glorious than the shallot?" he said, and tasted the first pour of the wine. He told me that he lived on Central Park West in New York City, and from his stories, it seemed that he spent most of his time reading, drinking, and entertaining one "rascal" of a Latino boyfriend after another. He also had an apartment in London, and he came to Paris several times a year on his way to Rome.

Our shared sexuality never really became a subject, although he did ask me several times if I'd met the writer Edmund White, who was then living in Paris. I had, but our fledgling friendship had stalled after he'd made a pass at my boyfriend. Amusingly eccentric, Joe was good company, but it still puzzled me that I couldn't place him in Quogue. The last time I'd been there was the summer my grandmothers had sent my parents on a three-week cruise around the Mediterranean, hoping it would mend their marriage. While they were away, we kids stayed with my paternal grandmother. Joe had clearly been there, though, since he reminisced about our epic Monopoly games and my grandmother's witty stories of her travels in India, Egypt, and Iran.

"I think Bart was one of the best-looking men I've ever seen," Joe said, referring to my second cousin, who had been hired by my grandmother to take me and my brother John to the beach every day that long-ago summer. Bart got his beauty — the nose of a Roman emperor, the thick raven-black hair, the green eyes and high cheekbones — from his Argentine mother. I remembered the hot, still summer nights when we left all our windows open. I had lain in bed, burning with envy as I listened to the giggles of the pretty blonde au pair girl (there would be a number of these) Bart brought back to the apartment over the garage.

"There was so much sex in that house in Quogue," Joe said.

"Well, maybe for Bart."

Joe snorted. "No, for everyone. You could just walk down that long hall upstairs and go into any bedroom and find someone to have sex with."

I laughed. "I don't think so, Joe. The only people in the house during the week were us children and my grandmother and Eddie, her housekeeper, which didn't exactly make it a den of iniquity."

"No, Alec, there was a lot of sex in that house."

I decided he'd had too much to drink, got the check, and walked him back to his hotel. On the way, we chatted about his trip to Italy the next day. When we got to the door of his hotel, I gave him a kiss on each of his steak-like whiskery cheeks and told him to have a good time in Italy.

"Good night, Joe."

"Good night, Alec." He put his hand on my shoulder and squeezed it. "You might not remember it, but there was lots of sex in Quogue."

It was a warm moonlit summer night in Paris, so I decided I'd walk home. I was passing the Louvre when the shock hit me as immediately as a glass dropping onto the floor. I started shaking and thought I'd be sick. Then I ran, faster and faster, over a bridge, down one street and then another. I didn't want to remember, but I couldn't stop my mind.

My bedroom door opened and closed so quickly, I couldn't see who'd come in. Beard burn on my eyelid. A fat, wine-soured tongue forced into my mouth. He yanked down my pajamas and started rubbing my genitals. He climbed on top of me, crushing me so that I could barely breathe, bucking harder and harder against my groin with his pants pulled down, his hand pressed hard over my lips, cutting them on my teeth. I tasted blood. He bucked and bucked and then pushed down very hard a final time, and shuddered. The bedsprings creaked. In the dark, I heard him buckling his belt. He mussed my hair and said, "Good night, Alec."

When he'd finally gone, I waited in terror for a few minutes, afraid he'd come back or was hiding somewhere. Then I ran half-way down the backstairs to the kitchen, stopped, and screamed. Eddie came rushing up from the kitchen and took me in her arms. She immediately knew what had happened. Finally, she led me downstairs to the kitchen and, using a cotton ball, put something on my cut lip. It stung.

"Goodness sakes, what's going on in here?" It was my grand-mother.

"It was that bad man, Mrs. Lobrano."

My grandmother sat down at the kitchen table, dropping her head into her hands. Eddie put me in a hot bath with Epsom salts and gave me a mug of hot milk with something in it. I slept for a very long time but started crying again every time I woke up.

There was a suite of shadowy days in bed. Eddie brought me scrambled eggs, sandwiches, soup, cookies, and glasses of milk on a tray, and I ate almost nothing. When I finally did get up, the piteous solicitude I saw in every adult face in that house was unbearable. "Are you feeling a little bit better?" my grand-mother nervously asked me every time she came in to see me, and I rolled over to look at the wall and wouldn't answer.

Every day for a week, I climbed out the window leading to a short, flat part of the roof that surrounded a big dormer win-dow. I sat there for hours, watching my brothers and sister play-ing croquet, Bart mowing the lawn, Eddie hanging the laun-dry to dry. I picked at the sandy finish of the asphalt shingles for hours, swinging my legs over the eaves, but I never moved farther. I just sat there, toying with the temptation of gravity and surprised by how invisible I was to everyone in the green yard below.

Finally, I stopped running, leaned against a wall, and was sick. I started crying so violently that I shook even harder. When a startled stranger asked me if I was all right, I began running again. As soon as I got home, I called my mother.

"I had dinner with Joe McCrindle tonight. What happened in Quogue that summer that you and Dad went away?" I said, my voice shaking.

"You saw Joe?" I could tell from her tone that she was shocked.

"Why didn't you ever tell me or talk to me about it?"

"Oh, dear. Oh, dear. Well . . . we hoped you'd forget, and it seemed best to let sleeping dogs lie."

"But what exactly happened?"

There was a pause. Then she said, "Something inappropriate."

"So you found out about this when you came back from your cruise and came to pick us up?"

"Yes."

"And what did you do?"

"Well, we took you out for a nice lunch. Do you remember how much you used to like Hawaiian Punch?"

"Oh, for God's sake, Mom! Did you take me to a doctor or a psychiatrist or something?"

"Your father didn't think it was necessary. And your grandmother was very upset. No one wanted any trouble with the police. You know this was why your aunt broke off with Joe."

"I, I just can't believe that you didn't do anything to help me. Someone molested me, and it was all just swept under the rug."

"Well, darling, there wasn't really anything to be done. We just hoped that time would heal everything, and it did, because you've turned out so well."

"I just can't, I can't even begin . . ."

"Well, I guess I'm just a terrible mother." She sounded weepy.

"No, you're not, Mom."

"I am. I'm just a terrible mother. Everything's my fault, always."

"I have to go now."

"Everything's always my fault."

"Good night, Mom."

I took one of the powerful sleeping pills Leoš had given me to help me sleep on the bus, but I was still overwhelmed by revulsion. It occurred to me that the occasion I recalled probably wasn't the only time Joe had come into my bedroom. Rather, it was just the time he got caught.

When I woke up the next morning, though, I felt guilty for having upset my mother. I also felt a sort of a queasy relief. Maybe this was why I'd always felt so skittish about physical intimacy, which I often found smothering.

My mother called again a day later. "I've been thinking about what we talked about the last time we spoke," she said.

"Yes."

"And I think that event may be a reason why you love food so much."

"What?"

"You were such a sensitive little boy, and I think that eating delicious things probably made you feel better, don't you?"

"Oh, Mom. That's so crazy, I just don't even know what to say to you."

"I'm very sorry about what happened," she said piteously.

"It wasn't your fault, Mom."

We were silent for a little while.

"So what did you have for dinner tonight? Something delicious, I hope."

I mumbled something about langoustines. I was just about to hang up when my mother spoke again.

"By the way, darling, do you know when you'll next be back in New York?"

I didn't.

"Well, let me know when you do, because Ruth Reichl

—you know, the lady who's the restaurant critic for the *New York Times*—would like to meet you. Her mother is a friend of Phyllis Feinberg, and when I played bridge with Phyllis the other day, she told me Ruth liked the article you wrote about some Spanish chef and wants to meet you."

17

RUTH

On a hot August morning, I sat on a bench on the edge of Central Park and watched the doorman, in his stone-gray suit and stiff cap decorated with gold braid, on the other side of Fifth Avenue. Within the square of public pavement measured by a peaked forest-green canvas awning, this solid man cheerfully greeted a succession of deliverymen, nurse-maids with baby carriages, and everyone else who entered or exited the limestone building through the doors he guarded. It was his routine I envied at that moment; with the start of every shift at this expensive building, he pretty much knew what the day might hold.

In my life, every day was different, and I mostly thrived on this unpredictability. This morning, though, I was unnerved, knowing that I'd have a single chance to make a good impression on the famed writer and editor Ruth Reichl. With my mother as the go-between, Ruth had invited us to join her for lunch at Le Régence, the gastronomic restaurant at the Hôtel Plaza Athénée on the Upper East Side, which she would be reviewing. The reservation had been made in the name of my mother's friend Mrs. Feinberg, who would also join us, and my mother and I had agreed to meet up beforehand. This was my idea. I needed to set some boundaries for the meal.

A yellow taxi stopped across the street, and I stood up and

waved as my mother got out. She crossed the street, and we sat down together on the bench.

"That color is very unflattering," she said of my new olive-green linen jacket. "It makes you look faded and rather feminine."

"Oh, nice to see you too," I said.

She lit a long dark-brown More menthol cigarette and started complaining about how my father hadn't given her any money after his mother had died. In her eyes, he should have used some of his inheritance to repay what he'd lost of her money when he'd built a textile factory in North Carolina, which had failed.

"I wish you children would speak to him about it," she said. The death of her own mother had removed the major impediment to my mother's freedom — my Bostonian grandmother did not believe in divorce. Ever since her passing, contact between my parents had been strained and sporadic.

Finally, I spoke. "Thank you for arranging this lunch, Mom, but before we go, just bear in mind that this is a professional situation for me, and not a purely social one. So please don't tell any embarrassing stories about me as a child. And please don't call me Andy." When I went to college, I'd shed the confusing family nickname.

She relit her cigarette.

"Also, please don't smoke at the table. I've heard Ruth hates cigarettes. Since she'll be there to eat as a professional, smoking would be rude."

My mother stared impassively at the traffic coming down the avenue. I glanced at my watch. It was time to head for the hotel.

Ruth and Mrs. Feinberg were already seated when we arrived, and as soon as we joined them at the table, my mother asked the waiter for an ashtray.

Ruth's Mexican woven bookbag was slung over the back of her ornate Louis XIII armchair, and her thick black hair was pulled back in an amber plastic clip. "I don't know how you can see with your bangs in your eyes like that," my mother said to her. I winced. But during the polite and inevitably stilted conversation that began our meal, Ruth was warm, smart, and funny.

After the waiter brought our menus, I followed the customary etiquette among restaurant reviewers and asked Ruth if there was something she wanted me to try.

"Thanks, Alec. Would you mind having the corn ravioli with shrimp and cheese and then the halibut with duxelles?"

I nodded.

"So tell me what's going on in Paris these days, Alec," she prompted me.

I told her about La Régalade and the modern bistro movement, explaining that it was a really exciting time to be in Paris because everything was changing.

"That sounds fascinating," she said. "But what's happening to the old-fashioned bistros?"

"Wouldn't it be nice to have a conversation everyone else could be part of?" my mother asked.

Ruth cocked her head. "I'm reading *Charming Billy* by Alice McDermott, Barbara," she said. "Beautiful writing and a very strong story. And what are you reading?"

"You know, Ruth, Andy has always been a very good writer. I remember when he wrote an essay in the second grade about watching an old farmhouse being torn down, and he described how sad it was to see the faded floral wallpaper of a half-demolished bedroom in broad daylight," said my mother, lighting a cigarette just as our first courses were served.

A hard, burning button erupted on my forehead, an itchy hive. I wanted to scratch it, but refrained. It seemed to be traveling slowly from one side of my face to the other. I was sweating profusely.

"What do you think of the ravioli, Alec?" Ruth asked.

"I like the idea of using sweet corn in the heart of an

American summer, but the dish doesn't really come together for me because the flavors don't interact," I replied.

"You sound rather pretentious to me," said my mother.

"What are some of your favorite meals since you've lived in France?" Ruth asked.

"A lot of my favorites have happened in places you don't find in guidebooks," I told her, and added that one of the annual assignments I most enjoyed was writing an article on a different region of France each year for the elegant annual magazine published by the French Tourist Office in New York. I'd follow the itinerary arranged by the regional tourist office. This project, which I'd worked on for six years running, had given me an invaluable geographic, gastronomic, and historical knowledge of regions I'd surely never have visited otherwise. I'd traveled thousands of miles on the back roads, eating foods I couldn't have found in Paris and learning about the country up close. And I had some spectacular meals in very unlikely places.

The year I was covering the Rhône-Alps region, which includes most of the Rhône Valley and the Savoie, I found myself in Vals-les-Bains in the Ardèche. Many French spa towns have an aura of medicinal gloom, but Vals immediately struck me as a cheerful sort of place, and I liked the tidy, old-fashioned spa-goers' hotel where I was booked for the night. Going downstairs for dinner, though, I had limited expectations. The tight budget dictated by the tourist office meant that my meals were rarely stellar events.

In the dining room crisp white tablecloths were spread over solid oak tables, and tied-back drapes made of heavy brown damask hung in the three large half-moon windows. The only other guests were a silent middle-aged couple eating soup and an old man reading a book folded open on his table while he methodically cut up his omelette with a knife and fork. Sitting by one of the windows, I had a view of the boxes of geraniums on the other side of the glass, and beyond that, the mists rising from a torrent hidden in a tree-lined ravine.

A smiling woman with a mahogany bob and beautiful green eyes brought me a basket of bread and a little dish of green olives. She introduced herself as Madame Cervadoni and poured me a glass of white wine, explaining that it was a Côtes du Vivarais. "We make some nice little wines in the Ardèche, but few people know of them outside the region," she added. The wine was flinty and refreshing.

My first course was a superb terrine of cèpes, which had a musky perfume and a foxy flavor. When I complimented the dish, Madame Cervadoni said, "I made it myself. It's my grandmother's recipe." Next came caillettes ardéchoises, little patties of ground pork, pork liver, and chopped Swiss chard wrapped in lacy doilies of white caul fat, grilled and served with salad. The caillettes were unctuous with the chard, giving a grassy flavor to the rich blend of meats. I ate all four of them. Madame Cervadoni had made these as well, and I was touched by her earnest desire to please.

She refilled my wineglass regularly — a change from the usual two-pour meals I was accustomed to during these assignments. She chatted eagerly about the cooking and produce of the Ardèche, telling me the region is famous for its chestnuts, which were once made into flour for bread but could also be transformed into a sweet puree to spread on toast or use in desserts — notably Mont Blanc, a swirl of riced candied chestnuts topped with a tiny summit of whipped cream. Its name comes from the famous peak in the Alps.

By now I was sated and happy, but Madame Cervadoni returned with a roasted tenderloin of pork garnished with peeled roasted chestnuts and baby onions and a sauce with a bright spine of aged vinegar. She placed the casserole on the table and served me generously. The floury chestnuts, a variation on potatoes, played up the juicy meat, and the sauce had a deep, earthy resonance beyond the provocative acidity of the vinegar used to deglaze the cooking juices.

"That forest taste comes from the water I soaked the dried mushrooms in," she explained. "I filter it and save it for use in sauces or to make rice and pasta."

I didn't want to disappoint her, but I knew I could never eat the whole pork loin, so when she next came to the table, I asked her if I could have the rest to eat the following day.

"Of course! I will make you a picnic!"

After a beautiful chestnut soufflé with preserved apricots in its center, I refused her offer of coffee and homemade cookies. She insisted I taste some of the plum eau-de-vie she had distilled herself, and with the windows of my room wide open, I fell asleep listening to the hidden waterfall in the forest nearby and thinking a single thought. Paul Bocuse was right: most women cook to show love, while most men cook to show off how much they know in the kitchen.

"That meal sounds fabulous, Alec," said Ruth.

"Andy's favorite foods when he was little were Cheez Doodles and Sara Lee German Chocolate Cake," my mother chimed in. Ruth glanced at me and rolled her eyes.

After lunch, I walked my mother to Park Avenue and hailed her a cab to Grand Central Station. "You should be ashamed of yourself for trying to sabotage that meal," I told her before I slammed the door to the cab. She avoided my eyes and closed the cab door without a word.

Later in the day, I called Ruth to thank her for lunch, and she started laughing.

"Faced with so much torture, you were wonderful, Alec," she told me. "How long are you in town? Do you want to have dinner with us tonight?"

I joined her and some television producer friends from Los Angeles, and over dinner we dissected the catastrophic lunch.

Ruth told me she'd perversely enjoyed it because my mother reminded her of hers, and it had been fascinating to see someone else coping with the wanton misbehavior of a parent who'd acted like a puppy digging up a just-planted garden.

"The hive in the middle of your forehead moved back and forth like some kind of Indian marriage dot," she said, laughing, and we left the table as new friends with a lot in common —our complicated mothers and our love of good food, travel, and writing.

"Alec, please stay in touch," she said, waiting for her car service on the street corner after dinner. "Some interesting things will be happening soon. And by the way, that's a really great jacket. The olive color looks good on you."

Maybe the past ten years of hard work as a freelancer would finally pay off. Maybe I'd even be able to stop writing for guidebooks, including the single most stupefying project I'd ever taken on—my recent stint as the editor of the *Zagat Paris* guide. The job involved producing hundreds of jaunty editorial pellets that covered a restaurant's cuisine, decor, service, and cost, while remaining faithful to computer-generated numerical scores for each category and using as many quotes from survey responders as possible, in four or five lines. The task was torturously precise and mind-meltingly dull.

I'd done stories about Paris chefs and restaurants for *Food & Wine, Bon Appétit*, the *Guardian* in London, and other publications, but I still hadn't found an outlet that would allow me to share what I knew, in my own voice and style. I wanted to bring together everything I'd learned about France, French food, and reviewing restaurants, but I hadn't found a means to do that. I yearned to break out of the straitjacket format of reviews for *Time Out*; they were too short for deeper observation. If people read a restaurant review to get an authoritative gastronomic judgment, *Time Out* was just barely adequate; its reviews didn't offer quite enough depth to help a person decide whether a particular place would be enjoyable. In addition to information about its food, readers want a sense of a restaurant's personality, a creation of both the chef and the clientele. Who went to this restaurant, and why? I wanted to write reviews that would help people see, hear, and smell a restaurant before they walked through its door.

I had come to see restaurant reviews as little paintings that would show you everything about a given table by means of dozens of sharp details, strokes of color, and a revealing perspective (my particular point of view). I wanted to write reviews that revealed Paris as precisely and poignantly as Pieter Bruegel's canvases revealed sixteenth-century Flanders, as in his magnificent painting *The Harvesters*. It depicts a bunch of exhausted peasants having a picnic lunch, surrounded by the freshly scythed shocks of wheat they'd produced. A vast toast-colored field in the background awaits their further efforts. A viewer can sense the flavors, sounds, and physical textures of the scene.

For me, every restaurant in Paris was like a little theater that revealed something about the character and the sociology of the city, and France itself. Some places did so with special finesse and depth of feeling. I thought of my most recent meal at Au Bon Saint Pourçain, the Saint-Germain bistro I'd promised my friends I'd never write about. When you stepped through the heavy red-velvet curtains at the door, you entered a sort of private club where everyone looked up, expecting to recognize you, and if they didn't, that made you both suspect and interesting. This was the place the gallery owners and book editors, who lived in big inherited apartments around the place Saint-Sulpice or along the boulevard Saint-Germain, came when they were hungry and didn't want to cook, which was often; their weekends were spent in the country and they worked too late to shop. Here, you could eat when you didn't want to go to a restaurant but needed to relax, where you could take foreign friends for an honest experience of a Paris they'd never find on their own, where you could eat long-simmered dishes like veal stew with green olives or braised beef with carrots—homey meals your mother never cooked, but your maid might have. The food was good, but no one paid very much attention to it. The wine was cheap, and the beetle-browed waiter François would give you a cigarette from a pack behind the bar if you decided to renege on your vow to swear off tobacco for a night.

This was a place where you'd see the neighbors you liked and those you didn't, and there was a permanent fuzz of neighborhood gossip in the air, which was recreational but never nasty. Had she had a facelift? Was that his daughter or his mistress? The last time I'd been there with my friend Judy, we'd sat next to a pair of middle-aged blonde divorcées who were complaining about their ex-husbands. After a bottle of wine their severity dissolved, and they ended up giggling together. François poured them a last glass on the house to clinch the change of mood.

"I slept with the lifeguard at the Club Med I just went to in Senegal," one of them confided.

"Good for you. You have to start somewhere, don't you?" her friend replied.

Occasionally there'd be a movie star, maybe Catherine Deneuve or Leslie Caron, and people would smile at them politely but never address them directly, because it just wasn't done. If you came here, you knew the rules.

Then there were the exciting new places where the room and the crowd didn't much matter because you came to eat. My favorite was Le Baratin, a hole-in-the-wall in scruffy Belleville, the then rundown working-class neighborhood on the northern edge of Paris where Edith Piaf was born. The chef, Raquel Carena, an elfin Argentine woman, herself brought out the food she cooked, and it was as shockingly good as it was lusty and deceptively simple, like coarsely chopped garnet-colored tuna tartare tossed with fat sweet pitted black cherries from the Basque Country, a pinch of fleur de sel—those wispy crystals gathered from the salt pans in the Guérande—and a drizzle of very green olive oil. Or veal cheeks braised with tomatoes, red peppers, and saffron, a dish from the lost world the cook had come from, a provincial city on the Pampas; Carena told me it looked like the Loire Valley. Her cooking was deeply personal and profoundly creative, and it came from her heart.

This was the secret food that few people knew existed in Paris, and I was desperate to write about it.

18

THE TWO GIFTS

The next time I saw Ruth Reichl, she had just become editor in chief of *Gourmet* magazine. I called her to say I'd soon be in New York, and she invited me to lunch at the Four Seasons. When we arrived at this luminous preserve of power and privilege, with its famous rippling swag curtains of beaded metal chain, a hush fell over the room. New York was a food-obsessed city, and Ruth was a celebrity. We were led to a corner table in the corral where the regulars were seated.

Because of the absence of my mother, this lunch took on a different mood. The conversation was cooler and more incisive and assessing, like an interview of some kind. Ruth was studying me with a mixture of amusement and skepticism, and I was studying her in the same way.

We ate fiddlehead ferns and sautéed Hudson River shad roe, two profoundly American wild but delicate foods I'd never had before. When I told Ruth how much I liked the sylvan flavor of the crunchy coiled ferns in brown butter and the sweet lakewater taste of the roe, she replied, "I love American food."

"I do too."

"But you chose to live in France."

"It's because I've lived in France for such a long time that I can appreciate American food as much as I do," I replied.

She nodded. "I'm sure that's true, actually." She asked me a lot of questions. "So who are the most important food critics in France right now?"

In 1999, the two most respected food French critics were Jean-Claude Ribaut at *Le monde* and François Simon at *Le figaro*. They were very good writers and widely thought to be fair. I added that I personally liked Simon better because he was witty and occasionally lethal.

"In what way?" Ruth asked.

"He once described a meal at Guy Savoy as a 'three-star crucifixion.'"

French food writing had until recently been rather pompous and patently partial because it was driven by the bellows of big egos and bourgeois conservatism. But now the rise of a new generation of food writers was shaking things up. These upstarts were irreverent and funny; they spanked the traditional conventions of Gallic gastronomic criticism and thumbed their noses at the *Michelin Guide*.

"That sounds interesting, might make a good story," Ruth said. "And what about you, Alec—how do you judge a restaurant?"

I told her what mattered most to me was the food, especially the quality of the produce and the chef's execution and originality. After that came the service and the atmosphere, and last, the decor. "I'd rather have a brilliant meal in a truck stop than a mediocre one in a gold-leafed dining room with crystal chandeliers," I said.

"Me too," she replied.

Ruth announced that she'd always hated the nouvelle cuisine of the 1970s and '80s because of its prissy plating and tiny portions. I agreed about the irritating fiddliness of this style, but I defended the young chefs of the new modern-bistro movement in Paris, who had salvaged its best ideas.

She challenged me. "Like what?"

I was intimidated by her question but also excited. It was

exhilarating to have such a serious conversation about food. I made it brief, telling her that these young Turks built flavor by using *jus,* or deeply reduced stocks, instead of sauces made with cream and butter. They also loved fresh herbs, citrus, and shorter cooking times, which preserved the natural flavors of the food.

"What about Ferran Adrià? Is Spain the new France?"

"A meal at El Bulli is kind of like a night in handcuffs at a Catalan S & M club. You have no choice but to blindly submit to a chef whose goal is to tease you into his own kinky idea of ecstasy."

"So did you like it?" she kidded.

I told her I did, but that once was enough.

Suddenly, I realized I was speaking spontaneously rather than trying to deliver what I thought might be the right or smart answer. I liked Ruth a lot, and I was beginning to trust her too.

We had a rhubarb dessert, and Ruth talked about being editor of *Gourmet.* "It's sort of like taking over as captain of the *Queen Mary,*" she said with a sigh. "I want to make the magazine less stuffy and elitist and more approachable. I think younger readers find its posture of relentless expertise boring and irritating."

I agreed. For me, wit and humor were the missing ingredients in American food magazines.

"Alec, I want you to do a story for me, but not about France for the first one. Do you have any ideas?"

I did. Marrakech. The Moroccan city was taking off again, and I loved Moroccan cooking — a poetry written with spices. I'd spent hours wandering in the dappled dusty shade of its souks, with their potent scents — dung, diesel, orange flowers, bread baking, and meat grilling. I'd stopped worrying about getting lost because that was the whole point of visiting this teeming ancient desert city surrounded by thick red ramparts.

"I love that idea," Ruth said. "Do it!"

While walking Ruth back to her office, I told her I'd

known her father, the courtly Ernst Reichl, a distinguished typeface designer who had sublet a round office in the turret of a building on lower Fifth Avenue where I had once worked for a few months. Soft-spoken and impeccably dressed, Mr. Reichl radiated an Old World elegance and civility that I envied.

"Yeah, my dad was great," Ruth said. "But he never understood my love of food, which I think he found kind of embarrassing." She shrugged, and I laughed. I could have said exactly the same thing about my father.

Ruth loved the Marrakech story, and a few months later, Jocelyn Zuckerman, a *Gourmet* editor, came through Paris and asked me to dinner with her and her husband, Bill. I had to get up early for a flight to the United States the following morning, but I accepted anyway. Over dinner, Jocelyn explained that Bill Sertl, who'd become *Gourmet*'s travel editor, had suggested to Ruth that I become the magazine's Paris correspondent. Ruth had signed off on the idea, which would mean I'd do a monthly memo on the latest news in Paris and France, suggest story ideas, and also write articles. I'd receive a regular monthly stipend and be on the masthead. I accepted immediately. I was so happy, I couldn't sleep that night.

I was now *Gourmet*'s man in Paris. I was thrilled and flattered but also humbled and intimidated. I hoped I could live up to the job.

Very early the next day, I kissed Bruno's warm forehead in the darkness of our bedroom and spent the next twelve hours in the plane, ecstatically musing about how much my life had changed in such a short time.

Bruno and I had met in a bar six months earlier when I'd gone to meet a Scottish friend for a Christmas drink before he headed back to the Orkney Islands to stay with his mother for the holiday. In the small smoky room, I'd been listening to my pal's beery grumbling when I suddenly noticed a handsome man with a beautiful smile at the end of the bar. I couldn't tell if he was looking at me or not, but every time I glanced his way again, he was still there and still beaming.

He looked like a nice guy, which made me nervous. For the past couple of years I'd sworn off relationships after the devastating discovery that Leoš, the Czech doctor I'd been besotted with, had another boyfriend on the side in Prague. Since I seemed incapable of making good choices in my personal life, I'd decided to focus on my work and friends instead. It had been a long time since I'd seen anyone for more than a couple of dates.

When I next looked down the bar, the smiling man had vanished. I went and looked in the side room, but there was no trace of him. For a minute I stood alone, looking out the picture window and wistfully thinking I'd missed my chance to meet him. Then I felt a tap on my shoulder.

"Are you looking for someone?" he said, with the same blazing smile, and introduced himself. Bruno had a thick head of chocolate-brown hair and topaz-colored eyes. He told me that he was the head financial officer for a major French metal-producing company and was originally from Valenciennes, a small city on France's border with Belgium. He was warm, funny, and very smart, and he also seemed kind. We dated for six months, and then Bruno moved into my tiny apartment on the rue du Bac. I'd never been happier.

Now I was on my way to spend a week with my father, who'd been living in Greenville, South Carolina, after the death of his second wife. For his seventieth birthday I had suggested we make a trip together. I knew he'd never come to visit me in Paris, but perhaps he'd meet me in London to visit my brother John, or go to Nantucket, where we'd spent many family vacations. In the end, he chose Amelia Island, a golf resort I'd never heard of off the coast of northern Florida, near Jacksonville.

He'd selected it because his late wife, whom he married after my mother divorced him, had liked it.

It was early evening when my plane landed in the tawny light at Jacksonville International Airport, and I saw my father before he saw me. He was wearing a corn-colored polo shirt, a faded pair of madras patchwork shorts, ivory-colored wool socks that had shrunk from being washed too many times, and a pair of ancient Topsiders, his weekend shoes for as long as I could remember. He stood out in the crowd of people wearing T-shirts stenciled with parrots or palm trees or silly sayings, along with cargo shorts and flip-flops. Though worn, and even a little broken, his elegance was still conspicuous. He'd never again be the man in the khaki suit, blue oxford shirt, and raspberry-and-melon silk repp tie who'd once swept us across the huge limestone concourse of Grand Central Station on a memorable summer morning. It was so hot, most men had removed their jackets and had damp spots under their arms, but not him. Stepping off the train in a hurry — before his own workday started, he was handing us over to my aunt at Pennsylvania Station to take us to my grandmother's summer home on Long Island — he carried our brown leatherette suitcases, and we followed him. Even at 7 a.m., the city smelled of hot dogs, onions, cigar smoke, and greasy engines. Though I was walking as quickly as I could, almost trotting, I still saw the way that people looked at my father. Everyone — young, old; men, women — would stop what they were doing and just stare. He was that good-looking. It made me feel proud but awkward, which is the way I always felt around him.

"Hey, there. Nice to see you," he said. "Let's go." We hugged stiffly and then walked to his rental car in the humid subtropical night. We stopped at a traffic light, and I noticed that the pickup truck in front of us had a big decal of the Confederate flag and two rifles on a gun rack.

"Welcome to Dixie," my father said, and chuckled. He always put a good face on his exile, as he called it, but it made me sad. Along the roadside, trailer signs advertised some of the commodities, services, and entertainment available here: frozen catfish, discount dental care, and "Foxee Ladies!"

"Since the beef in France is so tough, I thought you'd want a good steak," said my father. "So I booked us at a place that a friend from Atlanta said is good." We drove along in silence for a few miles. "Muggy night," he said. I agreed and asked if there was any coffee at the apartment he'd rented for the week. He wasn't sure, so we stopped.

It was an odd experience to be with him under the fluorescent lighting of a vast American supermarket. I said, "Dad, this week is my treat. If you see something you'd like, just put in the cart." We decided to have bacon and eggs in the morning, and he picked up a pack of the store-brand bacon and a dozen eggs in a Styrofoam box. When he went off to look for a coffee cake, I exchanged the cheap bacon for something better.

He came back with a bottle of tangerine-flavored vodka. "What do you think this would taste like?"

"I don't know—put it in the cart and let's find out."

When we unloaded the cart at the checkout counter, I was surprised by some of the items we were buying: a lot of dog toys and a flea collar for his pet back home, some razor blades, a bottle of aspirin, and an outdoor light bulb, all of which he put into a separate bag while I signed the credit-card slip. "It'll save me some time to get this shopping done now," he said. He'd run through his inheritance by opening an ill-fated art gallery in Atlanta with his second wife.

The steakhouse had a happy hour, so we each had two fish-bowl-sized margaritas while waiting for our steaks. Each arrived on a little cutting board with a foil-wrapped baked potato and a few wilted salad leaves. I ordered a glass of red wine, and Dad drank beer.

"You boys need anything else?" said the waitress, her hands on her hips.

My mind reeled. My father and I shook our heads, and after she'd walked away, he said to me, "Well, if I was going to have a date tonight, I guess I could do a lot worse than you." He had understood. The waitress thought we were a couple.

When we stepped through the door of the rental apartment, my father said, "This place isn't done in the best of taste." It was furnished with rattan furniture painted white, nubby moss-green nylon wall-to-wall carpet, and framed prints of African wildlife and a Spanish dancer.

I put my bag in my bedroom and went out on the balcony for some air. The sliding door rolled open a minute later, and I heard ice cubes in a glass. "I thought you might like a little nightcap." He brought drinks for us both onto the balcony.

"So how are you, Dad?"

"Pretty good."

"Do you think you'll stay in Greenville?"

"It's OK, the weather's nice." He sipped his drink. "I'm afraid it's going to be a little rainy here tomorrow."

"Oh well, we can still go for a walk, maybe go out for lunch." I was too exhausted to chat for long. I poured the vodka tonic he'd made into the kitchen sink and went to bed.

When I woke, I smelled coffee and bacon. The first thing I saw when I opened my eyes was a pair of knees. "I thought you might like some breakfast in bed."

"Thanks, Dad. Why don't put it over on the dresser, and I'll get up in a minute."

There was something excruciatingly poignant in this gesture. This was the most solicitude I'd experienced from my father in my adult life. I ate the bacon, brushed the burned scrambled egg from the paper plate into the toilet, and took a fast shower. When I went into the kitchen, I saw the bottle of tangerine vodka on the counter. It looked like someone had driven a spike through its aluminum cap; it was punched open but not twisted off. I poured myself some coffee.

"That vodka's actually pretty good, but I couldn't get the cap off last night," said my father, who was reading a newspaper that appeared to be more of a collection of brightly printed advertising supplements than anything else. "I couldn't get the *Times;* the best I could do was the Atlanta paper," he said.

We walked all the way down the wide flat beach and out to the end of a very long pier, where an old Black man with grizzled white hair was sitting on a folding stool with a fishing pole and a plastic bucket.

"Catch anything today, sir?" my father said.

"You're the first one so far."

My father laughed. "Well, good luck to you then." We kept walking on the broad, flat beach. A ruffle of slack waves soaked the shoreline.

"I had some very good news the other day, Dad."

"Oh?"

"Yes. I've been asked to be the Paris editor for *Gourmet* magazine."

"Oh. Well, I guess that's good."

We strode in silence, and then he stopped to light a cigarette. His lighter snapped shut and he looked at me. "When did you become so interested in *food?*" he said. The way he emphasized the word *food* communicated a quizzical distaste.

I didn't know what to say. Most of my earliest memories arose from my taste buds, and my fascination with food had been the rudder of my life. But his skeptical question was tinged with the tone of jocular derision that was the closest he got to overtly expressing affection, so I found his words strangely fortifying. And anyway, I realized that I no longer needed his approval.

Over the next few days, we went to a movie, played miniature golf, and drove off the island to an antiques fair in a nearby town. He'd taken up this new interest with an improbable vengeance to please his second wife.

When it was time for me to fly home to Paris, he drove me to the airport. "Thanks a lot," he said, and patted me on the back as we parted.

I turned back to wave before I went through the sliding doors.

"Bon appétit!" he called, with a wry but not knowing smile. Since wryness is fermented from unexpressed emotion, I expect my parting smile to him looked pretty sardonic as well.

I never saw him again. But as my father's son, I love bacon, pizza, sharp Cheddar cheese, barbecued food, and even the occasional ill-advised shot of tangerine vodka as much as he did.

When the plane jolted off the runway, it jarred me out of the sadness I felt at leaving him and at our emotional reticence. I comforted myself with the idea that I had traveled a long way to show him I cared, and that somehow he had to know it. Then the plane pierced the thick clouds, it was light again, and I was suddenly very excited to be going home to write about Paris for *Gourmet.*

19

THE HARVEST

There were seventy-eight messages on my answering machine when I got back. I couldn't believe how quickly the press attachés of the city's most famous chefs had found out I'd become the new *Gourmet* correspondent. But it was the new generation of young chefs, the ones who were inventing a new French kitchen, that I wanted to write about—not the city's Michelin three-star chefs.

All over Paris, but especially in outlying residential neighborhoods little known to tourists, the new guard was cooking a bright, iconoclastic style of cuisine inspired by flavors from around the globe, something that had never existed before. I wanted to tell their stories and explain their cooking. Paris had quietly become the most gastronomically inventive city in the world again, and I knew it.

Ever since Camdeborde had launched the modern bistro movement, every year brought a new crop of remarkable restaurants. So I jumped into action when a friend called to tell me about an amazing meal she had, cooked by a monosyllabic chef with a Basque family name at a tiny new place in Montmartre called La Famille.

I went for dinner that night and loved the funky charm of this hole-in-the-wall place. It had a record player spinning vinyl disks, low lighting, and beat-up Scandinavian furniture probably found at a flea market somewhere. The laid-back, humorous staff gave the restaurant a loungelike atmosphere, more Californian than Parisian. I ordered a "gazpacho" of white peaches and tomatoes, and a steamed rolled chicken breast stuffed with coriander, haricots verts, poblano peppers, fresh corn, and queso fresco, with side garnishes of sumac-seasoned Israeli couscous and root-vegetable slaw. These dishes were delicate and succulent, with percussive cosmopolitan flavors that were leagues away from traditional French cooking.

When I went back to the restaurant the following day to chat with the chef, Iñaki Aizpitarte, he was sitting on the steps of his kitchen, peeling onions. I introduced myself and sat down on the stoop next to him, telling him I'd be glad to help him peel if he had a second paring knife. My suggestion broke the vacant faraway look on his long narrow face, and after he went inside and returned with a knife, I chatted with him as we shed onion-induced tears together.

"The idea of La Famille is just to have a good time. Most restaurants aren't fun, but they should be," he said. His voice trailed off into a distracted silence. I decided it would be better to let him speak freestyle than ask him questions, so I waited quietly, which seemed to surprise him.

"My cooking is sort of a *cuisine de vagabond*," he told me, a reflection of his travels in Latin America and the time he spent working as a line chef in Tel Aviv. "I like bright flavors, spices, and fresh herbs, and lots of texture and heat. My parents are Basque, and Basque cooking uses smoke as a flavor and likes pepper, but Latin American food pushes these flavors even harder." He was talking in a sort of trance. He had the aura of a lost child, and I could catch a glimpse of his exposed and untamed imagination, a gentle but chaotic crucible that had conjured up that superb white peach and tomato gazpacho and stuffed steamed chicken. Aizpitarte has since become one of the

most famous chefs in Paris at his own Michelin-starred Le Cha-
teaubriand in the 11th arrondissement.

I also wrote about chef Stéphane Jégo, a former sous-chef of
Camdeborde who bought L'Ami Jean, an old Basque restaurant,
and reworked its menu with earthy, modern bistro dishes like
Parmesan soup with bacon chunks, onion, chives, and croutons;
seared foie gras in smoked eel bouillon; and smoked-hay roasted
lamb. Another of my subjects was Daniel Rose, a very talented
young chef from Chicago who had opened a vest-pocket bistro called Spring a few steps from my front door in the 9th arrondissement. His delectable menu changed daily and ran to
dishes like grilled wild salmon with powdered beets and lentils and a brownie-style cake with spiced pumpkin puree. Rose
would go on to run Le Coucou, my favorite French restaurant
in New York City.

Then one beautiful October morning in 2009, a breathless reporter from Agence France Presse called to ask me to comment
on the news that *Gourmet* was closing. The question stunned
me. I declined, and hung up. I dove into the internet. The phone
rang several more times, with reporters I knew from two different London dailies calling for a comment on *Gourmet*'s demise. One of them later ran a story with the headline "America
Shocked by Condé Nast's Fallen Soufflé."

When I couldn't bear any more calls, I put on my coat and
went out. The minute I stepped through the heavy oak doors of
my building, I felt a little better. *Gourmet* was gone, but I still
had Paris. I didn't get two steps before I ran into the chef at a
local restaurant who told me he'd just received a crate of the
season's first scallops from Erquy, a port in the Côtes-d'Armor
department of Brittany, a good reason to come for dinner that
night. At my next stop, my novel-loving pharmacist told me
she'd almost finished reading a book she knew I'd love and
would put it under the counter for me for the next time I came

in. But it was a strain to be cheerful, and I had a lot of adrenaline to walk off.

With no destination in mind, I meandered through the neighborhood of elegant limestone zinc-roofed buildings in the heart of the city where I'd lived for over ten years. Crossing a street here, turning a corner there, I now knew Paris so well, I could walk most of it without a map. With every step, my shock resonated differently. What would I do now?

On a bench in the Jardin du Palais Royal, one of the most elegant and intimate places—it's sort of like an open-air salon, and though it's in the heart of the city, many people overlook it—I watched the fat gray pigeons, doubtless nourished by mountains of flaky crumbs from croissant and brioche pecked from the sidewalk terraces of nearby cafés, and envied them the oblivion of their gluttony. A fountain splattered and reassured, one of the eternal aural signals of being in a civilized place. Then the breeze shifted, and I caught a sharp sweet scent of flowering stock—that clobbering stink of tobacco, sweat, sex, and sugar, which seemed sharply funereal on that particular morning.

Then I continued my walk, anxious and sad but also heartened by the very rare pleasure of being out in the city in the middle of a beautiful autumn day instead of sitting at my computer in a T-shirt and sweatpants for hours on end, as I usually did. I crossed the Pont Neuf, stopped to admire the pewter-colored waters of the Seine, and headed up the rue Guénégaud, past one of my favorite buildings, in the Bauhaus style, with rounded casement windows, at the corner of the rue Mazarine. I continued through the busy crossroads of the Odéon, where the gutters had filled with bronze-colored leaves.

I wandered into the Jardin de Luxembourg to see the espaliered apple and pear trees and the beehives that furnish fruit and honey to the table of the senators in Le Sénat, and when I emerged at the southwest corner of the park, I realized I was hungry. There was some cold roast chicken in the fridge at home, but I had no appetite for solitude. Since the best cure for a fear of privation is sometimes a little extravagance, I decided to take myself out for a good lunch.

At Le Dôme, an expensive fish restaurant in Montparnasse, I sat down at a table set with a crisp white cloth on the sunny enclosed terrace. When the dapper black-jacketed maître d'hôtel arrived with the menu, I told him I already knew what I wanted.

"Good for you!" he said with the wry smile that's the stock-in-trade of the best Parisian maître d's, simultaneously teasing, mocking, and complicit in accomplishing the important task at hand, the pleasure of your meal. "So what would you like today, sir?"

I would have nine Spéciale n°3 Gillardeau oysters, a sole meunière, and a bottle of Saint-Aubin.

"What a perfect meal," said the maître d'hôtel. "Are you celebrating something?"

I paused.

"A death," I said.

"My condolences, and I think the wine will help," he said, and bowed briefly.

When a waiter brought me bread, butter, and a dish of tiny, sweet gray North Sea shrimp as an hors d'oeuvre, I told him I wasn't in a hurry.

"Understood, monsieur," he replied, pulling the cork out of the wine bottle and placing it on the table next to my napkin. The rich gold wine had a nose of beeswax and marzipan, and it was fat and silky, with a clean finish. The oysters arrived, and the architecture of the meal I'd constructed quieted my mind. The iodine-rich rush of the fleshy oysters braced me for the future, while the wine blunted my fear of it, and the melted butter the sole had bathed in was soft balm for my sadness.

I didn't have dessert, just a coffee, and then I walked home, leaving a half bottle of good wine behind me like a votive offering, the Parisian equivalent of dropping a penny into a wishing well. I knew the delicious Burgundy would make one of the waiters happy, or perhaps he'd gift it to another client the same way one had moved a half-finished bottle of expensive Bordeaux from the next table to mine after my neighbors had paid their bill and left, at the Brasserie Balzar in the Latin Quarter the first time I went there. To make sure I understood it was deliberate, my waiter had brought me a fresh glass, which he'd put down on the table with a theatrical wink.

Walking home after lunch, it suddenly struck me that, after living happily in a gilded cage for ten years, I would be able to write for other publications again. The terms of my *Gourmet* contract had forbidden me to publish pieces almost anywhere else. Now I'd fly on my own wings once more.

A year later, on a hot summer afternoon, I had an email from an editor at the weekend magazine of *Les echos*, France's largest and most widely read business newspaper, asking me if I would be free to come in for a meeting the following week about a possible editorial project. As soon as we sat down in the small conference room, one of the three editors asked me, "What was the best meal you've ever had in Paris, Alexandre?"

I knew they wanted a titillating story, so I told them one about a restaurant I expected many of them knew, Restaurant Alain Ducasse au Plaza Athénée, the Michelin three-star table of France's most famous gastronomic entrepreneur. The first thing that made this meal so memorable was the way Bruno and I had been welcomed by the supremely suave maître d'hôtel, Denis Courtiade. I explained that Courtiade was probably the best restaurant manager in Paris, with an instinctive knack for sizing up his clientele by seating them and then chatting with them for a few minutes. This allows him to determine who they are and what they want that evening. Then he communicates his "diagnosis" to his team, so they can deliver a charming made-to-measure experience and kid-glove service. The night I went to dinner with Bruno, Courtiade correctly intuited that it was an important occasion, and we wanted service that was amiable but efficient and unintrusive. While we were looking at the menu, the sommelier arrived with a bottle of Dom Pérignon Vintage 2008 Champagne.

"Monsieur Courtiade would like to offer you a glass of Champagne to congratulate you on this special evening," he said. After we'd been served, I toasted Bruno on the tenth anniversary of our meeting. Across the room, Monsieur Courtiade smiled and dipped his head. How on earth did he know?

The meal began when chef Christophe Moret sent out one of the most beautiful things I've ever eaten: a starter of poached langoustines napped with raw-milk crème fraîche and ornamented with shiny black commas of caviar. The acidulousness of the cream pampered the firm, sweet flesh of the crustaceans, and the caviar was the fuse that lit the potent sensuality of this seemingly innocent composition. My main course was a square chunk of firm but still pearly sole sitting in a silky marinière sauce dotted with tiny clams, whelks, barnacles, and squid carved into tiny rolled "flowers"; the sole tantalized with its taut flesh and fertile saline taste. And finally, dessert: caillé de brebis (fresh sheep's-milk cheese), caramel poivre (peppered caramel sauce), and miel d'arbousier (strawberry-tree honey). A deceptively simple dish with potent flavors on a soft saddle of just-set sheep's-milk custard, it seduced with its smells of the human life cycle—milk, the soft skin of an elderly man or a newborn baby, cowhide (first pair of shoes), tobacco (adolescence), musk, and a whiff of something ripe shading to rot.

At the end of the meal, I thanked Courtiade for the Champagne and asked him how he'd known our dinner was a special one. "You both radiated a great happiness, and your posture once you'd sat down was that of two people alone in the world," he said, and shook hands with us before sending us out into the night with the restaurant's very thoughtful parting gift to dinner guests: a loaf of freshly baked bread for breakfast.

The editors nodded and smiled as I spoke, and when I'd finished, one of them said, "We like the way you write about food and the way you tell a story, Alexandre, so would you like to do our restaurant column, in French, of course?" I accepted the offer immediately, and we came to an agreement: I would write a weekly column reviewing new restaurants, mostly in Paris but also important openings elsewhere in France and sometimes abroad.

Back on the street after the meeting, I was thunderstruck. I thought I was being called in for some sort of a special project and I had left as the prestigious paper's restaurant critic. My wonderment was laced with cold panic. The new job was very flattering, but what had I gotten myself into?

When Bruno came home that night, he was pleased for me but somewhat wary. "Will you write in English, and then they'll translate you?"

"No, they want me to write in French."

"Your spoken French is fluent, Alec, but you don't write in French very often. I think it could be very challenging for you." This observation irritated me, but he was right, of course. I knew the column would be hard work, but I was quietly proud that a prestigious French publication had judged my knowledge of Gallic gastronomy and culture not only worthy of its pages but of an expert caliber. And I was determined that my written French would rise to the occasion, no matter how hard I had to work at it.

I was shy about telling people about my new job, though, because doing so seemed boastful. This self-doubt, I knew, kept the blade of my ability sharp. Still, every time I thought about my new gig, I had to pinch myself, because the plot seemed so totally improbable: suburban Connecticut guy becomes restaurant critic of a leading French newspaper.

"You do know, *mon cher*, there will be long knives out for you in every direction," one of my oldest French friends advised me when she invited me out for a congratulatory glass of Champagne. "It's a very prestigious and visible job, and many people will be jealous. You know — why did they give the job to a foreigner? What does he know? All of that. You'll have to be very careful. You can't make any factual mistakes, and you must begin the column on tiptoes. What I mean is, be sparingly critical without being too provocative until you've won the confidence of the newspaper's readership," she said, which was good advice.

On the one hand I'd worked for an internationally famous food magazine, and on the other, I knew many French people would assume that I could never write about their food with any real authority because I was a foreigner, and worse, an American. If the French were flattered by the American adulation of Gallic gastronomy, they also found this attitude puerile and exasperatingly colonial. To be sure, a few foreigners, like the painter, writer, and wine connoisseur Richard Olney, had persisted and gotten a pat on the head — in Olney's case, a column in the prestigious magazine *Cuisines et vins de France* in 1962. Olney and the food writer Patricia Wells, when she was restaurant critic for the *International Herald Tribune*, were showcased as eccentric but harmless exceptions to the prevailing gastronomic benightedness of Americans. Like M.F.K. Fisher, Elizabeth David, Alice Waters, and dozens of other Anglophone food writers, including me, they had been transformed by their exposure to and subsequent ardor for French culinary culture. But ultimately, their Achilles' heel was that they weren't French, which meant that their judgments were, for many Gallic readers, more picturesque than convincing.

I thought of the question that other Americans I met while traveling often asked me. Astonished and sometimes taken aback when I told them I'd lived in France for over thirty years, many of them asked if I considered myself French. The answer to this question was no: my education and imagination had been nourished by the English language and the American values of egalitarianism, politeness, skepticism of official authority, and modesty. A vital part of me had actually become French, though — my palate. I had spent three decades learning about French produce and developing a now instinctive preference for the subtlety of great Gallic cooking. I'd also acquired the expertise of being able to appreciate and evaluate the skill that went into creating a dish even if I myself didn't like it.

My evolution reminded me of a conversation I'd once had with the *Los Angeles Times* food writer Jonathan Gold when he'd come to Paris to do a story. "The really interesting food in the world today is found in the United States in strip malls, truck stops, and airports, and in Asia and Latin America," he declared the first time we met for dinner. "We don't need to get in a plane and fly over here to feather-dust our balls anymore, because we've got great food at home."

I told him that despite seeing France challenged by other countries, I believed the culinary benchmark of the Western world would always be Gallic gastronomy. Why? Because no other Western country has such amazing produce, such a high level of historical gastronomic literacy, and such a fiercely exigent system of culinary education, which is the best in the whole world. The gestalt of Gaul's gastronomic excellence isn't confined to the bourgeoisie as it is in many other countries. Rather, it cuts across all social classes. The French care as much about the excellence of their chefs' sauce-making and knife skills as they do about their movie stars or sports teams. And all of the Gauls love to eat.

Over the next seven months, I labored over my reviews, covering a pair of new restaurants in Bordeaux, one in the Faroe Islands, the dining room in the luxury hotel created from the villa of the glass designer René Lalique in Alsace, and many places in Paris. As Bruno had predicted, the columns took me much longer to write than I'd anticipated—it could easily take a couple of days to produce enough copy to fill half a page of the newspaper. I was constantly challenged and often frustrated by the difficulty of rendering wit and humor in another language, especially since the trip wires of laughter in France are so different from what makes me smile: wry, dry wit.

One morning when I turned my computer on, I found an email from my editor at *Les echos,* telling me that due to budget constraints, they had decided to bring the food column in-house to be done by someone on their staff. I was both disappointed and relieved. I knew the column I'd written had been well received, although I had ruffled the feathers of more than one chef by being more pointedly critical than was customary. Only a handful of French food writers offer direct unvarnished criticism. The press attachés and public relations agencies representing chefs and restaurants are powerful, and they have a muting effect on most writers, whose work is often more reportorial than critical. Since the paper was paying for my meals, however, I was obligated to be honest, but I was also aware that some calls I made were controversial.

By the end of the day, the news had inspired an unexpected serenity that had nothing to do with the fact that I'd reached the summit of restaurant writing in Paris.

On the messy desk in my Paris office is a faded snapshot of a boy standing under a cactus, squinting. I remember that morning in Mexico as though it were yesterday afternoon, the fine red dust in the air, the smell of woodsmoke, the distant barking of dogs. I had been snapping a photo of a large lizard with my Kodak camera when Mr. Shaw startled me.

"Good morning, Alec."

"Good morning, Mr. Shaw."

"I told you to call me Joe, Alec. Can't you just please call me Joe?" His eyes were bloodshot.

I nodded.

"Why don't I take a picture of you, Alec?"

"No, thanks," I said.

"Someday you might like to have one," he said, and took the camera from me. "Go stand under that cactus."

The ground crunched under my sneakers as I walked over to it.

"Now step out of the shade a little bit, and take your hands out of your pockets. Don't stand so stiff, and how's about a smile?" After taking the picture, he handed me my camera, stepped back, opened his fly, took out his penis, and pissed a strong yellow arc that wet the dust between us.

When the photos from my camping trip were developed, my mother and I picked them up at the drugstore and sat on a couch in the living room to look at them together. There were dozens and dozens, and eventually my mother started shuffling through them faster than I could comment on them, until finally we came to the end. She cocked her head and looked at me. "All of those pictures, and only one of your friend Tiny Rosen and just one of you," she'd said, confused but not angry. "It's as if you became invisible for two months."

I hadn't seen those photos for years until the day I signed for them at the post office a few months after my job at *Les echos* ended. My mother had sent them when she moved into the retirement home. I found them unsettling at first, but then I came across the picture of that little boy standing under a cactus, me. I stared at him for a long time, and I liked him, so I put the photo on my desk to keep an eye on him.

MY LITTLE BLACK BOOK

Here are my thirty favorite Paris restaurants, a selection that ranges from wallet-walloping special-occasion splurges to bistros I go to often, plus some simple places for an affordable casual meal. (Average price is for a three-course à la carte meal without wine.) You can find more addresses in Paris and other places in France at www.alexanderlobrano.com.

L'AMARANTE

As chef Christophe Philippe brilliantly proves at his stylishly austere corner bistro near the Bastille, a lot of the best French cooking is achieved by treating outstanding produce with simplicity. Start with the Basque pork terrine or the foie gras, continue with the roast duck or whole veal sweetbread, and finish up with the swooningly good chocolate mousse made from funky, smoky chocolate from São Tomé et Príncipe.

4 rue Biscornet, 12th arrondissement. Tel. (33) 07-67-33-21-25.
Métro: Bastille.
Open Fri.–Tues.
www.amarante.paris
Average 60 euros.

L'ARPÈGE

Many people, including me, have a love-hate relationship with chef Alain Passard's vaunted Left Bank restaurant. Staff can be inexcusably haughty, and it's shockingly expensive. But every time I go back, I'm astonished all over again by the transcendent beauty of Passard's mostly vegetarian cooking. He works almost exclusively with produce from his own farms to create dishes like cèpe mushrooms with lemon and a vol-au-vent (puff pastry case) filled with baby peas, turnips, and snow peas in a cream sauce stung by Côtes du Jura wine.

84 rue de Varenne, 7th arrondissement. Tel. (33) 01-47-05-09-06.
Métro: Varenne.
Open Mon.–Fri.
www.alain-passard.com
Average 350 euros.

L'ASSIETTE

The brawny excellence of chef David Rathgeber's bistro cooking draws a devoted crowd of discerning regulars to this pretty restaurant with a painted nineteenth-century glass ceiling, on a quiet side street in a residential part of Left Bank Montparnasse. His rabbit terrine, cassoulet, and pan-sautéed sea bream with a grenobloise garnish and an emulsion of Comté cheese are outstanding. The crème caramel is one of the best in Paris, or go ahead and be tempted by the lemon mille-feuille or the chocolate tart with Grand Marnier ice cream instead.

181 rue du Château, 14th arrondissement. Tel. (33) 01-43-22-64-86.
Métro: Pernety or Gaîté.
Open Wed.–Sun.
www.restaurant-lassiette.com
Average 60 euros.

L'ASTRANCE

Even after more than twenty years of cooking magnificent modern French haute cuisine in a minuscule kitchen, the guilelessness that is chef Pascal Barbot's gastronomic signature remains unchanged. Every dish has a freshness and sincerity that is disarmingly poignant, including signatures such as his mille-feuille of raw sliced button mushrooms; verjus-marinated foie gras with hazelnut oil and roasted lemon paste; and tartare of veal with oysters, cockles, and dashi.

32 rue de Longchamp, 16th arrondissement. Tel. (33) 01-40-50-84-40.
Métro: Passy.
Open Tues.–Fri.
www.astrancerestaurant.com
Tasting menus 250 euros, 170 euros, 95 euros (lunch).

LES ARLOTS

This very popular hole-in-the-wall bistro near the Gare du Nord is proof that the real gastronomic glory of Paris is found in the city's neighborhood restaurants. Chef Thomas Brachet's blackboard menu changes daily but consistently offers delicious, reasonably priced market-driven dishes like a salad of green beans, apricots, speck, and fresh almonds; stuffed cabbage; and John Dory meunière with vegetable accras (beignets).

136 rue du Faubourg Poissonnière, 10th arrondissement.
Tel. (33) 01-42-82-92-01.
Métro: Gare du Nord.
Open Tues.–Sat.
www.facebook.com/lesarlots
Average 45 euros.

LE BARATIN

Argentine-born Raquel Carena is one of the most passionate cooks in Paris. In her little bistro in Belleville, on the northern edge of the city, she humbly serves up some of the capital's most original, personal, and deeply satisfying food to an eager international crowd of regulars who include famous chefs — this is where many of them come on their nights off. She cooks from instinct and intuition to create dishes like mackerel tartare with smoked vinegar or rabbit and mushroom ragout with red-wine sauce.

3 rue Jouye-Rouve, 19th arrondissement. Tel. (33) 01-43-49-39-70.
Métro: Pyrénées.
Open Tues.–Sat.
Average 60 euros.

LA BOURSE ET LA VIE

Chicago-born chef Daniel Rose's vest-pocket bistro near La Bourse (the former French stock exchange) consistently delivers some of the best traditional formal French cooking, also known as *cuisine bourgeoise,* of any Paris restaurant. The menu changes regularly but runs to dishes like foie gras–topped artichoke hearts, sea bream with sauce Foyot (béarnaise with veal demi-glace), and a bliss-inducing chocolate mousse.

12 rue Vivienne, 2nd arrondissement. Tel. (33) 01-42-60-08-83.
Métro: Bourse.
Open Mon.–Fri.
www.labourselavie.com
Average 60 euros.

LE CADORET

Belleville, the old working-class district where Edith Piaf was born, is one of the last authentically bohemian neighborhoods in Paris. This gives it a rough charm, but the other reason Parisians flock here is for excellent, reasonably priced restaurants like the cheerful bistro run by the brother-and-sister team Léa and Louis-Marie Fleuriot in a former corner café. He runs the dining room while she cooks a produce-centered chalkboard menu, which changes daily. It features homey Gallic comfort food like mussels in creamy, saffron-spiked bisque; haddock in coriander court-bouillon with mushrooms and potato puree; and an eggy crème caramel.

1 rue Pradier, 19th arrondissement. Tel. (33) 01-53-21-92-13.
Métro: Pyrénées.
Open Tues.–Sat.

www.facebook.com/Le-cadoret-142920366465634
Average 35 euros.

CHEZ L'AMI JEAN

Chef Stéphane Jégo's good-times Left Bank bistro occupies the dark-wood-paneled, 1930s vintage premises of a former Basque pub popular with rugby players. If the delicate, reverential way he cooks seafood reveals his Breton origin (Bretons love fish), the compass of the kitchen is his intense love of southwestern French farmhouse food. Dishes like Parmesan soup with bacon, onions, chives, and croutons; luscious beef and carrot stew; and lamb roasted in smoked hay show off his technique and imagination.
27 rue Malar, 7th arrondissement. Tel. (33) 01-47-05-86-89.
Métro: La Tour–Maubourg.
Open Tues.–Sat.
www.lamijean.fr
Average 60 euros.

CLAMATO

Chef Bertrand Grébaut's small-plates seafood bar is a great address for a casual but deeply satisfying off-the-cuff meal of imaginatively prepared, sustainably harvested fish and shellfish. The menu changes daily and might include cockles in smoked vinegar butter; sea bream carpaccio with pumpkin and coriander; or a whole sea bass with béarnaise sauce. No reservations, so go early or late.
40 rue de Charonne, 11th arrondissement. Tel. (33) 01-43-72-74-53.
Métro: Charonne.
Open daily.
www.clamato-charonne.fr
Average 50 euros.

COMICE

Canadian chef Noam Gedalof and his wife, the sommelier Etheliya Hananova, have created a charming restaurant with an elegant contemporary decor, warm service, consistently excellent contemporary French cooking, and a great wine list. The menu evolves regularly but features lyrical dishes like duck foie gras with hazelnuts, strawberries, balsamic, and black pepper or butter-poached lobster with sweet-pea and mascarpone ravioli.

31 avenue de Versailles, 16th arrondissement. Tel. (33) 01-42-15-55-70.
Métro: Jasmin or Mirabeau/Eglise d'Auteuil.
Open Tues.–Sat.
www.comice.paris
Average 130 euros.

FRENCHIE

Since it opened ten years ago in Le Sentier, Paris's old garment district, chef Gregory Marchand's modern French bistro has become one of the city's best and most popular contemporary restaurants. Marchand's cooking is precise, cosmopolitan, and intelligently creative, as seen in dishes like roasted guinea hen with butter beans, morels, and grilled peaches or spelt risotto made with fish fumet and topped with crabmeat.

5 rue du Nil, 2nd arrondissement. Tel. (33) 01-40-39-96-19.
Métro: Sentier.
Open Mon.–Fri.
www.frenchie-ruedunil.com
Average 88 euros, 50 euros (lunch).

LE GRAND RESTAURANT

A few steps from L'Elysées, the home of the French president, chef Jean-François Piège's intimate contemporary French restaurant has a striking open kitchen and an elegant modern dining room with an atrium roof. The reason it's always booked solid is that Piège, one of the most technically well-drilled chefs in France, also has a nimble and often puckish culinary imagination, which delivers dishes that are as witty as they are delicious. Among the most memorable are a beet baked in seaweed, sauced with a deeply reduced chicken bouillon and beurre noisette, and topped with caviar; and veal sweetbread cooked on walnut shells with salsify, stewed parsley, and a truffle reduction made with walnut wine. The eight-course Le Grand Dessert is spectacular too.

7 rue d'Aguesseau, 8th arrondissement. Tel. (33) 01-53-05-00-00.
Métro: Madeleine.
Open Mon.–Fri.
www.jeanfrancoispiege.com
Prix-fixe menus 306 euros, 256 euros, 116 euros (lunch).

HUÎTRERIE RÉGIS

This tiny, no-reservations shop-front raw bar in the heart of Saint-Germain-des-Prés serves some of the very best oysters in Paris. They're delivered daily from Yves Papin, a producer in the Marennes-Oléron region of the Charente Maritime on France's Atlantic coast, and from Cadoret in Riec-sur-Bélon in Brittany.

3 rue de Montfaucon, 6th arrondissement. Tel. (33) 01-44-41-10-07.
Métro: Saint-Sulpice.
Open daily.
www.huitrerie-regis.com
Average 45 euros.

JOSÉPHINE CHEZ DUMONET

One of the last and most authentic old-fashioned bistros in Paris serves the city's best boeuf bourguignon and other beautifully pre-pared dishes, including confit de canard, cassoulet, and steak tar-tare. The Grand Marnier soufflé for dessert should not be missed. Drink the cheapest Bordeaux on the wine list — most of the regu-lars quaff it.

117 rue du Cherche-Midi, 6th arrondissement. Tel. (33) 01-45-48-52-40.
Métro: Duroc.
Open Mon.–Fri.
www.facebook.com/chezdumonetjosephine/
Average 75 euros.

JUVENILE'S

Originally founded by the Scottish expat and esteemed vinophile Tim Johnston, this warm, friendly bistrot à vins is now run by his daughter Margaux and her French husband, Romain Roudeau, a very talented cook. This is the perfect place to come when you want a relaxed meal of really good French comfort food and a great bottle of wine without the hassle of making reservations months in advance, getting dressed up, or spending a fortune. Expect dishes like celery soup with cockles and chives with whipped cream; roasted octopus with Greek yogurt, spiced chickpeas, puntarelle, kumquat, and mint; duckling fillet with Swiss chard and chestnuts; and sea bream with beets, turnips, and cabbage in a béarnaise emulsion.

47 rue de Richelieu, 1st arrondissement. Tel. (33) 01-42-97-46-49.
Métro: Palais Royal–Musée du Louvre.
Open Tues.–Sat.
www.juvenileswinebar.com
Average 55 euros.

MAISON PAR SOTA ATSUMI

After winning a reputation for spectacular contemporary French cooking, Japanese-born chef Sota Atsumi recently opened this restaurant, one of the most original in Paris for a long time. Guests dine on a regularly changing prix-fixe menu at a table d'hôte in front of the open kitchen, where Atsumi and his team work. Expect dishes like veal tartare with cèpes and haddock; roasted monkfish with squid ink; and a golden pithiviers—a short-crust pastry tourte, filled with duck, foie gras, and spinach garnished with quince puree.

3 rue Saint-Hubert, 11th arrondissement. Tel. (33) 01-43-38-61-95.
Métro: Saint-Maur.
Open Wed.–Sun.
www.maison-sota.com
Average 140 euros, 95 euros, 55 euros (lunch).

MOKONUTS

It's worth traveling to this little shop front for some of the best casual dining in Paris from a regularly changing menu that shows off just how cosmopolitan the city is today. Omar Koreitem, a Franco-Lebanese chef, and Japanese-born Moko Hirayama run this friendly café-bakery. He does the savory dishes, such as potato galette with sea urchin and cabbage cress or bonito with spring tabbouleh, while she's the talented baker who produces superb fennel, pickled lemon, and almond cookies and a flourless chocolate layer cake with coffee-mascarpone cream.

5 rue Saint-Bernard, 11th arrondissement. Tel. (33) 06-11-95-59-12.
Métro: Faidherbe-Chaligny.
Open Mon.–Fri.
www.facebook.com/Mokonuts
Average 35 euros.

PANTAGRUEL

The most exciting thing about my work as a Paris food writer is the sudden gastronomic vertigo of discovering a brilliant new restaurant, chef, or food producer. This is what happened when I went to chef Jason Gouzy's small, simple restaurant in Le Sentier, Paris's old garment district, for the first time in December 2019. Gouzy's food was so earnest and stunningly good, at once young and aspiring but profoundly anchored in French gastronomic tradition and culinary logic, that the meal was spellbinding. The smoked parsnip with trout roe and turmeric emulsion and the beef cheek with squid's ink and red-wine sauce are poetry to muse on. Gouzy has a huge future before him.

24 rue du Sentier, 2nd arrondissement. Tel. (33) 01-73-74-77-28.
Métro: Grands Boulevards or Bourse.
Open Tues.–Sat.
www.restaurant-pantagruel.com
Average 65 euros.

RESTAURANT ARNAUD NICOLAS

Nicolas is a charcutier by trade and an MOF (Maître Ouvrier de France, a coveted government award that recognizes the country's best artisans), so the pâtés and tourtes served as starters in his stylish low-key restaurant are stunningly good, especially the pâté en croûte of chicken and foie gras. Beautifully cooked main courses run to cod with grenobloise sauce to a succulent daube of beef cheeks. Don't miss the baba au rhum for dessert.

6 avenue de la Bourdonnais, 7th arrondissement.
Tel. (33) 01-45-55-59-59.
Métro: Ecole Militaire.
Open Mon.-Sat.
www.arnaudnicolas.paris
Average 70 euros.

RESTAURANT DAVID TOUTAIN

Normandy-born chef David Toutain, one of the most talented young chefs in the city, is part of a rising generation that is inventing a future for French haute cuisine. His Left Bank restaurant has a ryokan-like decor of bare wood tables and white walls, and this stylish rusticity informs his luminescent, mostly vegetarian cooking too, which includes dishes like foie gras with mandarin oranges and pumpkin; scallops garnished with lardo di Colonnata; and smoked eel with black sesame and Granny Smith apple.

29 rue Surcouf, 7th arrondissement. Tel. (33) 01-45-50-11-10.
Métro: Invalides.
Open Mon.-Fri.
www.davidtoutain.com
Tasting menus from 250 euros, 170 euros, 130 euros.

LE RIGAMAROLE

Proof that Paris has become as deliciously international as Los Angeles, London, or New York is found at this excellent and very original restaurant in the 11th arrondissement, that swath of eastern Paris that has become the city's incubator for innovative restaurants by young chefs. Franco-American chef Robert Compagnon's small-plates menu of tempura, yakitori cooked over binchotan charcoal, and freshly made pastas evolves constantly but is light, bright, fresh, and full of flavor. Taiwanese-American pastry chef Jessica Yang does superb desserts like chocolate fondant with praline and buckwheat ice cream.

10 rue du Grand-Prieuré, 11th arrondissement. Tel. (33) 01-71-24-58-44.
Métro: Oberkampf.
Open Wed.–Sun., dinner only.
www.lerigmarole.com
Average 60 euros.

ROOSTER

Marseille-born chef Frédéric Duca's delightful modern French bistro showcases his personal and deliciously earthy Provençal-influenced cooking style, including dishes like pissaladière topped with red mullet and roast shoulder of lamb. Duca cooked at the New York City branch of Racines, the Paris bistrot à vins, for several years and says that the experience of the food in this heaving multiethnic metropolis emboldened him to do modern riffs on traditional French and Provençal recipes.

137 rue Cardinet, 17th arrondissement. Tel. (33) 01-45-79-91-48.
Métro: Villiers. Open Mon.–Fri.
www.rooster-restaurant.com
Average 65 euros.

LA SCÈNE

The exceptionally talented Stéphanie Le Quellec is one of the chefs who are reinvigorating French haute cuisine for the twenty-first century as an experience that's less stilted and more joyous and affordable. Her cooking, served in her intimate subterranean dining room, is stunningly good, including poached langoustines with buckwheat and a blanc-manger quenelle of their claw meat; veal sweetbreads with roasted cauliflower and harissa; and a ganache of Criollo chocolate from Venezuela, made with olive oil.

32 avenue Matignon, 8th arrondissement. Tel. (33) 01-42-65-05-61.
Métro: Miromesnil.
Open Mon.–Fri.
www.la-scene.paris
Average 150 euros.

SEPTIME

With a bohemian chic worthy of Bloomsbury, chef Bertrand Grébaut's beautiful restaurant in an outlying neighborhood just may be my favorite restaurant in Paris right now. Why? The service is charming, the prices are fair, and the regularly evolving produce-driven contemporary French cooking is humbly exquisite. The menu changes regularly, with cameo-like dishes like a roasted sunchoke slicked with grilled hazelnut sauce and topped with caviar, or venison medallions with Kerala pepper, fermented turnips, and a black-garlic-enriched jus.

80 rue de Charonne, 11th arrondissement. Tel. (33) 01-43-67-38-29.
Métro: Charonne.
Open Mon.–Fri.
www.septime-charonne.fr
Prix-fixe menus 95 euros (dinner), 60 euros (lunch).

SUBSTANCE

This stylish bistro, with one of the best Champagne lists in Paris, is the showcase for the cooking of Matthias Marc, one of the city's most talented young chefs. Marc's cooking is as technically flawless as it is intriguingly creative, as seen in dishes like squid's-ink gnocchi with a smoked egg-yolk condiment, pickled watercress sauce, and a jus de morteau; and John Dory on a bed of quinoa with pickled celeriac, fried capers, and a cardamom-flavored sabayon.

18 rue de Chaillot, 16th arrondissement, Tel. (33) 01-47-20-08-90.
Métro: Iéna.
www.substance.paris
Average 80 euros; prix-fixe menus 95 euros, 75 euros, 39 euros (lunch).

LA TOUR D'ARGENT

Chefs come and go at this venerable time capsule of a restaurant, which is perched on the bank of the Seine and said to have opened in 1582. For a sexy rush of vintage, postwar Parisian glamour, this very expensive place remains unmatched, and the subtle, sensuous, neoclassical cooking of chef Yannick Franques is as dazzling as the views over Paris from a table next to one of the picture-window walls. The most famous dish here is the roast duckling served as two different courses — roasted and plated with a sauce of its own blood with pommes soufflés, and then the bird's boned thighs with foie gras and black pudding. The famous bird, for which every customer receives a numbered postcard as a souvenir, is superb, but the 105-euro three-course lunch menu, which changes regularly, is one of the best buys in Paris and a less onerous way of tasting this legendary table.
17 quai de la Tournelle, 5th arrondissement. Tel. (33) 01-43-54-23-31.
Métro: Maubert-Mutualité.
Open Tues.–Sat.
www.tourdargent.com
Lunch menu 105 euros; prix-fixe menus 290 euros, 340 euros; average à la carte 325 euros.

LE TRAIN BLEU

Ever since chef Michel Rostang and his daughters took over the kitchen, this magnificent restaurant has become an excellent destination even if you're not catching a train at the Gare de Lyon, where it's located. The sumptuous belle epoque decor is the main attraction, but the roast leg of lamb carved tableside and the steak tartare are solid choices for a good meal.

Place Louis-Armand, 12th arrondissement. Tel. (33) 01-43-43-09-06.
Métro: Gare de Lyon.
Open daily.
www.le-train-bleu.com
Average 80 euros.

VERJUS

New Orleans–born, Boston-bred chef Braden Perkins opened this casually chic duplex restaurant overlooking a side street next to the Palais-Royal nine years ago, and his idiosyncratic, contemporary, French-accented American bistro cooking just gets better and better. Expect dishes like grilled Basque pork belly with semolina gnocchi, pajori (Korean-style green onion salad), and apple labne (drained yogurt); and buckwheat cake with curd cheese, chestnut honey, and marinated cherries.

52 rue de Richelieu, 1st arrondissement. Tel. (33) 01-42-97-54-40.
Métro: Palais-Royal.
Open Mon.–Fri., dinner only.
www.verjusparis.com
Prix-fixe menu 78 euros.

ZE KITCHEN GALERIE

Chef William Ledeuil is hugely gifted. His love of cooking is so sincere, he's never been tempted to do food television or food endorsements or to franchise his talent. Instead, he's created a superb trio of Left Bank restaurants, and each expresses a different facet of his gastronomy — Kitchen Ter(re) serves pastas made with heirloom grains, KGB is his casual dining restaurant, and Ze Kitchen Galerie is the stylish art-gallery-like dining room in which to discover his intriguingly Asian-inflected contemporary French cooking. Think Iberian pork and smoked eel in mushroom consommé with a nori tartare; chicken with a Persian lime and mostarda condiment; and caramelized passion fruit with lemongrass sorbet.

4 rue des Grands Augustins, 6th arrondissement.
Tel. (33) 01-44-32-00-32.
Métro: Odéon.
Open Mon.–Fri.
www.zekitchengalerie.fr
Prix-fixe menus 98 euros, 85 euros (dinner); 72 euros, 48 euros,
41 euros (lunch).